LEAVING SHANGRILA

LEAVING SHANGRILA

the True Story *of a* Girl,
Her Transformation
and Her Eventual Escape

Isabelle Gecils

New York

LEAVING SHANGRILA

the True Story *of a* Girl, Her Transformation *and* Her Eventual Escape

© 2016 Isabelle Gecils.

Published in New York, New York, by Morgan James Publishing. Morgan James and The Entrepreneurial Publisher are trademarks of Morgan James, LLC. www.MorganJamesPublishing.com

The Morgan James Speakers Group can bring authors to your live event. For more information or to book an event visit The Morgan James Speakers Group at www.TheMorganJamesSpeakersGroup.com.

Shelfie

A **free** eBook edition is available with the purchase of this print book.

CLEARLY PRINT YOUR NAME ABOVE IN UPPER CASE

Instructions to claim your free eBook edition:
1. Download the Shelfie app for Android or iOS
2. Write your name in **UPPER CASE** above
3. Use the Shelfie app to submit a photo
4. Download your eBook to any device

ISBN 978-1-63047-684-7 paperback
ISBN 978-1-63047-685-4 eBook
Library of Congress Control Number:
2015909838

Cover Design by:
Rachel Lopez
www.r2cdesign.com

Interior Design by:
Bonnie Bushman
bonnie@caboodlegraphics.com

In an effort to support local communities and raise awareness and funds, Morgan James Publishing donates a percentage of all book sales for the life of each book to Habitat for Humanity Peninsula and Greater Williamsburg.

Get involved today, visit
www.MorganJamesBuilds.com

Habitat
for Humanity®
Peninsula and
Greater Williamsburg
Building Partner

To Adrian and Logan,
for inspiring the telling of this story

TABLE OF CONTENTS

	Prologue	1
Chapter 1	Not Sons	7
Chapter 2	Belonging	9
Chapter 3	First Escape	13
Chapter 4	Turning Point	15
Chapter 5	Arriving in Shangrila	20
Chapter 6	Regret	23
Chapter 7	Path to the Round House	29
Chapter 8	Building of a City	34
Chapter 9	Lover Left Behind	41
Chapter 10	New Life	49
Chapter 11	Myth of the Cult	54
Chapter 12	Dobby	59
Chapter 13	Playdates	61
Chapter 14	Lies	64
Chapter 15	Stepmother	66
Chapter 16	School Choices	73
Chapter 17	Smarts	78
Chapter 18	A Prison But in Name	83

Chapter 19	Windows to the World	88
Chapter 20	Money	91
Chapter 21	Postman	98
Chapter 22	Escaping From My Life	107
Chapter 23	Call For Help	112
Chapter 24	Coming of the New Messiah	113
Chapter 25	First Domino Falling	119
Chapter 26	Olympics	124
Chapter 27	Father	130
Chapter 28	Way Out	138
Chapter 29	Breaking Away	142
Chapter 30	Wrong Side of History	147
Chapter 31	Farewell	160
Chapter 32	The Move	165
Chapter 33	Retiro	170
Chapter 34	Afternoons	178
Chapter 35	High School	181
Chapter 36	Visitor	184
Chapter 37	The Bus	191
Chapter 38	Night Owl	198
Chapter 39	Membership	204
Chapter 40	Boyfriend	213
Chapter 41	Breakup	221
Chapter 42	Caught	226
Chapter 43	Discovery	232
Chapter 44	Summer Vacation	239
Chapter 45	The Exam	248
Chapter 46	Rural	258
Chapter 47	Invitation	265
Chapter 48	Change	267
Chapter 49	Campaign to Go Back	280
Chapter 50	The Return	286
Chapter 51	Next Semester	289

Chapter 52   The Lie That Ended All Lies   299
Chapter 53   Leaving Shangrila   304

              Epilogue   *311*
              Acknowledgements   *314*
              About the Author   *319*

I did lie. But what I remember is omitting the truth,
never outright lying. Simply because nobody ever asked.

PROLOGUE

My entire class staged a school play, except that, unlike everybody else, I watched it rather than act in it. Joining the theater troop required almost daily rehearsals at one of my classmates' lavish colonial homes near school. I was not invited to join the group. They already knew I would not come.

At the school grounds, my classmates cracked jokes about what happened during their afternoons together. They perched on one another as they traded stories and exchanged hugs. I heard about the English classes they took after school, their boat trips around the bays of Rio de Janeiro, the excited chatter that accompanied field trips I was never allowed to join. When the entire class decided to spend a lightly chaperoned weekend in Cabo Frio, a town with white, sandy beaches and coconut trees lining the boardwalks, my jealousy meter spiked. For two months, that is all anyone talked about. Since I did not even receive an invitation, nobody spoke with me.

I felt lonely observing them. I longed to be as adored as were the two most popular girls in my class: Isabela and Flavia. Isabela, despite the discolored white spots all over her skin due to type 1 diabetes, was the reigning queen. The boys swooned over Flavia, two years older than the rest of us although she repeated third and fifth grade due to her poor academic performance.

I observed these two girls, searching for what it was about them that made them special. Yes, they were both beautiful. While their beauty may have helped with their popularity, it surely was not the main factor, as there were other pretty girls too. I decided that what they had in common, what nobody else had, was that they were the best athletes in my class, even perhaps the best in all of the school.

Isabela and Flavia were always the ones everybody wanted to have on their team and as their friend. They were either team captain or the first pick. They seemed to try harder than everybody else. So I thought that if I truly focused on sports, then I could be just like them. If only I could excel on the handball field—as girls did not play soccer, despite the madness surrounding the most popular sport in Brazil—then maybe, just maybe, my social standing could change too. I made a plan. One day, I would be just as great as these two. One day, I would be chosen first.

At the beginning of each week, the P.E. teacher assigned two captains. They, in turn, each picked a team for the week. We played handball on Tuesdays, volleyball on Thursdays. And every week, for the past three years, I was the captain's last, grudgingly chosen pick. I knew why. Had I been captain, I would have chosen myself last too.

I did not score any goals in handball. My throws were either too weak or out of bounds. Knowing this, my team did not bother passing the ball to me. I spent the game playing defense, barely succeeding at blocking the other team's powerhouse players as they demolished the team I was on. When an opponent charged towards me dribbling the ball, I got out of the way. In volleyball, I removed my thick glasses for fear they'd be broken, and as a result, I could not see the ball coming to hit me in the face.

I did not particularly enjoy playing sports. However, to change my standing in the team-selection pecking order, I practiced with a purpose. During games, I became more aggressive. I wore my glasses. I reached for the goal, whereas before I simply stood on the sidelines. I blocked more aggressively too—even if it meant pulling my opponent's shirt or hair—no matter that this often led to a penalty against my team. During these early weeks, I returned home with two broken eye glasses, earned a couple of red cards, and made my teammates angry.

At home, after completing my homework, I begged my two sisters to play ball with me. They did play, but not for long. When they grew tired, I threw the ball against the wall, attempting to increase my arm strength. When my arms felt tired, I ran around the farm to increase my speed and reflexes by dodging a pretend ball. At night, as I drifted to sleep, I prayed silently so that my sisters would not hear me plead: "God, please, make me be chosen first."

As weeks turned into months, I became quite adept at catching the ball as it ricocheted from the wall towards me. I was no longer chosen last. That horrible fate was bestowed on a shy and almost as awkward classmate who had the extra disadvantage of being overweight, which slowed her down compared to me; I was slight and scrawny. Yet, despite months of effort, I did not score any more than before, did not throw the ball any harder or more accurately, and hardly touched the ball at all. Since I often increased the penalty count with my new, more aggressive tactics, the coach had me sit out whenever there was an odd number of players.

A year into this futile attempt, I felt a deep sense of disappointment but realized the foolishness of pursuing an utterly impossible dream. Maybe one had to be content with their lot in life, I concluded. Any attempts to try to change who one was, or what one wanted, were futile. Feeling defeated and deflated and knowing that, despite any effort, the sports court was not a place for me, I talked myself out of my goal. I stopped practicing in the afternoons. I removed my glasses again during games. I accepted that I was not meant to be popular and that the world where my classmates lived did not belong to me.

I hated my life. I hated going home where there was nothing to do and nobody to play with. I hated how different we were—with our round house, with our religious meetings, with our inability to do anything other than go to school. Not knowing what to do to change any of it, I returned to my routine, finding friendship in books and getting all my validation from my grades.

Two months later, I felt sick.

My head and muscles hurt; my nose was running; and I coughed uncontrollably. I barely slept. My mother suggested I stay home. No matter how sick I felt, I would never choose to stay home with my stepfather lurking around. Anywhere was better than home. Despite my illness, I dragged myself to school that day. It was a Tuesday, which meant handball day. That morning, I walked to the handball court, hoping my swollen eyes and drippy nose would help me avoid playing at all.

"Coach, I am sick," I said with narrowed eyes. "Can I sit out the game today?"

"Being sick isn't enough reason not to play," the P.E. teacher said, not even bothering to look at me. "So, go play."

Although students never questioned the decisions of a professor, I protested feebly.

He dismissed me again, treating me as a little pest who could not be taken seriously.

"Here is what you will go do," he told me. "Your team needs a goalie. Go defend it," he said, pointing towards the goal. The regular goalie was also sick that day, but unlike me, she had the good sense to stay at home.

Off to guard the goal post I went, grateful at least that I did not have to run or be pushed around on the court. I hoped that a strong team defense would prevent me from having to exert much effort. My teammates groaned and shook their heads in disbelief as they saw me standing in front of the goal, mumbling that the team had already lost. The opposing team congratulated themselves before the whistle blew. "This will be easy," they bragged within earshot, ensuring I knew they considered themselves to have already clinched victory. Having me guard the goal was the same as having no goalie at all.

A surge of anger and despondency bubbled up within me upon hearing their snickers. I felt tired of always being at the bottom of the totem pole, tired of feeling ridiculed and different. I puffed my chest as if this would make me larger, ignoring how painful it felt to take deep breaths.

My team's defense did not keep its end of the bargain. The balls from the opposing team flew towards the goal at unreasonable speeds, from what appeared to be impossible angles. Yet, I blocked them out. I blocked every single ball that came towards me. I shielded that goal as if my life depended on it. At the end of the game, my team won by a landslide.

Not used to the taste of victory, I did not distinguish the elation I felt from the confusion at this unexpected turn of events. My dumbfounded classmates looked at me as if they saw me for the first time, trying to make sense of what had just happened.

They, and I, were in awe.

My feat as the goalie made the gossip circuit and by the following week, despite some lingering doubt about my abilities, I was picked third in the line-up. I had jumped seven places in one week! This was better than an improvement; it was a major victory!

At the sound of the whistle, the players moved. I tried to concentrate. Not feeling as angry as I did the previous week, my confidence waned even before the game started. But I wasn't playing for the game. I was playing for my dream, my rank in the social pecking order, and my desire that for once, people would pay attention to me.

Nobody pierced my defense of the goal. My team won again.

Two weeks later, the captains planned the team selection for the school's annual Olympic Games. The teams played together for two months in preparation for the week-long competition, held at a sports complex where all the parents—and the large, extended families that most Brazilians had—watched the games. The Olympics was the talk of the school.

My class split the girls into teams; these teams would play both handball and volleyball. The P.E. teacher selected the team captains. To my utter surprise, Isabela was not one of them. Thus, there was a possibility that Flavia and Isabela, the two best players, could be on the same team together. And that, I was sure, would lock in victory for whichever team they were a part of. I hoped that I would be chosen, even if last, to the better team. It was obvious to me that the opposing team would have no chance and would simply be crushed.

There was an air of excitement and nervousness at the school playground as the captains readied themselves to make their picks. Flavia was one of the captains. Ana Cristina, a strong but not stellar player, was the captain of the opposing team. After a coin toss, Ana Cristina was first to select players.

"I want Isabelle," she said pointing at me.

She clearly meant Isabela, with an "a", and not me, with the French spelling of a name most Brazilians did not get right. It made no sense to me that she would have chosen otherwise. So I did not budge.

"You heard her, Isabelle," the coach said, tapping me on my shoulder. "Hurry up and move to Ana Cristina's side."

I was too stunned to hear the loud murmur emanating from the cluster of the other girls at this unexpected choice. This could not be right. I thought Ana Cristina had been crazy to select me. This choice guaranteed that Flavia would pick Isabela next. Ana Cristina's team would be decimated. No team could win against the two stronger players.

I looked at Ana Cristina with panic in my face and shook my head. "Don't do it," I whispered. "Pick Isabela first."

She looked at me, puzzled.

"Why?" she asked

"Get the next strongest player. Don't let them be on the same team. Worry about the goalkeeper later!" I stated, with a modicum of desperation in my voice.

She stared at me with a serious frown on her face and gestured impatiently, beckoning me.

"Isabelle, just come over here."

As I walked, she spoke loudly enough for all the other girls to hear. "If I do not choose you, Flavia will. Then my team will not ever have the slightest chance. Nobody can score when you are defending that goal. You are the most important player here and the one I want on my team."

Still stunned, I moved next to Ana Cristina as the selection continued until all girls were sorted into teams. Once I got past my horror that we would now face Flavia and Isabela together, I remembered my wish made months earlier, the one I gave up so easily, about being chosen first. Yet, even in my wildest dreams, I had never expected that it would happen during the most important and visible athletic event of the school year. I felt an unfamiliar feeling of elation fill my chest. I felt I could burst. A broad smile spread across my face. I went home, screaming with joy: "I was chosen first! I was really chosen first!"

And for the first time in my life, I believed I was good at something.

Chapter 1

NOT SONS

My parents learned of our sex upon our birth. When Nathalie, my older sister, was born, she had the same translucent, green eyes that belonged to my mother.

"Is it a boy?" was my mother's first question upon the birth of her child.

"She is a beautiful girl!" Grandmother Mathilda said.

"She has eyes just as yours!" Grandfather Isidore exclaimed.

"Oh," my mother sighed, feeling disappointed.

My mother had originally planned to raise her child on her own, without help. Yet, she soon hired a nanny to look after my sister and a maid to care for the house. She also called upon my grandparents for help, spending most of her days at their apartment in Rio de Janeiro and staying there whenever my father was traveling the world for his work.

Within the same year, my mother got pregnant again.

At the time of my birth, my mother posed the same question to her parents as they swiped the sweaty hair off her forehead and the doctor sutured her stomach from the C-section.

"Is it a boy?" she asked, wanting to know my sex.

"No, she is a girl," my grandmother said cautiously. "She is beautiful and healthy!"

"Another girl?" my mother asked, not hiding the disappointment that I was not a boy. As my mother later told me, she looked at me and commented, "At least she has green eyes," as if the color of my eyes were compensation for the disappointment of my sex.

"When you were born, Isa," my mother said as she told me this story, "I asked my parents before I even saw you whether you were a boy. By the time your sister Catherine arrived, I did not even have to ask! Your Grandmother Mathilda knew better than to allow me to feel disappointed again, so she preempted my question by telling me Catherine was a girl. She even chose your baby sister's name!"

"Congratulations. Catherine is beautiful, and she has green eyes!" my grandmother said before my mother could ask about the sex of her third child or comment on the color of her eyes.

Chapter 2

BELONGING

With three daughters born within a little over three years, my father stopped his technical training as a software programmer to find employment to support his growing family. He worked at IBM, a job that not enabled him to support his family, but also ensured he would do so while avoiding the chaos of a house full of crying babies. This job took him to far-flung places around the world, leaving my stay-at-home mother, my sisters, and me behind. Our living conditions reflected his increased success at this new job. Our young family moved out from my grandparents' miniscule, two-bedroom apartment close to the famed Copacabana beach, to a penthouse in Laranjeiras, an upscale neighborhood in Rio de Janeiro, with an unparalleled view of our leafy, urban neighborhood.

With my father rarely at home, my mother relied on her parents, a maid, and a nanny to help her get through the day. Despite her relative abundance of time and freedom, she found little to occupy herself. She did not have friends, nor did she try to make them. The nanny took us to the park, denying my mother the opportunity to meet other mothers and their children. She spent her days hovering next to us and the nanny, seeing my sisters and I play with dolls and crayons, a constant reminder that she did not have sons. She felt ill at ease with her children and alone without her husband. Ultimately, she mostly lived a life without purpose. Bouts of loneliness and feelings of irrelevance permeated her days, along with the pervasive sense she did not belong anywhere.

Each pregnancy took a toll on her health and on her motivation to care for herself. Her once petite frame grew increasingly large. Long, frizzy strands replaced her once coiffed, coquettish hair. Fitted Parisian suits gave way to boxy dresses.

My mother did not attempt to find work to fill her long days—despite my father's frequent suggestions.

"I cannot work," she answered. "I am ill."

Nobody quite knew what her illnesses were. She complained of constant vertigo, fatigue, and headaches, preferring to retire to her bedroom for most of the day. At my father's and grandmother's request, she met with doctors to address the concerns about her declining state of health. The doctors repeatedly said she was healthy and there was nothing wrong with her. My mother soon stopped seeking medical help.

Grandmother Mathilda sighed at the sight of her unkempt daughter. "If you only knew how beautiful your mother once was," she often told me wistfully, her voice tinged with the disappointment and self-recrimination over where she could have gone wrong. How did she let her precious jewel of a daughter become such a rough stone?

In their insistence to help her, my mother felt the disapproval of her parents and her absent husband. Realizing that she would not fulfill her search for belonging through her daughters, husband, or parents, she ventured out to other places, places to which she would have been wiser not to venture.

Brazil was a highly superstitious place, with the majority of its vast population self-declared as church-going Catholics. Yet, whether they attended church on Sundays or not, it did not preclude a significant percentage of the population from also engaging in all sorts of other religious and superstitious practices. Brazilians routinely sought quick fixes for their troubles from those who claimed they could fix anything: a wayward lover could be brought home; an unrequited love could turn around; a terminal disease could be cured.

Testimonials abounded about how someone's life was transformed upon throwing offerings into the ocean, pinning cushions, or placing oneself in the middle of a circle while enlightened souls chanted incantations. It was commonplace to stumble on offerings with flowers, voodoo-type dolls, rice, candles, and all kinds of miscellaneous objects required for such practices on street corners or buried in the sand on the beaches. Brazilians, when walking past these offerings, made the sign of the cross and gave a wide berth so as not to become adversely affected by the surrounding dark magic.

Not surprisingly, there were entire organizations that espoused all kinds of superstitions and religious admonitions, pouncing on and welcoming those who were weak, lost, unloved, or in desperate need of a solution to their ills. Whether these organizations offered love, cures, or wellbeing was debatable—but they certainly offered an irresistible sense of belonging and purpose.

My mother found solace in such a gathering in Rio de Janeiro. With this new group of people, she felt understood and loved. They told her that her illness and overall malaise were real, a result of negative energy that entered her aura and was struggling to leave, thus rendering her sick. They offered to help her clear her aura of all its negativity and darkness. They never mentioned her unkempt appearance. They did not ask her to change at all. At the end of their meetings, they insisted she return. Feeling loved, accepted, and understood just the way she was, she acquiesced and returned weekly at first. Soon, it was every couple of days. She had finally found acceptance and a purpose. Seeing how much benefit she derived from this group, she set out to clean her aura. And soon, she wanted to cleanse others.

She spoke of this new group to my father and my grandparents. They did not share her excitement about this newly found religious expression. My father, having erased all vestiges of his Jewish roots by insisting that his daughters attend Catholic school, shunned religion. He had seen first-hand how religious affiliation only served to decimate one's family, his own parents having experienced persecution during World War II. My mother initially asked my father to accompany her to these religious meetings. He refused. My father ridiculed the premise of this new religion. Concerned, he redoubled his efforts to encourage my mother to see a doctor to devise a medical treatment plan so her physical, and now mental health, could improve.

"I already found a way to heal," my mother noted, refusing any advice to seek medical help. "It is you who needs help," she retorted. "You have a dark aura around you."

My parents reached an impasse. Not surprisingly, my mother's newly acquired religious and spiritual zeal caused a rift. Rather than address this rift, my mother turned to her religious group to fulfill all the emotional needs her family did not provide. At the meetings, she not only found a sense of belonging, she also found a lover.

Chapter 3

FIRST ESCAPE

*C*ome with me," a man said as he reached for my hand.

I looked back towards my mother and my two sisters who were a few yards away, playing on the large sidewalks that flanked Copacabana Beach.

"I cannot," I answered. "I need to ask my mother."

"There is no need to ask your mother," the tall man said with a sugary tone. "Come, I have a bonbon for you."

The bonbon tempted me. But I recalled the warnings that I should not talk to strangers. My eyes watered. I felt fear, but it was tempered by the desire to eat the promised bonbon.

"I need to ask my mother," I reluctantly said again.

The man betrayed his impatience and moved towards me, grabbing my arms. I screamed.

My mother, who had been distracted shopping among the street stalls that lined the broad sidewalk, looked my way. Sensing something was wrong, she left my two sisters behind as she quickly moved towards me. The man, realizing that his window of opportunity to snatch me had closed, disappeared among the crowd. I saw my mother's concerned, flustered face through the tears that freely flowed on my chubby cheeks.

"I could have lost you!" my mother said while hugging me tightly. She stared into my eyes, her tears now matching mine. "I will always protect you," she said while caressing my hair. She put her lips close to my face and whispered, "I promise."

It was not a promise she kept.

Chapter 4

TURNING POINT

*M*y mother hid her affair for four years from my father, as well as from me as I do not have early memories of Lauro. The only vague recollection I have of my mother's lover was when she closed the sliding doors that separated the living room from the rest of the apartment one day while the short, compact figure of a man stood next to her.

My father's promotion to the management ranks of IBM brought us to Sao Paulo, a concrete-jungle megalopolis that was a six hour drive—which, to my mother, was just as remote as moving to the other side of the world—from Rio. My mother resisted this move.

"We can't go. My parents will be too far away," she said.

"We will come visit them often," my father, always ready with a practical retort, replied.

"But they help me with the children; I need them around all the time. And they need to see the girls grow up," my mother protested.

"We have a maid. We have a nanny. Surely that's enough," my father retorted, frustrated. "We need to move because my job is what keeps paying for all the help. I can't be a manager if we stay in Rio."

"But I need to attend my meetings for my healing," she continued.

"We will find you doctors in Sao Paulo."

My mother, unable to state she did not want to be away from her lover, followed her husband to our new, whitewashed home on the outskirts of the largest city in Brazil.

Beyond a limited recollection of the smell of freshly baked bread my kindergarten class once prepared, the only memory I have of our year-long stay in Sao Paulo was my mother forgetting to pick me up one day at school. The school day ended in the early afternoon, and we typically returned home straight after. As the hours passed, I was left alone on the school grounds after all the other students had left.

"Where is your mother?" the principal asked me.

"I don't know," I said.

"Did she say she would be late today?" she asked.

I shook my head. The school had tried unsuccessfully to reach my mother by phone.

"Who else can come pick you up?"

"No one," I said.

There was no one. My grandparents lived in Rio. I had no idea whether my father was in town or traveling, but either way, I did not know how to contact him. My sisters were not at the same school, and I did not know where they might be.

The principal brought me to her office and offered me a bag of popcorn, which I gleefully accepted. I did not feel worried, but rather happy for the opportunity to play with friends and indulge in snacks. As the day turned into night, however, I felt distressed. At about seven o'clock, my mother arrived, flustered, profusely apologizing to the principal, but providing no excuse about her tardiness.

I never learned why she forgot me that day.

A few days later, we moved back to Rio de Janeiro.

We settled in a penthouse apartment and resumed our lives as if nothing had been interrupted by the year we spent in Sao Paulo. I resumed attending the Lycée Français, a French private school in the heart of the city. My father, as always, was absent most of the time. On the rare occasions he was around, he hardly paid attention to my sisters and me.

"The fact that your father wouldn't play with you or hug you made me wish that you had a different father," my mother once told me.

Finding herself again unhappy, but now with the threat of my father's career taking her away from her lover and her religious gatherings, my mother must have thought that time was ripe for a change. She must have thought her lover could compensate for the shortcomings of my father's aloof parenting style.

One afternoon a few days later, the movers came and swiftly cleaned our large apartment of our belongings and most of its furniture. My sisters and I did not understand what was happening as we returned from school, but we did notice that the house was void of our furniture, clothes, and toys.

"Where are all of our things?" I asked, surprised. How large our apartment looked now that it was empty!

"We are going on a trip," my mother simply said.

As we readied ourselves to exit the apartment, my mother stood in front of the fireplace in the now-empty living room, with its gleaming, hardwood floors, holding a white envelope in her hand. She slowly placed it on the fireplace mantel, lingering over the letter and rearranging it a couple of times, moving it so that it stood right in the center of the mantel piece in the darkened room. Now, whoever came through the sliding doors would immediately see the letter.

Within the envelope was a note, one that must have completely shocked my father, communicating that their marriage was over. In the letter, she also noted that we could not yet disclose our destination, but that she would contact my father—when she felt ready. She did not indicate how long this might take.

Later that week, my exhausted and jet-lagged father must have opened the door to his apartment, expecting to see his loud family greet him. Instead, he found an empty house.

"Let's go!" Lauro, whom I noticed for the first time, commanded, prompting us to move along and snapping my mother's gaze from the letter.

My mother closed the sliding door, and we all crammed into a small car, along with a few bags of our clothes. My sisters and I did not know our destination. We were not used to asking questions anyway.

We had never been on a road trip besides the move to and from Sao Paulo earlier that year, so this outing seemed to be an adventure. The tall buildings and the urban environment we lived in transformed into an industrial zone as we drove over the large, main thoroughfare that linked Rio de Janeiro with the rest of Brazil. The road, flanked by industrial parks and then by miles and miles of favelas, Brazilian slums, was packed with trucks and buses. It was so different from our leafy neighborhood. Here, masses of youth prowled the roads, despite the car-packed mayhem, offering water bottles or to wash car windows. They were dressed in rags, and they swarmed the roads.

Eventually, we left this mass of humanity as the car climbed a mountain highway that became increasingly lush and twisty. The favelas gave way to broad leaves and a dense forest. There were a handful of people manning mountain shacks along the way, offering coconut water and wooden, carved tools.

"Where are we going?" Nathalie asked.

"You will see when we arrive there," my mother answered.

Lauro mostly stayed quiet as he drove us up the mountain road. My sisters and I looked out of the car window, marveling about this whole new world we had never seen before.

After about one hour, we stopped in front of a white iron gate. There was a wooden sign next to the gate bell with "Shangrila" written in ornate lettering. Lauro greeted the man who opened the gates as if he were someone familiar, giving him a pat on the back.

We parked the car and walked over a grassy patch towards a large house. Rather than enter this large house, we climbed side steps to a round house placed just above it, on what should have been its roof. As my mother ushered us in, I noticed some of our furniture.

"Our couch is here!" Nathalie exclaimed.

"What is our couch doing here?" I asked, puzzled, turning to my mother.

My mother and Lauro stood in the center of the cramped living room that had our piano, our couch, and lots of boxes.

"This is your new home!" my mother cheerfully said, as if unveiling a special present.

"Will we live here?" I asked, still confused.

"Yes. Isn't it great?" she said

"What about our apartment?"

"We no longer live there. We live here," she repeated.

"What about Pappy? Will he know to find us here when he arrives home?" I asked.

My mother, stood beaming next to a man whose complexion resembled that of the indigenous Indians who live in the forest. He also had their short stature and almond shaped eyes; unlike Indians, however, his eyes were green, like ours.

Lauro came from the state of Acre in the western extreme of northern Brazil, bordering the Amazon forest. Acre is so sparsely populated that it was rare to meet someone who hailed from the state. Brazilians uncharitably call it the "end of Brazil." Thus, although Brazil is a veritable mix of people of all colors, Lauro did not quite look like anyone we had ever seen.

"Lauro is your new father," my mother told us, presenting her lover to us.

My sisters and I opened our mouths wide, not quite understanding what my mother meant. The three of us looked at him, then to my mother, and finally to each other, betraying confusion and a little bit of fear, not fully understanding how a stranger could take such an important role in our lives. How could this man that we may have seen once or twice before suddenly become our father? I was six years old. I felt confused, but I could not articulate what I felt. Neither could I understand what my mother was saying. My first thought was that something awful must have happened to my father.

"What happened to Pappy?" I asked, fearful of the answer, feeling a deep knot on my stomach.

"He hasn't been a father to you," she responded curtly, hardening the tone of her voice. "Now you will see what it is like to have a real father."

Chapter 5

ARRIVING IN SHANGRILA

hangrila was meant to be a vacation retreat. There were no phones in the house or, as far as I could tell, anywhere in the whole region either. Phone lines had not yet made their way to this remote area. To communicate, the few neighbors knocked on each other's doors, which they did often when the small supermarket that served the area ran out of supplies before weekly deliveries restocked it. There was no bus service. The area had a few vacation homes interspersed in the hills and the beginning of slums that housed the caretakers of these homes. The only businesses there, besides the small supermarket, were a bar and a church.

Shangrila became a make-shift farm more by accident than by design. It was a weekend getaway for its owners, who stayed in the house below ours. The property itself was a bit of a commune. The owner of Shangrila thought others might also want to use his family's weekend getaway to escape the oppressive heat and humidity of Rio de Janeiro. He built small homes on the property that he rented to people who preferred the mild weather and coolness of the mountain air—or to people like my family, who wanted to disappear from mainstream society.

Our house was completely round. Why our landlord built a round house on top of his own sprawling, rectangular one remained a mystery. Our living quarters occupied half of the circle, with all rooms shaped like pie slices, leaving wide gaps between the furniture and the walls.

A large room facing the highway took the other half of the round house, with the original intent to serve as a party hall. Tall columns protruded towards a raised roof in the center of the house, allowing light and air in. A staircase to the top hugged the wall, leading to a spectacular view of the lush, surrounding mountains and the valley below.

From the windows of our pie-shaped bedroom, we could see the canopy of trees that surrounded the property and beyond that, an imposing mountain range bordering the valley that stood in front of our house. Everywhere we looked, there was greenery, lushness, and fertility. Thunderstorms occurred frequently, causing the familiar, earthy smell in the late afternoons, resulting from the wet soil that was quickly dried by tropical air.

Surrounded by fertile soils and abundant rain, tons of fruits and vegetables grew on the property. The fruit trees sprouted illogically, allowed to grow where they may. A huge avocado tree, taller than our second-story perch, provided shade and plenty of fruit. The fruits were so abundant that they fell to the floor below in a big splat, spreading their green mess on the rocky paths and making walking and bike riding slippery and treacherous. The mangos and papaya trees were so heavy with fruit that their limbs lowered a few inches at the height of the growing season. Cocoa trees abounded, as did an endless supply of sugar canes. We had but to extend our hands—or climb the trees—to feast on the bounty of fruits and vegetables. If we wanted a pineapple, we simply went outside to grab one. Bananas were so easily reachable that we never stored them in the house. We spent countless afternoons following the landlord's gardener around as he whacked through the dense vegetation surrounding the property. We loved to sink our teeth into the morsels of juicy sugar cane stalks. He used his large machete to remove the thick, dark skin surrounding its center and then let us feast. We chewed down the stalks, letting all the juices stick on our hands, mouths, and clothes as we hungrily drank in the sweetness. The landlord dammed a pond deep in the forest, creating a make-shift pool for humid days.

Then there were the animals. Animal pens housed chickens, ducks, and pigs. A kennel lodged multiple dogs, whose purpose was to guard the property at night and, apparently, to make deafening noises with their incessant barking as they protested their confinement during the day. Snakes and bats were regular visitors, as were countless insects, moths, and butterflies, which surrounded the lamps and light bulbs at night. None of the many windows that abutted the circumference of the house had screens. The windows remained open through the night as it was the only way to cool off. The butterflies and moths descended en masse immediately after sunset, placing themselves around the incandescent lamps that stood high on the walls, touching the light and warmth. The mass of insects stayed around the lamps until we turned off the lights. We did not fear them. Insects and moths were just part of the landscape. By morning, when the symphony of wild birds woke us up, all insects were gone, flying back outdoors to enjoy the warm day as the sun rose.

During the day, there were tons of opportunities to get dirty and muddy and to be free. We tromped into the large yard that had no boundaries on its mountain sides and descended into a deep canyon, allowing us to explore as far and wide as we wanted.

Shangrila could have been our Shangri-La.

Instead, it was a prison.

Chapter 6
REGRET

Shangrila's distance and isolation suited my mother.

"You should feel grateful that we now live here," my mother said when we complained that we missed Rio or my father. "Growing up in the jungle is how kids should be raised. Besides, Rio is dangerous, chaotic, and loud. I need to be here so that I can recover from my illnesses."

Yet, my mother still refused to see a doctor, choosing instead to sleep, meditate, and pray in her search for healing. On the rare occasions when my sisters or I got sick, the doctors came on house calls, their bags brimming with medicine and medical instruments. Despite her frequent complaints about her health, the doctor never once was summoned to check on my mother. In general, my sisters and I hardly saw our mother as she spent a considerable part of the day in her room, laying on her bed because she felt dizzy or tired. A cleaning lady cooked simple meals for us. Otherwise, we were mostly left on our own.

Lauro quickly filled the vacuum my mother had created by her illness and disinterest. With nobody to rein him in, he barked orders as soon as we set foot on Shangrila. Some orders were necessary to keep the household in order. Most, however, were completely unreasonable. Despite having a cleaning lady, he constantly asked us to clean what the maid had already done. We were not allowed to enter the half of the house that he planned to turn into a temple and were strictly forbidden from taking the circular steps up to the roof. Whenever he had visitors, we were not to speak to them.

At the religious meetings where he met my mother, Lauro was just one more person among many worshippers. In remote Shangrila, he grabbed power by placing a leadership mantle on himself.

"I have a mission to accomplish," he often said. "I will be answering God's call."

"What mission is that?" I asked.

"I will father the next Jesus," he said.

Lauro was not much of a conversationalist. Whenever he talked, it was to tell someone what to do or to state some truth, such as "I am the chosen one." His favorite phrase was, "You must do as I tell you, not as I do." This was especially true on occasions where he barked an order that we were sure he would not follow himself. He never engaged in conversation long enough for anyone to question his certainty about his role in the world. He expected those who knew of him and his importance to profess total obedience and adoration, the same way Catholic Brazilians worshipped the true son of God.

"Yes, he is, indeed," my mother confirmed before we could question the veracity of these claims. "His destiny is to father the next Jesus," she would say, nodding her head.

"Mom," I questioned, "if Lauro was meant to father a boy, how come Catherine is a girl?"

My mother slapped me for this question.

"Don't be insolent," she said.

I soon learned not to ask too many questions—even when most things did not make sense.

In order to establish himself as the next Messiah, Lauro needed to create a following. Shortly after we arrived in Shangrila, worshippers trickled to our house to attend meetings on Wednesday nights.

My mother did not engage in setting up these meetings, choosing instead to spend her days locked in her bedroom. On the rare occasions when she woke up from the stupor of her illness and the dizzying pace at which our lives were changing, my mom must have realized that her new situation was not quite an improvement from the life she had before. She must have realized moving to Shangrila was a mistake and that she should leave while she could. It dawned on her that she followed a control freak, who made everyone miserable with his grandiose plans that did not seem all that coherent. She had a change of heart.

Swallowing her pride, about two months after our move to Shangrila, my mother asked my grandparents, during one of their visits, to contact my father to tell him where he could find us. She invited him to see his daughters and to a meeting to talk about the future.

Within the week, my sisters and I ran towards our father as he arrived at Shangrila's front gate. After a brief hello, he walked the tree-lined path that led to the stairs to the round house to talk with my mother. We followed, but my mother told us to go back to the yard and stay there until she called us.

My parents talked for about an hour. Despite our curiosity, any attempts my sisters and I made to hear their discussion were met by a closed door.

My mother later told me what transpired. She admitted to my father that she erred in moving to Shangrila. She neglected, however, to point out that she had a lover and that her relationship with Lauro was not a momentary weakness, but an affair she had carried on for years. Wanting to give my father the assurance that she would easily end this misguided adventure, she admitted to making a poor choice, but insisted that she had learned her lesson. In short, she wanted a chance to work on their marriage—a chance she never took in the past ten years.

My mother would not admit whether she believed in anything she claimed. She would say anything she thought would lead her back to the life she had rejected because it was infinitely better than the one she now lived.

"We are a family. We should stay together," my mother pleaded with the finality of a done deal. Our suitcases, packed and lined up in the living room, were at the ready so that my father could simply drive us back to Rio de Janeiro at the end of that conversation.

"We stopped being a family the day you decided to leave!" my father curtly responded.

Until that moment, my mother held the illusion that my father would do whatever it took to keep the family together, a conclusion based on years of him dutifully following her whims. She thought she could, at any time, revert the damage her lack of forethought caused. She counted on my father's strong sense of duty and responsibility. Resuming their marriage was her poorly conceived fallback plan as she had not anticipated needing one.

If the circumstances had been different, perhaps my father would have considered her plea. He perhaps would have even forgiven her, and our family could have remained as one.

There was, however, an unexpected wrinkle to my mother's regret-fueled plans to leave Shangrila. By the time my mother realized the foolishness of her decision, within the short weeks since their separation, my father had met Carroll.

Carroll was an American who came to Brazil to lead a training class for computer programmers at IBM that my father attended. Although Carroll lived in New York, she transferred to the IBM Sao Paulo offices shortly after meeting my father. Now that Carroll moved countries to be with him, my father thought it was an acceptable compromise to move back to Sao Paulo, where both his and Carroll's career could progress. He had already vacated our penthouse in Rio de Janeiro and rented a house in Sao Paulo that he would share with Carroll.

Therefore, my father heard my mother's pleas for reconciliation with the cool detachment that characterized his interactions with just about anyone. "I now have a responsibility towards Carroll," he responded to my mother when she asked him to reconsider his decision for the sake of his children.

"To a woman you just met? What about your responsibility towards your daughters?"

"Children of divorce don't suffer."

"Of course they do!" my mother said, purposely forgetting that she was the one who caused their separation.

"No, they don't!" he insisted.

"How would you know?" she asked sarcastically.

"Carroll told me so," he said to my stunned mother, who laughed at the idea that a woman who did not have children would know what is best for them.

"She knows," my father continued, "because her parents are divorced, and she told me she did not suffer."

Not quite expecting this rejection, my mother still did not relent. My mother pleaded, "If you don't do it for me, at least do it for the children."

"They will be fine," my father stated. My father stormed out of the house without saying goodbye. My mother recognized, too late and with utter disbelief, that my father had had enough and that she had put herself and her children on a path from which she could not turn away. She was too weak and too heartbroken to fight it. We would stay in Shangrila.

My father, visibly upset, met us in the yard as he walked towards his car.

"Are we going home, Pappy?" I asked.

"This is your home now," he said and quickly left.

My mother soon forgot that it was she who betrayed and left my father first. My father's choice of creating a life with Carroll hurt my mother deeply. She ensured my sisters and I would never forget that Carroll was nothing more than my father's mistress. Constantly reminding us that my father was a bastard who abandoned his daughters, she insisted that it was my father—not she or her lover—who bore the responsibility for the misery of our lives.

My father's rejection of her plea for reconciliation hurt deeply for another reason. Brazilians, being a deeply religious people, frowned on divorces, which were not sanctioned by the Catholic Church. Surely, a divorced couple was so because the woman must have brought that shame upon the family. Women were supposed to endure bad marriages. Affairs, typically those carried on by the husband, were common place, and it wasn't enough reason to break up a marriage. It happened all the time, and the Brazilian way to deal with it was to turn a blind eye until the husband got tired of his mistress once she demanded more than he wanted to give. Nobody divorced in Brazil. And where relationships did end, the women surely must have caused their husbands to leave them.

Despite the deep cultural resistance, the law allowing divorces was enacted in 1975. Thus, my French parents had the dubious honor of being the fifth couple to divorce in all of Brazil and the first in the city of Petropolis.

Divorced women were quickly shunned in the deeply religious and male-dominated society. Thus, her divorced status filled my mother with shame. The resulting outcome was a complete withdrawal from the world at large. Her shame at being divorced was just too great. Thus, she devised a plan. If she told the world that Lauro was, indeed, our father, then nobody would think of her as a divorced woman. Better yet, if she did not interact with anyone, then she would not feel judged or blamed. She figured her withdrawal from the world would not have many adverse consequences. She knew that Lauro would step in and be the parent that she either refused to be or was incapable of being.

Lauro wasted no time taking advantage of the role that life, and my mother's weakness, gave him.

Chapter 7

PATH TO THE ROUND HOUSE

*B*efore she fell ill, my mother often spoke of her childhood in France and the tumultuous journey that led her to Brazil. She often spoke with a sense of longing, betraying a regret for not having particularly lived a life she wanted and for carrying within her unfulfilled dreams.

There was not much to do in Shangrila. The farm abutted a lush highway connecting vibrant Rio de Janeiro with colonial Petropolis, a smaller city where Brazil's former emperor once vacationed in its cool and lush mountains. When we were not playing outdoors—collecting the abundance of fruit weighing down trees, taking care of chickens, ducks, and dogs, or trying to kill snakes—we passed the time hearing my mother tell stories of her past, stories she often repeated with greater detail each time, as to ensure we fully understood the extent of our family's struggles.

"Did you know that Grandmother Mathilda never knew her birth date?" my mother asked.

"Really?" I asked, surprised. "How can one not know the day of her birth?"

"Well, in Egypt people did not register births. There were so many children, and many died young because they were poor and ill," my mother responded.

"Was Grandma Mathilda poor and ill?" I asked.

"Yes, they were very poor. Grandma started working when she was fourteen years old to help support the family. See, it is the job of the children to help support the family too!" she said, looking at me.

My sisters and I looked concerned about the hardships our grandmother may have experienced.

"I see you are concerned, but you need not be," my mother said. "It ended well; we chose a birthday for her, and now she can celebrate like everybody else, one day each year."

And through these tidbits of information, we learned about the tortuous path my family took from remote lands on the other side of the world to Shangrila, our home on the little farm that was situated miles away from anywhere, in the jungles of Brazil.

Grandmother Mathilda met Isidore Hodara at work in her native Cairo, in Egypt, "Where civilization began," my grandmother often said.

My grandfather, born in Ankara, Turkey, hailed from a family of low economic means and too many children. Not having enough money to educate all their children, my great grandparents chose to invest their limited resources on Isidore's older brother, who moved to Paris to study medicine. With all the resources focused on the older son, Grandfather Isidore was left to fend for himself, which led to an unrelenting anger about not being the family's chosen one. Feeling neglected by his own family, he left the family home in Ankara on a whim and crossed the Black Sea to Egypt to try his luck in its sprawling capital, Cairo.

When he met my then fourteen-year-old grandmother, he promptly said he would marry her. And despite my grandmother's young age, that is what they did. Months later, they welcomed their first daughter, Paulette Hodara, my mother, into their lives.

Despite Grandfather Isidore's claims of an enviable work ethic at his Jesuit school, there were never good enough jobs and never enough money for his growing family, especially after my Uncle Sylvain was born two years later. Not having attended college, Isidore was simply one of the millions of uneducated Arab youth with limited economic prospects.

Cairo, the largest city in the Arab world and Africa, housed a million people within its sprawling city limits and additional millions in its suburbs. Cairo had an abundance of crowds, pollution, and violence, but a shortage of educational and economic opportunities, especially for foreign Turks. Cairo was in disarray because of World Word II. Although the ground wars occurred in Europe, Egypt experienced shortages of food and tools, as all that was of value was rerouted to Europe to support the war. Those who could leave Egypt did. Meanwhile, Isidore's brother who lived in Paris constantly wrote of his abundant life, despite the war. Through his brother, my grandfather found a way to move away from Cairo to seek better economic opportunities.

Upon arrival in Paris, my family settled in the brother's apartment until Isidore could find a job. My grandmother, young and inexperienced, now had two toddlers and soon would have a third child. She did not work. The end of World War II signaled promises of abundant economic opportunities as France picked itself up from the German invasion and resulting destruction. Yet, as an uneducated Arab, Isidore had difficulties finding meaningful work. When he could not sit for exams that would open employment opportunities, he walked around the cobblestone streets of Paris, knocking on doors, practically begging for people to give him a chance. His persistence paid off. He obtained a job as a door-to-door salesman, trolling various sorts of equipment, including lamps and typewriters.

Despite the lack of progress in my family's economic prospects, my grandfather felt wealthy in ways money could not buy. He had in my mother an unusually beautiful child, with a large set of clear, sparkling green eyes. No one else in the family had eyes of such color, and my grandfather never tired of mentioning my mother's beauty.

"I can see your soul when I look into your eyes, Cherie," my grandfather often said when doting upon my mother.

"I could do no wrong with my father," my mother told me. "He was so tough and strict with Sylvain and then with my baby sister, Simone. But me, he treated me as a precious princess! I always got what was the best, and what was left went to my brother and sister."

Isidore worked tirelessly, yet his earnings were so limited that the only difference between his life in Egypt and in France was that in Cairo at least he felt a sense of belonging. In Paris, he was an Arab with limited prospects. His ego suffered seeing his brother, now a doctor, so successful and so needed in the immediate aftermath of the war. He witnessed how his brother's living conditions improved along with his success, while his own life remained lackluster. After three years, Isidore moved my family to Nice, in the south of France, seeking better luck, sunshine, and some distance from his doctor brother. In Nice, Isidore got a job selling large motors to other businesses.

The Hodaras life in Nice was relatively modest. They lived in a simple house and sent their kids to school nicely dressed. They put their past behind them, and for all intents and purposes, the family became French, in their ways and love of country. Arabic was no longer their primary language, as my grandparents spoke only French with their children so that they would better assimilate in their new country. My family almost forgot their Arab roots.

The French people, however, constantly reminded them of where they came from. The French taunted my family frequently about their origins—at work, around the neighborhood, and especially at school.

"Odeur de rat," my mother's classmates shouted at her in fits of laughter. The family name, Hodara, converted nicely in French to the moniker that meant "the smell of rats." It did not escape my grandparents that the French think of some immigrants groups as pests, as rodents, as rats.

My mother and her siblings often returned from school crying whenever the epithet was hurled in their faces at school, reminding them of their rightful place in the pecking order of French life.

"We are French!" my mother protested feebly, as she did not remember any other life that she may have lived before the move to France.

"We are!" my grandmother agreed.

"How come my friends keep telling me I smell like a rat?" my mother asked.

"They are not your friends," Grandfather Isidore said bitterly.

"They will stop. You will see. That is only the joke of the moment," Grandmother Mathilda said in a more conciliatory tone.

"A very bad joke," Isidore said.

But it did not stop. As the jeering continued, the family's outsider status in the country they loved hurt their pride deeply.

"We are not rats!" Isidore exclaimed when anger claimed the best of him.

Grandfather Isidore's indignant stance was not restricted to wanting to protect his children from bullying. While Isidore did work, his heritage prevented him from getting promotions and other opportunities. He had two seemingly insurmountable challenges. The first was his lack of education. In France, one's school determined which employment exams he could take. The exams established which jobs one could apply for. In short, education determined one's economic destiny. Thus, my grandfather had to be content with where he was and hope for no more.

Lack of education was not even the most significant obstacle. My family was also considered illegal immigrants. To obtain meaningful work, they needed to become French citizens.

Understanding these requirements, Isidore applied for French citizenship five years after his arrival in Paris, as per the protocols at the time. His first attempt was denied. He tried again. And was denied again. He tried every two years. Every two years, he received a rejection, which wounded his pride and self-esteem.

He persevered out of pride, but mostly because there was no other choice. At least my mother and Uncle Sylvain had Egyptian passports. Aunt Simone was "sans terre," a term coined for those who did not have a claim to any land. She had been born in France, as such she was not Egyptian. But no one in her family was French, so she could not claim citizenship in her country of birth.

Isidore felt increasingly stuck.

Soon his love of France turned into hate.

My mother and her siblings did not know any different and did not share Isidore's change of heart. Despite the constant jeering at school, France was home for them. It was all they knew. It was where they studied, played, worked, and loved. Life was perhaps challenging, but as any proper French person, they felt they lived in the best country in the world. They did not foresee any possibility of or need for a change.

Chapter 8

BUILDING OF A CITY

$\mathcal{I}$n the late 1950s, Rio de Janeiro was Brazil's capital. The city, located in the southeastern portion of the country, along its famed shores, housed the majority of Brazilians. Brazil is a vast country, with a landmass larger than that of the continental United States. Yet, hardly anyone ventured out from the coast to the center of this dry, hot country. Despite its size, most of the country was desolate, undeveloped, and sparsely populated.

The president of Brazil at the time, Juscelino Kubitschek, was set on mining the natural resources that existed in the middle of that vast land. He looked at the map of Brazil and, sight unseen, selected a location exactly in the middle of the country.

"Here is where we will build a new capital!" he told his government, pointing his finger on the center of the map. From this new city, to be called Brasilia, the distance to the four corners of the country—north, south, east, or west—will be exactly the same.

Intent on achieving this vision, the president launched a competition for the design of a city to rise from the flat, dusty, and hot uninhabited land. This new city would enable a shift in the population centers, increase access to natural resources, and decrease distances between far-flung places. Brazil spared no resources to make this plan a reality.

Aspiring architects submitted more than fifty-five hundred designs in the competition for building the new capital. Brasilia was built in forty-one months, in the shape of an airplane. The suburbs of the city were located on the wings of the airplane. The cockpit housed the buildings for the Senate and other governing bodies. The commercial areas made up the rest of the body of the plane. The unveiling of the new city, in April of 1960, ended Rio de Janeiro's position as the country's capital, which it had held for more than two hundred years since the 1700s.

Naturally, significant resources, engineering know-how, and people were required to build a city from scratch. Brazil, at the time, did not have the expertise nor the machinery for such an undertaking. So it reached beyond its borders to acquire equipment and expertise wherever it could. Given that there were not sufficient numbers of qualified Brazilians for this massive project, the country cast a wide net outside its border. Brazil opened its doors wide for anyone who could make its dream of building the capital city a reality.

That is where the fate of this new city and the fate of my family intersected.

Brazilian businessmen travelled to Nice, a French city known for its great engineering capabilities. Their search for large equipment and motors led them to the company where Grandfather Isidore worked. Isidore's curiosity peaked as the Brazilian scouts milled around, so he inquired about this grand plan for a city. The idea that a city would arise out of nothing seemed incredibly futuristic.

"France would never build a city from nothing!" Isidore marveled to his family, referring to France's zeal in preserving its own history, keeping the future at bay. "The Brazilians can be so visionary!"

The Brazilian businessmen told Isidore tales of easy jobs and easier living. The clincher was the assurance that Brazil, in its need to recruit skilled people and obtain capital for the expansion plans, was offering citizenship. All one had to do was ask for it—even those without much formal education, as was the case with my grandfather. Highly doubtful of this claim, Isidore visited the Brazilian consulate in Paris to inquire about receiving the citizenship for himself and his family. Within a week, all five of them, Isidore, Mathilda, and their three children, had Brazilian passports.

"We are going to be part of history!" Isidore exclaimed through tears of joy to his family as he waved their new passports. "They built a city out of dust. We will build our lives out of dust too," he joyously cried upon receiving their new passports.

"We will need to leave France," Grandmother Mathilda said, concerned, "and everything we know. This is our home."

"France is not our home," Isidore said bitterly. "The French do not want us here. And this," he said, waving the passports, "this is our golden ticket to a respectable life. We will leave the humiliation we suffer among the French, who never let us forget we are Arabs. I will show them how proud I am to be Arab. We are going to a country full of possibilities while they stay here rotting and clinging to their past."

It was not as if my grandmother, mother, or her siblings could do much to protest this significant change in their lives. They followed my grandfather's plan because that is what children, even adult ones, did. They followed their parents.

"It never occurred to me to stay," my mother later explained, when I asked her why she did not stay behind in France. "Besides, what would I do? I failed twice to pass the baccalaureate." The baccalaureate was the standard test given to high school students for acceptance into the French university system. "I was twenty years old, but I did not want, nor did I plan, to work."

Rather than study or work, my mother spent her days traipsing around Nice, looking fashionably French, content to be loved by her boyfriend and by her family. She was also content to let others make decisions for her.

"I had Jean-Robert," my mother continued. "If he had asked me to marry him, I would have stayed," my mother said with a deep sigh.

Yet, he had not asked her to marry him in the days preceding her departure. "I was sure Jean-Robert wanted to marry me, but that he was waiting until the last minute so he could dramatically propose to me on the dock as the ship was about to leave. I just knew Jean-Robert would come and surprise me," she trailed off wistfully.

Jean-Robert was her boyfriend of two years, from whom she was inseparable. "I spent days planning how to tell my parents that I would not board the ship once Jean-Robert came to fetch me at the port."

Not aware of my mother's plans to be swept off her feet, my grandfather sold all the family's furniture and belongings to purchase one-way tickets to cross the Atlantic. The five of them stuffed the limited items they each had left into a few suitcases.

Jean-Robert did not accompany my mother to the port. He was not present as the family loaded their small suitcases and as they walked the platform that separated them from land and their life in France. My mother scanned the large crowds, expecting to see Jean-Robert among the throngs that milled about. Finally, the blare of the siren called all passengers to board. "I felt pain in the core of my stomach," my mother said. "I desperately searched the crowds, willing my eyes to see Jean-Robert's handsome face. I felt sure he'd be there. I felt sure I did not see him because he must have gotten lost in the crowd. There was no way that he would not have come."

The ship set sail, rendering the crowds smaller until they disappeared on the horizon a few minutes after the raising of the anchor. My mother unleashed a torrent of tears as she realized that the choice to follow her parents to a foreign land was then made for her. Grandmother Mathilda held her tight, thinking that my mother's despair was due to the fear of an unknown place and future, not because she wished to stay behind.

"I cried during the entire two-week trip across the ocean," my mother said. "When I realized I would not see Jean-Robert again, I thought I would die!"

Yet she did not die.

Upon landing in Brazil, she wrote a letter to her boyfriend as soon as she disembarked in Rio de Janeiro in 1960, asking why he had not come, worried that something, other than his own choice, must have prevented him from seeing her off.

Jean-Robert did not reply.

As the hope of hearing from her boyfriend faded, my mother joined her family in their intention to build a new life in Rio.

It was not as easy as Isidore had pictured. The plentiful jobs they expected did not materialize. Brasilia had been inaugurated, thus the work opportunities there dried up. The opportunities in Rio de Janeiro, never known as a thriving economic place, were dwindling too.

At least in France, my family understood the reasons why they experienced economic hardship. In Brazil, there existed a byzantine code for finding a job, renting a place, or doing anything. It was not about the rules anyway. It was about who one knew and how expensive the bribes were. My family knew no one, having arrived in Rio with little more than hope that their lives would just miraculously work out. Instead, the family found itself in a foreign country, where they did not speak the language, did not have jobs, and did not have friends. They did not know how to navigate a landscape mired in poverty, violence, and crushing humidity. They could not afford to pay bribes and did not understand how to go about doing so anyway. Having sold all they had to make the crossing, they simply did not have the means to return to France.

As soon as they landed in Rio de Janeiro, the family regretted their decision.

"I guess having a passport is just the beginning of another set of problems!" Grandmother Mathilda exclaimed in frustration while wiping her brow from the sweat caused by the searing heat and scratching the welts from mosquito bites. "We should go back to France on the next ship!"

Grandfather Isidore, always a hustler, assessed their situation. "Don't worry," he said, trying to calm the chorus of complaints emanating from his wife and children once they realized that Brazil was not an improvement from their life in Nice. "We created a life in France; we will create a life here too."

He had good intentions, but in reality, my grandfather could not create much of anything. Shortly after their arrival in Rio de Janeiro, Isidore felt a sharp pain in his back. He had liver disease. Instead of looking for a job, he went to the emergency room and underwent surgery. His recovery took months.

It fell on my mother and Uncle Sylvain, then, respectively twenty and eighteen years-old, to support the family. Grandmother Mathilda claimed she was too old to learn Portuguese and to work, plus she needed to care for my aunt, then eleven years old, and for her sick husband.

Out of necessity, my mother got the first job she held in her life, along with her brother, at a bookstore in downtown Rio de Janeiro. Each was paid half the minimum wage. Between the two of them, they earned one meager, minimum-wage salary. By any standard, this was not sufficient to support a family of five.

Yet, they carried on for a few months. My mother, hating the bookstore, eventually found work as a teacher at the Lycee Français, a French-immersion private school where she tutored the children of diplomats who struggled with French.

Isidore recovered from his illness after a few months. He could no longer work as a door-to-door salesman, primarily because of his inability to speak Portuguese fluently, but his weakened health also posed a problem. Foreigners were a rarity in Brazil, and where there were any, they were mostly Spanish-speaking people from nearby Argentina.

Eventually, Isidore took a desk job at a government agency that processed income taxes, checking their accuracy. Neither his nationality nor his accent prevented him from sitting behind a desk crunching numbers. Despite being far from one, he called himself an economist, a profession he proudly described when anyone asked what he did for a living. While Isidore did not hold a glamorous job, for the first time in his life, he felt a sense of stability in his professional life. He finally got citizenship for himself and for his family, and they were no longer ridiculed, nor discriminated against, for being Arabs. His salary was modest, but it was enough to afford a miniscule, two-bedroom apartment a couple of blocks from the famed Copacabana Beach. Isidore was finally happy, or at least, he was content enough with his life and his decisions.

Mathilda, my mother, my aunt, and uncle thought otherwise. They complained about the monotony of eating rice and beans every single day, the suffocating humidity that engulfed Rio over the summer months, and the immense economic disparity among the population. Such disparity created a deprived underclass who preyed on the possessions of those who appeared to have anything worth stealing. It was unsafe to step out by oneself, which limited how often the family could spend time outside. None of them spoke a word of Portuguese when they first arrived. They had left all their friends behind in France.

Even Mathilda, normally supportive of and compliant with her husband's decisions, felt unhappy. While Isidore openly mocked France, the rest of the family searched for any kind of experience that would tie them to France as they adjusted to this new, hot, humid, and unsafe land. Since they did not have the financial wherewithal to go back to France, they did the next closest thing. They joined the Alliance Française, which provided French citizens living in Rio de Janeiro a meeting place, as well as social events where one could consume French food, drink French wine, watch French movies, and meet French people—such as my father.

Chapter 9

LOVER LEFT BEHIND

I often thought of Jean-Robert, even though he did not write back when we arrived in Brazil," my mother told me when she steered the conversation towards her former boyfriend. "I thought about the many reasons why this could be. I did not understand. So I felt alone in Brazil, and your father seemed so interested in me. Plus, your father and I were in the same station in life. We both had just arrived in Brazil, and he understood what it was like to feel out of place."

The only commonality between my father and Jean-Robert was that they were both French. My father's green eyes, curly, light hair, and fair complexion was the opposite of Jean-Robert's dark figure. My father was quiet and reserved. Jean-Robert was surrounded by friends and women.

My father was smitten with my mother.

"I would catch your father simply staring at me," my mother told me. "It mostly made me feel uncomfortable. Yet, he was nice and kind. And I felt so alone. More than anything, I did not want to feel alone."

They kept each other company, attending events at the Alliance Française. My grandparents became fond of him as they noted how helpful my father was to them and how solicitous he behaved towards my mother. My father, mostly alone in Brazil, became a frequent guest at my grandparents' apartment for meals and conversation.

Soon, they all fell into a comfortable routine.

In his letters back to his family in France, my father described Rio de Janeiro as a fascinating place. He wrote about his experiences enthusiastically, perhaps some of it colored by being in love. These letters inspired my grandparents Laja and Rachmiel, as well as his sister, Aunt Paule, to move to Brazil. Rachmiel had developed arthritis. The drizzly, cold Paris weather caused his joints to hurt. They all thought that the tropical heat of Brazil would serve him well, so the entire family moved to Rio de Janeiro.

None of them, however, understood, once they arrived in Rio, what had so attracted my father to this place. Grandfather Rachmiel detested the humidity, the food, and the lack of security. Plus, his health deteriorated as his left leg became swollen due to a blood clot. He acquired an infection that would not heal. My father's French family was appalled at the poor quality of health care in Brazil, compared to what they previously had in France. Not trusting the quality of medical care in the tropical jungles of Brazil, nor the heat, poverty, or lack of safety, the Gecils swiftly returned to France after a few months, calling Brazil a godforsaken place. Rachmiel demanded that my father accompany the family back to France in this moment of family crisis. The Algerian War had also ended, and my father had to return to France sooner or later to complete his mandatory military service.

My father said goodbye to my mother to accompany his own family back to France.

"We will meet again. I assure you," he said as he departed.

"When?" my mother asked, this time witnessing her boyfriend leave her to board a ship that would cross the Atlantic Ocean.

"I don't know when," my father admitted, "but I will do what I can to see you again."

They both knew that my father's return was unlikely as obligations to his family in France would keep him in Europe. My parents had no concrete plans to reunite.

Once back in France, Grandfather Rachmiel's leg infection festered, and soon after, he had it amputated. He walked with a prosthetic leg and resumed working. Soon after, another blood clot formed, and this time it traveled to his brain, causing a stroke that left him paralyzed and unable to speak. It fell to my father to support the family. Thus, he postponed his plans to return to Brazil to help his family settle. Grandmother Laja, who had not worked in twenty years, took up a job sewing clothes. Aunt Paule found a job as a secretary. Not knowing what to do next and heeding the protests from Grandmother Laja against his return to Brazil, my father registered for the mandatory two years of military service, which he spent in a peace-time assignment in Germany and Switzerland. He sent his modest military wages back to my grandmother and aunt.

In his army barracks, my father wrote to my mother to pass the time. His quiet nature, honed from years of listening to the horrors of the war, made him shun conversation and become more of an observer. What he did not do with words, however, he did in writing. He wrote lovely letters to my mother, using cursive handwriting on long sentences that I hardly recognized as belonging to my father, who, by the time I came to know him, wrote in brief sentences using block letters. These letters described the incredible landscapes of Switzerland, my father's profound dislike for the army, and his bottomless love for my mother.

There was often a two-week delay from the time my father mailed a letter to when my mother received it. Often it would be two or three months between the times they exchanged letters. My mother no longer considered herself in a relationship with my father, but she enjoyed receiving these letters as they broke the monotony of her life.

More than a year after my father's return to France, my mother received a letter with a French stamp addressed to her, but on it, the handwriting was familiar, though now a distant memory. She held her breath momentarily and heard her heartbeat accelerate as she recognized the penmanship of her former lover, Jean-Robert, whom she had left behind three years earlier. While she had not forgotten him, she had, after so many years, accepted that he had forgotten her. Or at least she thought so since he had never before responded to her letters.

Chere Paulette,

I threw your address in the ocean once I received your first letter. I never thought I would survive the pain of your departure. I thought I would die of despair. I wanted to forget you and the pain you caused me when you boarded the ship that took you away from me.

I write now because I met your cousin at a café in Nice. We spoke longingly of you, and she gave me your address.

I, many times, wished I had been a stronger man to have held on to you. With love, Jean-Robert

This letter erased all my mother's previous efforts to forget her former lover. It was impossible to avoid comparing the passionately written letter from Jean-Robert with the much more restrained ones sent by my father. Irrespective of what role my father had in her heart, the unexpected letter from Jean-Robert rekindled the buried passion my mother felt for him. The man she had always loved also loved her back! Yet, an ocean separated them. She needed to see Jean-Robert. She needed to return to France to reconnect with the love of her life.

My mother did not have many available options. She did not earn enough to pay for a return trip to France. My grandparents were not supportive of the idea of her return, especially because they approved of my father and knew he had been corresponding with her. Not finding an immediate solution, my mother's despair from being stuck in Brazil grew. She promptly wrote back to Jean-Robert, confessing how much she loved him still.

Not enough time passed for Jean-Robert to write back before suddenly an unexpected opportunity materialized. My mother was serving as a French language tutor for the daughters of a diplomat, and the family planned to return to France. They offered that my mother accompany them to ease their daughters' transition.

"Move to France with us," they offered. "This way, you can continue tutoring our daughters. It will be so hard for them to adapt to France and to have to speak French fluently. They need someone with whom they can speak Portuguese during their adjustment period."

My mother could not believe her luck.

"Yes, of course," she said, without reflecting on what she was doing, not bothering to check with her parents, my father, or anyone else. My mother had found a path to return to France. And she would let no one stand in her way.

Within a few weeks, she accompanied the French family to Paris.

Once my father learned my mother was unexpectedly in France, he promptly took a week-long leave from the army to welcome her. Joyfully believing that my mother returned to France to resume their relationship, my father introduced her as his fiancée, despite never formally asking my mother to marry him.

My mother did not correct him. Yet, sensing that this impending marriage was moving faster than she could manage, she planned to visit Nice as soon as possible. She longed to see Jean-Robert again, before it was too late.

"I will go to Nice," my mother told my father.

"Would you want me to accompany you and meet your family?" my father asked.

"No!" she quickly responded. "It's been so long since I saw my cousins; I want to spend some time with them alone."

She contacted her cousins and close girlfriends, mostly because she did not know how to find Jean-Robert and hoped one of them would have a phone number for him. Her cousins did provide my mother with the number she sought. Once she had this prized information in her hand, she called her former boyfriend during an afternoon when the family with whom she lived left for an outing.

Jean-Robert answered the phone, and my mother blurted out, "Jean-Robert, I am back,"

"Paulette?" Jean-Robert asked, tentatively, recognizing a voice he had not heard in years.

"Yes, it's me!" she said. "I accompanied a French family, whose daughters I tutored in Brazil, on their return to Paris. They wanted me to come with them."

"I know," he replied.

"You do?" my mother asked, puzzled.

"Yes, your cousin told me."

My mother questioned to herself why, then, Jean-Robert had not tried to contact her as she had arrived in France at least a week earlier. Yet, she did not ask him. Instead, they agreed to meet at the train station upon my mother's arrival in Nice the following week.

My mother, excited about this long dreamed of reunion, wore her best dress, drenched herself in perfume, and boarded the train that would take her to her lover. Throughout the long journey to Nice, she daydreamed what she would say and how she would behave once they finally met again.

As the train pulled into the station, my mother expectantly looked upon the crowd gathered on the platform, remembering that she had done this once before when she first left France years ago. Again, she scanned the crowds for a glimpse of the man she hoped to see.

And, as then, she did not see the face she longed to find.

She remained on the platform, hoping that Jean-Robert was late, or that he met the wrong train. Yet, after a few minutes, she felt too embarrassed to stand there alone and walked towards the lobby, hoping that perhaps Jean-Robert would have chosen to meet her there. Eventually, panic stricken and highly disappointed, she realized that he would not come.

She boarded the bus towards her cousin's house and promptly cried for hours. Trying to console her, the cousin suggested that she call Jean-Robert, listing numerous scenarios that may have prevented him from coming to the train station—all of which had nothing to do with an active choice of not coming: "Surely something happened that prevented him from being there, and he must be just as worried as you are;" "perhaps he mixed up the day or time of your arrival;" "maybe there was an accident." My mother clung to these theories, and some hope bubbled within her. Feeling too distraught to do anything about it, she asked her cousin to call Jean-Robert.

"Call him," my mother pleaded with her cousin.

"Should it not be you who calls him instead?" she retorted.

"No . . . I feel too distressed."

Jean-Robert answered the phone within the first couple of rings, which made my mother cry even more. Not able to explain his absence, he asked whether he could speak with my mother.

"She feels too distraught to speak with you," the cousin answered. "Why don't you come visit us here?" She wisely shielded my mother from the chance of being stood up at yet another rendezvous.

Jean-Robert visited the next day. That first meeting, in the cousin's presence, felt constrained and awkward. Jean-Robert stayed for tea, then left.

He returned the next day, on his own volition.

This time, they met alone and talked more freely. She learned that Jean-Robert had a girlfriend. While that information hurt her, she chose to ignore it, knowing that the memory of their love, even years later, was stronger than whatever feelings he could harbor for the current girlfriend. She neglected to mention my father's existence. Jean-Robert stayed a little longer this time, but still left after tea.

The third day, they met outside the house, away from the prying eyes of my mother's family. They met at a café to share an aperitif, then walked around the park. My mother, sensing that Jean-Robert was not fully present, mentioned she was engaged to my father.

"I told Jean-Robert I would marry Pierre because I wanted him to realize he would lose me if he did not leave his girlfriend and profess his love to me!"

Defying my mother's expectations, Jean-Robert was momentarily stunned.

He finally replied, "Well, if you have a fiancée, then surely he is waiting for you."

Rather than beg my mother for her love, he instead accompanied her back to her cousin's house. Flustered that her plan backfired, my mother began sobbing again, unsure about what to do to make him love her.

"Stop crying. Your crying makes you unattractive," Jean-Robert said.

They parted with a cursory goodbye once he dropped my mother off at her cousin's doorstep.

He did not return for a visit for the rest of the week.

My mother felt disconsolate.

Upon her departure to Paris, she contacted Jean-Robert one more time, wanting to say goodbye. Jean-Robert offered to accompany her to the train station, which he did this time.

As my mother turned to him to say what she expected to be a brief goodbye, what she found instead was a man hungry for her love. They kissed intensely for several minutes.

"That was the most memorable moment of my life!" my mother later told me of that tear-laden, kiss-covered, emotional parting at the train station.

"Goodbye forever, my love," were the last words Jean-Robert uttered to my heartbroken mother.

Once in Paris, she resumed planning her marriage to my father. Yet, unable to forget Jean-Robert, she mailed him a wedding invitation, on the back of which she wrote, "I want to marry you instead."

She harbored the hope that this note would bring Jean-Robert to Paris and that after he declared his love for her, she could then cancel her nuptials.

"I always thought that Jean-Robert would burst through the church doors to stop me from marrying," she confessed to me once. "Until the very last minute, I looked at the door, wishing he would come, that he would say, 'Stop! Marry me instead!'"

But on the day of her marriage to my father, Jean-Robert was nowhere to be seen. Sobbing again, tears which the Gecils family attributed to the emotion of the moment, my mother promised to love and honor my father and their marriage forever.

Amid her tears, my mother realized that there was a bright side. Upon her marriage, she became a French citizen. She adopted a new name: Paulette Gecils. She called France home once more. With a new name, long-dreamed of citizenship, and married status, no one could ever tell her that she did not belong. No one would ever tell her again that she smelled of rats.

Chapter 10

NEW LIFE

*M*y parents settled in Paris. Both completed high school, but never went to college, thus they had limited economic prospects. At the time of their marriage, my mother was coquettish, petite, and dressed within the norms of the highly fashionable youth in Paris. There is not a single picture of my mother during her early twenties where she was not perfectly dressed in a suit, with her black, shiny hair perfectly coifed and framing her gleaming, translucent eyes.

My mother worked at Air France, the French national airline, at an office along the famed Champs-Elysees, the most fashionable area of Paris. My mother's job supported the family and paid for my father's tuition. My father, intent on making up for his educational shortcomings, registered at a technical school to learn how to become a software programmer.

Upon learning of her pregnancy, however, my mother promptly stopped working, claiming that Air France fired her. My mother believed growing a child in her womb was hard enough work. As such, she had no intention to seek another job. "My job is to grow my child," she said.

Now that my mother no longer supported my father's education, he took a part-time job while attending school. My mother, idle during the day without work nor my father's company and unable to cook even a simple meal, visited Grandmother Laja's apartment for lunch every day.

There, my mother expected to be treated as a guest, never offering to help—not with cooking or setting the table and most certainly not with cleaning up. Not surprisingly, this did not endear my mother to her in-laws. My mother increasingly felt poorly treated, and she felt the contempt her in-laws had towards her.

"I was tired, sick, and pregnant," my mother said when telling me this story. "Yet, they always complained that I did not help. I just could not help."

At the time, a wave of feminism was sweeping over France. Although she herself was a homemaker who had stayed home for twenty years until Grandfather Rachmiel could no longer support the family after his leg amputation, Laja firmly believed a woman should work. Laja now held a job as a seamstress, and Aunt Paule, who was the same age as my mother, worked as a secretary. While their jobs were modest, my grandmother and aunt felt proud to work, feeling at the forefront of the feminist movement, joining marches and protests for women's equality on the streets of Paris. They were appalled that while they fought for women's emancipation, their son and brother had married a woman who believed growing a baby was all the work a woman should do. Grandmother Laja and Aunt Paule derided my mother for her choice not to work and could not respect a woman who felt it her right to be catered to merely for being pretty or pregnant.

Their mutual dislike only grew. Tension mounted among the women in my family. The conversation around the lunch table often had veiled references to my mother's unemployed status and how she would serve everybody better by taking a job. When they were not focused on my mother's poor work ethic, the discussion centered on current affairs, one of which was the 1967 Israeli occupation of the Palestinian territories. War, in general, was a touchy subject within the family, given Grandmother Laja's strong opinions about what should or should not happen in a war. As Jews who survived World War II, the Gecils wholeheartedly supported Israel, identifying with its struggle for survival as a country and thinking it resembled the family's struggle, years ago, to survive the war.

"Of course Israel should take over these lands," Laja said. "Where are the Jews going to live? We are not welcome anywhere, not even in France."

My mother barely remembered her early months in Egypt. Yet, although she considered herself French, she felt loyal to her Arab origins. She wanted to participate in the conversation, yet she could not relate to Laja's indignant stance toward anyone who would challenge the Jews. My mother did not fully understand the Jewish struggle, much less the psychology behind Grandmother Laja's stance. Foolishly, she stated, "The Palestinians are driven from their home! The Jews have no right to do that. The Israelis must find their own home!"

"What do you know about being driven from your own home?" my grandmother bitterly asked, remembering that twice she was forced to leave her apartment in Paris during World War II, simply to survive.

My mother used my grandmother's experience against her. "Well, Laja, you didn't like being driven from your home during the war. Yet, the Jews in Israel are doing to the Palestinians exactly what the Germans did to you, and you support them," my mother said.

Laja dropped the utensils she held in mid-air, flabbergasted that my mother had just compared her people to Germans who exterminated millions of Jews. How could the Palestinians in any way compare to the monsters responsible for the demise of her family and for so much misery in general? She pushed herself away from the table, rising quickly, with eyes full of hatred and disgust towards my mother.

"You know nothing, you dirty Arab!" she exclaimed as she spit at my mother.

My mother had long realized that she was not welcome at Laja's home. Yet, she felt that because she was pregnant with the family's first grandchild, her in-laws would, at a minimum, respect her. She never expected to be insulted, much less spat at. She was Arab, indeed, yet Laja's hurling of "dirty Arab" brought back memories of the shame and struggles that she and my maternal grandparents lived through in Nice when they were regularly called dirty, ignorant rodents. Now it was her turn to feel appalled that she had married into a family who would treat her as the French had always done, as an outcast, as different, as dirty.

My mother began sobbing.

Grandmother Laja, angry and frustrated, did not tolerate my mother's frail emotions. Thus, Laja walked out of the house, slamming the door behind her, dramatizing just how upset she felt by that conversation. Laja may have expected my mother to follow her out of the apartment. Instead, my mother locked herself inside her in-laws' home. When Laja finished the cigarette she had smoked—while loudly complaining to a neighbor about her intolerable daughter-in-law—she returned to find her front door locked.

Laja banged on the door, screaming for my mother to open it, but to no avail. Aunt Paule came home after a couple of hours to find my grandmother sitting at her front door, with cigarette butts surrounding her. Aunt Paule tried, unsuccessfully, to reason with my mother. They then both waited until my father returned later that evening to pick up his wife, finding his irate mother and sister locked out of their own home by his ungrateful and spoiled wife.

My father had long realized his family did not embrace his choice of a wife. Yet, until then, he left the women to sort their animosities among themselves. Feeling torn between defending his wife and disrespecting his mother, my father had chosen silence, dealing with the situation by staying quiet and out of the way.

Now he no longer had that choice.

He knocked softly on the door.

"Paulette, it's me. Open the door!"

Upon hearing my father's voice, my mother opened the door and stared directly at my father. "We are moving!" she stated as she walked away towards the curb, without acknowledging my exhausted relatives.

My father told his family they would talk the following day and left to accompany my mother back to their home.

The next day, my mother wrote to my grandparents, Mathilda and Isidore, about the insult hurled at her. Mathilda and Isidore were overjoyed at the prospect of their first grandchild. They were also worried for my mother, having received numerous letters where my mother detailed her increased distress, amid tales of how unhappy and alone she felt in France. Frustrated that they were missing the experience of their first grandchild and concerned about how all the stress in France might be adversely affecting the pregnancy, they made an offer my mother found hard to resist.

"Come back to Brazil," they pleaded. "We will take care of you and your baby. You will be happy and loved here."

My mother weighed her options. In France, she felt hated and alone. In Brazil, she would be loved and understood. She would have help with her baby and a ready meal at Grandmother Mathilda's home.

Their offer proved irresistible. She must have known it would be challenging for her to return to France once she departed. But what had she built there? My mother's need to feel loved and accepted was infinitely deeper than her appreciation of fresh baguettes, French fashion, or a view of the Arc de Triomphe. She needed respite from feeling judged and hated for her inability to work due to her pregnancy. She wanted to have her child in peace. At five months pregnant, she packed her bags to board a flight back to Rio de Janeiro.

My father had no interest in leaving France. The only reason he liked Brazil before was because my mother lived there. Everyone in the Gecils family blamed Brazil's humidity and decrepit health infrastructure for making Rachmiel's health conditions worse, leading to his leg amputation, stroke, and eventual death—all bringing more hardship upon the Gecils family. They spoke so often about the horrible conditions in Brazil that my father could easily enumerate them: heat, insects, thieves, pollution, and the inefficiency of it all. Yet the most immediate, important, and immutable reason for hating that foreign land was that Brazil was not France.

My mother ignored my father's pleas for her to reconsider her decision to leave Paris. He tried to reassure her that he would protect her from his family, that this was all a phase. He assured her that once their child was born, she would no longer feel ill.

"If you don't accompany me to Brazil, I will go alone!" my mother said in answer to my father's pleas.

My father had a deep sense of duty and responsibility. He did not want to break up his family. Against his wishes, he resentfully followed his pregnant and indignant wife back to Rio de Janeiro.

Chapter 11

MYTH OF THE CULT

I always noticed we were different.

"Why do we live in a round house?" I asked my mother one day.

"Because we are special," she responded.

I thought she meant that we were different than other people.

We were the only people I ever met who had green eyes. All the neighbors, classmates, and even my grandparents had brown ones. We spoke French at home. The only time I had ever heard someone speak a language other than Portuguese were my grandparents, who spoke Arabic when they wanted to ensure my sisters and I would not understand what they said.

"How come other people don't understand us when we talk?"

"I already told you, Isa. We are not like everybody else. We are special. We truly are. We can speak many languages."

"How come people think we are weird?" I asked.

"Nobody thinks that," she said.

"Somebody called me weird at school today," I stated.

"Well, these people will likely go to hell."

I did not respond. Had I not been part of my family, I too would have thought we were weird. We were eccentric. We lived in a round house. We only left the house to attend school, returning home immediately after, never participating in school functions that did not include sitting in a classroom. But the biggest reason we stood out was because strange things happened at our round house. It was where religious meetings occurred.

"Do I have to go?" I asked my mom when I became old enough to find these weekly Wednesday meetings dull and dreadful.

"Yes, you do," my mother responded sternly.

No excuses were sufficient to miss meetings: not homework, not illness, not boredom. It was simply mandatory that my sisters and I attend—not only because my mother and stepfather expected us to, but because we feared what may happen if we did not.

By late afternoon on Wednesdays, people (often dressed in white) trickled into the house. They were young and old, rich and poor, black and white—along with the more common Brazilian mulattos. There were hardly any children besides my sisters and me. That it was a crowded room most weeks with about twenty-five to thirty-five people in attendance was in itself remarkable. With the exception of a few vacation homes near Shangrila, we were in the middle of nowhere as far as I could tell, along the lush highway that connected Rio de Janeiro to the remote mountain city of Petropolis. The nearest population center was at least fifty minutes away, through foggy, windy, treacherous, and poorly lit mountain roads. But come they did. They arrived silently, under the guise of whispering chatter and not enough laughter. Soon a small crowd congregated and took their seats.

The meetings were interminably long, often lasting more than two hours.

Once all the attendees silently settled on the chairs that together formed a tight circle within the large columns, Lauro rose up and stood in the middle, holding a book. On the cover was a large gate, apparently depicting the way to heaven. He read five or so pages of one of the twenty-seven *Rational Immunization* books. These volumes said nothing different from one another and seemed all the same, except the color of the gate on the cover. We were required to read these books outside the meetings too—all together, about thirteen thousand pages of utterly repetitive, insipid, boring, and useless text.

Lauro's monotone voice echoed through the large hall, yet I did not comprehend the meaning of the cryptic statements he often said. As he loudly placed the book down, another sound emanated from the room as chanting began. The words of the songs weren't discernible. I could not tell which language they were sung in, but it certainly was not Portuguese. Yet, the melody had a harmonious tone to it, initially. However, as the chanters elevated their voices and fell into a trance, the anticipation of what was to come made me recoil in fear. As the chanting got louder, invariably, somebody hissed, shouted, screamed, or cried. The rhythmic chanting did not stop—that is, until somebody moved. Somebody always moved, because if they did not, it would perhaps be possible that the chanting would never end. My mother rose often, hissing and moving her raised hands in parallel above her head; she called this gesture "vibrations."

As the hisser's convulsions began, the chanting continued at a steady cadence, never wavering, never stopping. Those who hissed stood up and shook, sometimes violently, in an entire body convulsion. Sometimes, they would stand still while waving their hands with a velocity intended for those shooing away evil. Sometimes they spoke in an unnaturally deep and loud voice, warning about some dire event about to befall humanity—or worse, about to befall one of us.

After a few minutes of this frisson and after delivering a warning, whoever shook the hardest fell with a loud thump, prostrated on the floor or his chair, exhausted from this ordeal, and helpless in having been possessed by some unknown spirit, or even by the dead. The others who remained seated nodded their approval, as if some truth had been revealed to them. The chanting stopped. The possessed ones, now free of their possessor, stood up and returned to their seats as if nothing happened.

As the scene concluded, Lauro's compact figure removed his reading glasses and preached.

"God has spoken," he started.

Typically, God spoke and we'd better listen—at the risk of some horrible atrocity if we dared not. Shell-shocked after witnessing one possessed by an evil spirit, all we did was nod our heads, promising total obedience.

"You are a privileged group," he then said with a half-smile, as we had the dubious luck of hearing from God himself, whose wrath was merciless.

On that note, the room fell silent, as people wondered what ill could befall them. It was the perfect transition to the meditation section of the meeting.

"Let us pray," Lauro said, beckoning us to close our eyes and remain silent, only listening to our breathing.

I did not know how to meditate.

"Clear your head of all thought," my mother tried to explain to me once. I tried, but it was impossible. Instead of clearing my mind of all thoughts, the dire warnings swirled around my head, creating a level of anxiety and fear that left me unable to relax.

I passed the time looking at my toes as they wiggled furiously; they were the only body part I could move without earning a lecture on my restlessness. Once I ensured all others had closed their eyes, I scanned the room, willing the time away and wishing it to pass more quickly so that the meeting would end. Unfortunately, before the meeting would end, I had to live through its most dreaded part. Before we adjourned, those around the circle reported what they "saw" during meditation. One by one, the meeting attendees reported spectacular visions, one more grandiose than the other, trusting that these visions reflected the depth of their spirituality.

The less spiritual had tamer visions: dots of bright lights or rainbows. Some were scary, including prophecies of horrendous ills about to befall the world, the country, our city, or one of us. I felt appalled by the creativity and insight that everyone else had. I, however, never saw anything. When it was my turn my mother always asked, "What did you see today, Isa?"

The answer was always the same: "Nothing."

"Try harder next time," she said with a passing glance, eager to move on to a person with higher levels of creativity.

"OK," I said as I shrugged my shoulders, both of us knowing that the following week, no vision would grace me.

Around the room most everybody else shared their colorful visions. As I heard what was said, I sulked, thinking, "What could be possibly wrong with me?"

Even my sisters, who were otherwise reasonable people, often had visions. I, however, always drew a blank.

After weeks, followed by months, followed by years, of no visions whatsoever, I figured it was about time I did see something. One Wednesday evening, as it was a common routine by now, my mother asked me again, "Any luck today, Isa?"

"Yes. I saw a faint, blue light," I made up.

My mother smiled broadly. Everyone else, so used to glancing past me as he or she learned about others' commitment to spiritual development, stared at me. Some were nodding, some smiling, but all communicated, through smiling eyes, joy that I could finally understand the depth of the experience. They thought I had been enlightened and had joined the ranks of the visionary, that there was some hope for me after all.

After meditation, Lauro raised his right hand as if giving God's blessing, and people stood up quietly and quickly left the room and the round house. The night when I lied about the vision of a blue dot, Lauro, my mother, and my sisters gathered around the table in our cramped kitchen.

"Here, Isa," my mother said, smiling, taking a cake out of the refrigerator and placing it in the middle. "You earned this today."

I wolfed down the unusually large slice of chocolate cake I received, not failing to note how small my sisters' slices were in comparison. The larger slice was meant to celebrate the opening of my spiritual self. My small family smiled towards me, and I felt the glow of being the center of attention. It was such a heady, unusual feeling that I sought to repeat it.

As I cleaned up the plates from the table, I wondered whether the visions of others were also lies, as mine had been.

"Who are the people who attend the meetings?" I asked my mother since I never directly spoke with any of them.

"People who are enlightened," she responded.

"Why do they come?"

"Because they want salvation."

"How come they have all kinds of visions?" I insisted.

"Well, they meditate, and they connect with God. So they see what God wants them to see. You saw a blue light today," she said, smiling. "Maybe your connection with God has increased."

Not wanting to admit I had concocted a blue light, I nodded my head and said goodnight.

DOBBY

*T*he several animals that roamed Shangrila did not belong to us. The farm had a kennel for guard dogs, a pen for chickens, an enclosure with a pond for ducks, as well as an enclosed area for pigs.

I adopted some of the animals as my own, although they technically never belonged to me. I named one of the ducks who survived long enough for me to feel attached to it before Lauro slaughtered the bird for a Christmas meal.

A stray cat often appeared at our house seeking food, yet he belonged to everybody, regularly making the rounds of the neighbors' homes. Wanting my own pet, I asked for a dog who would belong to me.

My family acquiesced. Dobby, a large dog resembling a German shepherd but fully black with piercing, yellow eyes, arrived in our lives. Tall, stately, and strong, Dobby came with conditions: I would be fully responsible for feeding and walking him, as well as collecting his waste.

I accepted these conditions and rejoiced in having my own dog.

Soon, though, Lauro appeared to want Dobby for himself. He often brought the dog with him to the roof tower, where I was not allowed to join. He frequently closed the door to the temple that separated half the house. The only way to have Dobby by my side would be to spend time on the temple side of the house, which frankly, I did not particularly enjoy doing. Even when I tried to lure him away, the dog stayed on the roof, where I was forbidden to go.

Dobby was increasingly my dog in name only. Not thinking that this was fair, I voiced my complaint.

"Dobby is my dog," I stated.

"I want him to be my dog," Lauro responded.

"What does that mean?" I asked.

"It means he will be mine and only mine."

"But he is mine!" I insisted.

"I will buy him from you."

"I don't want to sell him," I said.

"Then don't."

"But then you have to let him stay with me," I said.

Lauro did not respond. He continued to take the dog and close the door behind him so that I would not follow. When I tried to keep Dobby close to me or encouraged him to leave the temple room, Lauro screamed at me, demanding that the door to the temple room remain closed. He called Dobby towards him, even if I was hugging or caressing him.

Recognizing I had already lost Dobby, yet was still expected to feed him and clean after him, I acquiesced, deciding to sell the dog.

"I will sell Dobby to you," I said, feeling sad and defeated. "Here is my price." I stated my terms, willing to trade my dog for a new Barbie doll and a toy car.

Lauro brought me the toys I requested the next day.

"Dobby is mine now," Lauro said. "I do not want to see you playing with him."

"That means I will not collect his waste anymore either," I said.

"That's a deal," he responded.

From that day forward, I did not touch Dobby again.

Chapter 13

PLAYDATES

*W*hen we first arrived in Shangrila, the neighbors who vacationed in the nearby homes and who had girls of similar ages as my sisters and me invited us for playdates where we would spend the afternoon swimming in their pools and playing with their toys. On one of these playdates, I recall marveling at the large pool, fearing to use it as I did not know how to swim. I also felt astonished at the girl's room, a room just for herself, decorated as if a princess lived there. We met this family perhaps three times. Abruptly, we no longer received invitations.

Not understanding why we could not go on yet another playdate, I invited myself when I came across the girl's parents in the nearby bakery or at school.

"Can I come to your house?" I asked when they came to pick up their daughters at school.

They looked at me with downcast eyes, as if staring at a school girl was painful. "We are busy now," they would say, or, "We are going away for the weekend." When I suggested the following weekend, they said that they would be away for a long time.

I mentioned to my mother that I asked our neighbor to invite us to swim at their pool. "They are busy," I said, "but we can go when they return."

"Those people have negative energy; you cannot go to their home."

"But we visited them before," I stated.

"That was then. Now you will no longer go."

"Why not?"

My mother, not too coherently, explained that she tried to enlighten them by discussing the *Rational Immunization* books and by inviting them to join the Wednesday night religious meetings. When they refused, apparently a heated argument ensued. Now the neighbors no longer wanted us to visit them.

Trying to hide my disappointment, I instead asked, "How come everybody but us is a negative person?"

"They just are," she said.

"But how?" I insisted.

"Their aura is dark," she said ominously, as if this statement alone would instill deathly fear in me. "There is bad energy around them."

When I did not understand what she meant, she showed me a book full of images of tortured souls, with dark clouds surrounding their disfigured faces, which seemed to be yelling for help and salvation. Some pictures depicted devilish creatures around their bodies.

As my mother showed me these pictures, or spoke about others' bad auras, she attempted to rid herself of negative energy that must have hovered around us by the mere mention of it. She would vigorously move her hands from the upper arm to the opposite hand, as if to rid herself of some powder that accidently fell on her clothes.

"Do you want to be like them?" she asked me, jamming the scary pictures in front of me. "That is what will happen to you by daring to swim in their pool."

The pictures instilled fear in me. I shook my head, teary-eyed, and replied, "No, I don't want to be like them." Initially, I felt fearful of other people's dark aura and what effect it would have on me. I often emulated my mother's gesture of cleaning imaginary powder and darkness away from my arms.

However, the next time I saw the neighbors, assuming they had returned from their trip, I asked again, "You are back! Can I come to your house?"

"Maybe one day soon," they said, voices trailing, moving quickly away from me. They smiled faintly, patted my head, and stared at me with eyes I was too naïve to interpret as loaded with pity for me—and contempt for my parents.

"One day soon" never came, and their daughters, now former friends, overtly avoided me at school too. Neither enjoying that look of pity they gave me, nor wanting my mother to show me scary pictures, I stopped asking for playdates. I already knew the answer would be no. What was the point in asking anymore?

Without invitations to playdates and with my mother's illness used as a reason of why we had to remain at home, I only left the house to attend school. My father, who now lived in Sao Paulo, only visited once a quarter, and nobody else ever came. We did not go anywhere. The avenues that led to the outside world had shut down.

The only people who visited were my grandparents, irrespective of whether they felt welcomed. During their monthly visits, they sat in our cramped living room for an hour or two. Either Lauro or my mother, often both, were present. So while we did speak with our grandparents, we never did so freely.

Over time, whenever I asked again to go anywhere, rather than receive an explanation, I got slapped on my face. Lauro mostly, but sometimes my mother, slapped us for every little infraction, including turning on the TV without asking, playing any music besides classical, or even for no reason at all. I quickly learned the consequences of airing grievances, so my sisters and I learned to stay quietly out of the way and to obey. On the rare occasions when we strayed or questioned a course of action, Lauro employed the most powerful of all scare tactics, never said in front of my mother.

"If you don't do what I say, your mother will die!" Lauro paused for a minute and looked straight into my eyes. "Do you want your mother to die?"

I would nod my head no, with tears bubbling around my horrified and fearful downcast eyes.

"I did not hear you," Lauro taunted, shaking me when he did not hear a clear response.

"No," I answered more loudly.

"Yeah, I did not think so."

My situation was definitely challenging, but wouldn't it become worse if my mother died?

Chapter 14

LIES

*I*n their divorce settlement, my father agreed to pay my mother alimony and child support as long as she remained unmarried. Lauro thought he was above working for a living, that earning money was for less spiritually gifted people. Thus, he planned to live off my father's alimony payments. While my father may have felt obliged to support a struggling single mother with three young children, he would never agree to support her lover. Knowing this, Lauro and my mother hatched a plan. Lauro's existence was to remain a secret.

"You will tell your father that I am raising you alone," my mother clearly instructed.

"But you do not drive! Somebody needs to drive to go to the supermarket or to take us to school," I said. "What will I tell Pappy when he asks?"

"You will tell him we buy supplies at the local street vendor and that you take the van to go to school," she responded. "And your father does not care about you. He will not ask."

We nodded our heads.

"You will not tell your father about the cult," my mother continued. "That godless bastard would not understand."

The list of topics to keep hidden was long. My mother anticipated an answer for all the logistical complexities of living in such a remote place and instructed us what to say for any scenario.

Lauro hovered over us during these conversations, ensuring compliance either through force or fear.

It was not too difficult to keep secrets and ensure the details of our life stayed hidden. My father's move to Sao Paulo occurred within weeks of our move to Shangrila. As my mother had predicted, during his quarterly visits, he never once asked about our living situation. We never offered information, fearing punishment, a dark aura, and my mother's death.

Once Lauro and my mother felt reasonably confident that my sisters and I were brainwashed enough to keep secrets from my father, she asked us to keep these secrets from everyone.

"Do not ever tell anyone that I am divorced!" my mother said.

"But what do we say then when people ask about Pappy?" I asked.

"Pierre is not your father," she responded angrily. "He abandoned you to live with a slut."

"What do we say then?" I asked, puzzled.

"You will say that Lauro is your father," she said. Then came the most egregious order: "And from this moment forward, you will call him '*Dad*'."

Chapter 15

STEPMOTHER

*S*ao Paulo was a one-hour flight away, but despite my father's offers for us to visit, my mother forbade us to go. Thus it fell to my father to visit us. He coordinated his visits through my grandparents as they had a phone and we did not. In the absence of a phone, my father asked that we write to him. But we were also forbidden to write. Early attempts ended up burned in the fireplace.

My father's quarterly visit followed a predictable schedule. He arrived promptly at ten o'clock. We typically drove on the winding mountain road for a day-long visit to Petropolis, a small town with relatively limited entertainment choices. First, we stopped at the Park Cremerie, situated at the city gates and filled with parrots and other caged, exotic, tropical animals. We crossed red-painted bridges to access a small lake surrounded by German-inspired doll houses. We often rented paddleboats to maneuver under the bridge and take a closer look at the brightly painted houses. During hot days, we jumped in the public pool. I did not know how to swim, however, and mostly hung on the ledge. My father never joined us in the pool, and once we were old enough, he did not go on the paddleboats either, preferring to look at us from a distance.

At lunch time, we ate at my father's favorite restaurant, indulging in the Brazilian meat extravaganza known as churrasco. Waiters hovered around our table with huge chunks of sizzling barbeque meat on skewers, the air punctuated by the smell of charred meat that wafted through the restaurant. A buffet table held exquisite salads and fresh vegetables, which were common and abundant in Brazil.

The restaurant, while nice, was loud amidst the cacophony of waiters prancing around with skewers of meat and Brazilians drinking and eating in excess. We ate quietly, gorging on the abundant food, mumbling how delicious it was, and declaring how quickly we felt full. We hardly ever made an effort to learn more about one another's personal lives.

In the afternoons, we either watched a movie or visited the Imperial Palace where Brazil's former emperors took residence to escape the mid-summer heat. We also had little opportunity to talk as we moved from one palatial room to another, noting the signs throughout requesting that patrons whisper while on the premises. On the hour-long drive back to Shangrila, we felt exhausted and remained quiet too. My sisters and I often assumed we needed to stay quiet in the car. Whenever we drove with Lauro, he actively discouraged conversation or any noise, including music. Upon dropping us off in Shangrila around four o'clock, my father would open the trunk of his car, which was always brimming with gifts.

We would see him again in three months' time and would follow the exact same schedule of the day we just had.

Around the fourth visit, my father decided to introduce Carroll to my sisters and me.

"She is evil," my mother promptly said, upon learning that Carroll would join the visit.

At first, my sisters and I ignored this statement. My mother upped the challenge.

"If you loved me as your mother, you wouldn't go see that bitch," she said.

In the days preceding the visit, my mother wasted no opportunity to interject caustic criticism of Carroll and how it was our filial duty not to meet with her.

Despite the possible monotony of a day in Petropolis, my sisters and I loved my father's visit. It was our only opportunity to leave Shangrila, besides attending school. Evil stepmother or not, my sisters were not inclined to miss the opportunity to go out for the day, despite the ominous warnings about the dangers we faced being in Carroll's company.

As I had not yet met her, my mother's constant harping on Carroll shaped her image in my head. I felt conflicted. What if she was truly evil? I felt increasingly concerned about meeting her and about my exposure to her dark aura. I also thought that agreeing with my mother might perhaps buy me some of her sparse love and attention, which she spread equally among my sisters and me.

As the day of the visit arrived, I told my mother, "I will not meet Carroll."

She smiled broadly, showing the gap in her teeth, having lost a few by avoiding the dentist.

"Then you must truly love me!" she exclaimed loudly as she hugged me tightly, urging Nathalie and Catherine to make a similar choice and thus obtain her love and approval.

My sisters pretended I said nothing. Instead, they promptly ran to the yard to wait for my father's rental car to arrive at Shangrila's front gate.

Not seeing me with my sisters, my father made the unusual step to enter our house.

"Hi, Isa, let's go," he said after a cursory hug.

"I cannot go," I said.

"Why not?"

"I am feeling sick," I lied.

"Well, come say hello to Carroll at least," my father said jovially.

"I am really sick," I repeated, doubling over and rubbing my belly.

Now that he stood in front of me, I felt terrible. My belly did hurt as I felt a sharp pain in the pit of my stomach for this blatant lie. Suddenly, I longed to run towards him and join my sisters for the outing.

My mother stood next to me with a hand on my shoulder. Despite the longing, I did not feel I could move from the tight grip of my mother's hand, especially after stating earlier that I would stay home.

"You heard her," my mother said, addressing my father. "She said she will not go."

A cloud of sadness covered my father's dark green eyes. He raised his gaze towards my mother, understanding where my sickness came from. With a sigh, he turned around.

"Maybe next time," he said and left, without hugging me goodbye.

My mom promptly retired to her room.

I spent the entire day alone, staring at the clock, watching the minutes pass slowly, imagining what my family was doing. I knew that by eleven o'clock, they were at the Park Cremerie. By noon, they were eating copious amounts of meat at the churrascaria. By two o'clock, they were at the museum. The minutes seemed as long as hours. I paced all day and did nothing more than read a couple of books and watch the clock move slowly towards four o'clock, the usual time of our return.

In the afternoon, my father returned to the house to check on me.

"I am still sick," I lied again, hoping that the sadness in his eyes was not caused by my lies. He nodded his head, gave me a kiss, and left.

As soon as he left, I looked at my sisters expectantly, wanting to know all the details of the day. "Carroll is nice!" Catherine exclaimed as she recounted the day's adventures and the gifts they received or bought during their outing, which I, not having attended, did not get. My father knew that this display of generosity towards my sisters would not go unnoticed.

"Is there anything for me?" I asked as they showed me the gifts they received.

"I guess you needed to be there," Catherine responded.

It was the last time I ever missed a visit with my father.

Three months later, he returned with Carroll again. Even a real illness would not have prevented me from joining the outing. My mother's vitriol recommenced, but this time, I did not pay attention. It did not matter how evil Carroll was—and my sisters commented that she was actually nice. I wanted to leave the house, eat well, see my father, receive gifts, and not spend all day looking at the clock.

"It is nice to finally meet you, Isa," Carroll said, embracing me awkwardly upon our meeting.

She looked at me through the blue eyes that Brazilians thought all Americans had. She had shorn, short brown hair. She was heavier than I had expected and was wearing a t-shirt and baggy jeans. In contrast, my father was casually fashionable as he typically was, wearing a button-down dress shirt and smelling of cologne.

"Hi," I said curtly and took my spot in the middle seat of the car, noting to myself that nobody needed to take the middle seat when Carroll was not there.

We followed the typical schedule. We stopped first at Park Cremerie and rented paddleboats. We ate excessive amounts of food at the churrascaria. We visited the Imperial Palace in the afternoon. However, there was a notable change to our schedule at Carroll's request.

"Let's take the carriage horses around Petropolis so that Carroll can see the city," my father suggested, smiling to the four of us surrounding him. Outside the Imperial Palace, dilapidated horse-drawn carriages carried tourists over the historic, cobblestone streets of the town. The carriage's long benches, covered in red leather, faced one another and held three large people. My sisters sat on one side, Pappy and Carroll on the other.

"Isa, why don't you sit next to me?" Carroll asked me, smiling.

I sat between Carroll and my father. As the carriage meandered through the cobblestone streets that lined the center of the imperial city, we fell silent as all in the carriage looked outward to appreciate the scenery of the polluted river that divided the tree-lined street.

My opinion of Carroll had been formed long before we met. No matter what she did, no matter how nice she was to me that first day, I simply did not believe she could be nice. I would be betraying my mother otherwise. In my simplistic understanding of the dysfunctional dynamics of my parents' marriage, I blamed Carroll for our situation. She was the reason we lived in Shangrila. Had she not appeared in my father's life, he would have reconciled with my mother—or so my mother told me, multiple times.

I simply could not forgive her for being in our lives.

Carroll seemed content about how well the day was going. I reached towards her and caressed the length of her arm. She turned to me, smiling widely, believing that this gesture meant I accepted her presence in my life. I smiled back.

While smiling, I stopped caressing her and pinched her instead.

Her smile evaporated, replaced by a loud, "Ouch!"

Carroll slapped my arm back, as hard as an adult could covertly hit a child. It hurt.

I, however, did not utter a word; I was used to controlling my emotions when struck. My father noticed nothing, neither did my sisters. Yet, something monumental had just happened. The battle lines between Carroll and I were drawn.

Two years later, my father brought pictures of a handful of friends in what looked like a city hall and of the restaurant where my father celebrated his marriage to Carroll.

"I wanted you to be at our wedding, but your mother did not allow you to come," he said bitterly. Almost in the same sentence, he quickly added, "And now that we are married, we are moving to the United States."

My sisters and I were too stunned to say anything, so we stared at him wide-eyed, attempting to process what this news actually meant. After a pause, in which we all stared at one another in stunned silence, he added, almost as an afterthought, "I am building a better life for you."

That did not make sense. How was it that my father was building a better life for us, when he was effectively abandoning us?

Upon hearing that, I blurted, "Can I go with you then?"

"When you are old enough, you can."

"I am nine. Is that old enough?" I asked.

He did not answer. My father smiled and patted my head as if I had just said something funny and cute.

"I will still come to visit you every year," he said.

"But the United States is far!" I protested. Or, at least, I thought it was far. I had no idea how far it was.

"I will still come once a year," he repeated.

"One day a year?"

"Well, we see each other only four days a year now; it will not be that different," my father stated, speaking pragmatically.

The United States was on the other side of the world. He would simply be too far if I needed help. The fact that he already hardly visited us, despite living an hour's flight away, did not figure in my panic. At least now he could come if we had the courage to ask him. But once he moved, this possibility would vanish.

There was so much I wanted to say, but I could not organize my thoughts nor articulate the panic I felt at this news: *How are you going to come to the rescue if you are on the other side of the world? Who cares about the life you will build for us in the future? How about the present?*

If my father thought about the impact his departure would have on his children, he brushed it away.

Instead of voicing my hurt, I said nothing. I nodded my head and lunged towards him to hug my father goodbye. And just like that, he entered into his rental car and disappeared around the curvy mountain road a few seconds later, leaving my sisters and me behind, lost in the fallout of my parents' self-absorption.

Chapter 16

SCHOOL CHOICES

*O*nce Lauro had successfully ostracized us from our family and our neighbors, he set his sight on removing us from school.

There was too much out of his control in having us attend school. Rather than admit that this was a leak in his tightening noose, he adopted a different tactic. He complained loudly about school-related issues. The school, based in Petropolis, was too far. The van service was too expensive. It was too impractical for us to attend school in Petropolis. We needed to go to the local school, a public school with one room for multiple grades that educated the children of the maids who serviced the vacation homes in the area. Preferably, we were to be homeschooled. Or better yet, not schooled at all.

I learned later than my mother had agreed to this plan to end our education. This decision would have gone unnoticed, except that when my grandparents visited, they casually asked Nathalie how she liked school. We were still attending school at the time, but Nathalie was aware of the plan that we would stop attending soon.

"I love it, but soon we will no longer go to school," Nathalie said.

"How come?" Grandfather Isidore asked.

"Schools are terrible, dangerous places," Lauro responded instead.

Lauro's statement was not inaccurate. The public schools in Brazil, in general, were decrepit. The one next to our house had a single classroom for all the elementary grades. A vast number of slum-dwellers, who had no other choice, sent their children to this sub-par school. Since our neighborhood was a haven of weekend homes, the children of the well-off attended school in Rio or Petropolis.

Yet, Lauro did not mean that we should not attend public school. He meant that we should not go to any school at all.

My grandparents, until then, never appeared to question my mother's decisions, even as they witnessed these big shifts in our living situation. Even if they were concerned about Lauro's increased, adverse influence on our lives, they never raised the issue. My grandparents did not utter a word about the demise of my mother's marriage, her affair, the stealthy move to Shangrila, the religious meetings, or my mother's incredible transformation from an elegant woman to an overweight, unkempt one—until that moment, that is. The news that we would no longer attend school alarmed my grandparents.

"If the public schools are so terrible, obviously you will then send them to a private school in Petropolis instead," Grandfather Isidore stated.

"No. They are just not going at all," Lauro responded. "We live in the middle of the forest; there is no need here for the nonsense they talk about in school."

Isidore's unease grew, noting my mother said nothing, even though she was present. Feeling that there was more to this situation than the potential dangers of Brazil's public school, Isidore decided to intervene. To do so, he drew on the only weapon he had.

"If you don't send the girls to school, I will tell Pierre about you!" he threatened Lauro.

My grandparents acquiesced to my mother's request that Lauro's existence be kept a secret. They did not share with my father that my mother had a lover ruling her life and controlling their grandchildren's fate. It was not just their silence either. Aunt Simone and Uncle Sylvain also kept the secret of Lauro's existence, despite seeing my father every so often.

Lauro had not anticipated this threat. If my grandfather Isidore followed through with his threat, the alimony payments would surely stop. Although my mother and Lauro were not officially married, my father would consider them as much. A custody battle would possibly ensue, although that was unlikely, given my father's distaste for raising children, but my mother would not take that risk.

"It is not your place to tell me how to raise my daughters," Lauro said.

"They are not your daughters," Isidore retorted. "And that is not all," my grandfather continued, "not only you will send them to school, you will send them to the best school in Petropolis."

"We can't afford private school with the money Pierre sends us," my mother added in a more conciliatory tone. "Besides, Petropolis is so far; it would be a logistical nightmare to take them to school every day. They will have to wake up before sunrise just to arrive there on time!"

"Surely you will find a way," Isidore said. "I've done some research."

My grandfather, worrying about us living so remotely, had previously researched transportation options in and out of Shangrila. "There is a van that could take the girls to school," he stated. "I am sure that Pierre will cover the cost, but if he does not, I will help pay too."

As Isidore refuted Lauro's arguments, my stepfather must have weighed his desire to keep us away from the world against his distaste for actually having to work—or worse, having to answer to my father about his sinister plans. He must have realized he would not win, or that the price of winning would not be worth the victory. Either way, it was better not to ruffle feathers. Not sending us to school would invite too much scrutiny into what was happening within the round house. Despite their initial resistance, my mother and Lauro reluctantly relented.

And so my grandfather's wishes came to fruition. A few weeks later, I started fifth grade at the San Jose Institute, the most elite private school Petropolis had to offer.

Attending an elite school wasn't the solution for our isolation problems.

That first day, my mother sent us with instructions on what we were not supposed to say to our well-off classmates. She should not have worried. My classmates had no interest in me. They had known each other since kindergarten, and they had little interest in the new girl. Plus, we were so unlike any of them— wealthy, well-groomed, and normal—that I did not fit in from the start. In the previous couple of years, the only other children I had interacted with were my sisters, who shared the same bizarre life as mine. I had nothing to say that I thought could possibly interest anyone. So I remained quiet for the most part.

Nathalie and Catherine also struggled at first to fit in. Strangely, we never interacted with one another while at school. At home, we were each other's playmates—to a certain extent.

We lived in quite a socialist household. Everything had to be exactly the same for the three of us. If one of us received a toy, the other two received the same one, with the possible exception of being a different color. When purchasing clothes, we all got the same model, in different sizes. When we got a food treat, such as a candy bar, a meringue, or a slice of cake, we all got exactly the same quantity. Complaining about it would not give us more or less of anything. "It is what is fair," my mother would say.

Among ourselves, we did not think there was any fairness in receiving something we did not want, only because one of the sisters wanted it. So where we could, my sisters and I developed a barter system for food and clothing. In exchange for more of what my sisters had, especially food, I placed myself in the firing lines.

I took the lead in voicing complaints and asking my mother for things that we knew she would not give us. That seemed a fair trade with my sisters, who knew that asking for something my mother or Lauro were not inclined to give us typically resulted in punishment. I would have done it anyway, as I began to feel that somehow our life was not like the others, and I did not like all the rules imposed on us.

But I mostly did it for the immediate gratification.

Upon receiving my portion of a food treat, such as a candy bar, I devoured it at a fast clip. Then I looked at my sister Nathalie, widening my eyes as much as I could, our unspoken code that pleaded with her to give me a portion of her candy bar too. More often than not, she would give me half, either out of pity or just to stop me from bothering her.

Nathalie internalized others' emotions. She felt sorry that I was empty handed, notwithstanding the fact that I had already devoured a serving equal to what she had received. After a while, I did not even have to ask. She divided her loot in half and would just hand it to me. Nathalie, who was the skinniest of us three, delicately small boned and of a petite frame, simply watched me consume half of her portion of most everything.

Once I devoured whatever Nathalie gave me, I tried the same tactic on my baby sister Catherine. Catherine, however, knew better than to give me anything. Either she would eat her candy bar just as fast as I would or would pointedly refuse to give me even a crumb. Sometimes she would deliberately eat it slowly, just to see how long I could go without asking for a part of it. I never stopped asking since every so often she relented, giving me motivation to keep trying.

So we all created a symbiotic relationship. In general, I got more food rations, but the price I paid was to stick my neck out before anyone else did. My sisters did not challenge my position as the leader of our three-sister ring. Nathalie was more agreeable in accepting our repressed life, and Catherine was too young to know how to fight for her rights, but they knew I wouldn't shy away from a battle. They both willingly supported me in the battles I eventually waged in my family. They were happy to have me forge ahead so that they could follow. If it worked, it was great for them. If it did not, I'd be the one punished. So I learned that rules could be bent, provided that the rulers were unaware of it. I learned that if I asked, long enough and persistently enough, eventually I would prevail.

My position at the top of the sister pecking order did not come without a price. I always felt that Catherine and Nathalie had a closer bond with each other than they did with me. While I noticed it, I was mostly happy with our trade: more food and more power, even if it meant less bonding. Some of the bruises I gathered along the way seemed worth it. My sisters were all I had. Fighting for them ultimately meant fighting for what I wanted. Yet, despite how beneficial it would have been if we had really joined forces, we never became one another's confidants. We kept secrets among ourselves, too, aware that if we talked to each other, who knew? Our mother might die.

Chapter 17

SMARTS

My older sister Nathalie constantly heard she was beautiful. Grandfather Isidore held her in the same adoration he once held his first-born daughter, our mother. She heard it also from our neighbors and whoever glanced at her.

She, indeed, was beautiful, with large, green eyes, long legs, and a petite bone structure. My baby sister Catherine was pretty too, with a flowing, shiny, and straight mane that reached her lower back. Catherine's hair never went unnoticed or uncommented upon.

Despite hearing compliments on my sisters' beauty, nobody ever told me I was pretty. No one commented on my unruly, frizzy, curly hair; on my crooked teeth; on the thick glasses perched on my large nose. My mother cut my hair with a razor, ensuring my curly hair became a dried-up mop I did not know how to wear.

"Keep smoothing out your nose with your fingers," my mother frequently instructed me. "It is growing large; this way, your nose will grow thinner." She said this with the authority of someone who knows best. So I did, regularly, noting, however, that my nose did not turn finer as a result.

My family, more worried about nourishing our soul, did not pay attention to material possessions or physical beauty. Given that none of us attended social

78

events, my family did not understand the social status and pressure that comes from wearing the appropriate clothing and having a good cut for one's hair. My sisters and I owned a few, tattered items of clothing, stained with the mud we rolled in or the dirt from climbing trees to reach plump fruits. On the rare occasions my mother caught me brushing my hair in front of the mirror, she promptly said, "Stop being so vain." Often, she removed the brush I used in fruitless attempts to flatten my hair.

My front teeth, broken during a fall over cement steps, had grown back on top of one another. We only went to the dentist if a painful toothache developed. My father once asked me when I planned to have braces.

"I don't think I will," I responded. "Mom says that my teeth give me personality."

As I noticed how most of my classmates, indeed, had braces, I tried to emulate them by wrapping my teeth with aluminum foil, just to see what it was like to have braces and the prospect of a nice smile.

My mother laughed heartily when she saw that.

"Isa, you are so proud of your crooked teeth and glasses," my mother stated whenever I asked to have braces too. "You don't need braces."

Whenever people complimented my sisters' beauty, they somehow felt compelled to say something about me too. They looked at me, trying to find something positive to say about my appearance. But what was there to say? When words escaped them, most resorted to the next best choice in compliments.

"You, Isabelle, you are the smartest one!"

I heard I was smart so often that I began believing it.

I could not fix my nose, could not straighten my teeth, and could not convince my mother to use scissors instead of a razor to cut my hair. But I could certainly focus on using my brain.

Not having much to do outside of school, books became my companions. When I read all the books I could find in my house, even the dreaded, twenty-seven tomes of *Rational Immunization*, I went downstairs to the landlord's large library that flanked an entire wall of the glass-surrounded living room. With his permission, I borrowed his dusty books.

"You are the only one who ever reads these books," the landlord mentioned to me one day.

I took it as an admonition and proceeded to place the book back on his shelf. "No, don't put it back," he said. "You can pick a book here anytime you want."

"Really? Thank you!" I said, smiling, proceeding to take him up on his offer, then and many times over. I read school books multiple times too and was often lessons ahead of the class.

Soon all the reading translated into higher grades at school. I received the top grades in all classes, except for what I deemed more subjective classes, such as art. Try as I may, I had no artistic talent. Likewise, I earned lower marks in physical education, where it was a rare day when I was not chosen last for the volleyball and handball teams.

The San Jose Institute, espousing the theory that publicly ranking the students led them to try harder, posted every single grade and overall academic rank on the school board. Beginning at about sixth grade, my bolded name was always on top. Every two months, for the following three years, my bolded name remained on the number-one spot. A couple of students attempted to displace me and studied inordinately hard for most of a year. But nobody had as much time to study as I did, and I held on to the top of the academic perch.

Staying on top was not just a result of having more time to study, however. Receiving high grades was the only validation I ever received in my life. It filled me with pride and purpose. Seeing my name on the top of the list somehow made me accept feeling less than my classmates: less pretty, less popular, less athletic, less wealthy, and less able than anybody else. It did not matter that I did not have looks, sports skills, normal parents, or any friends. Others had all of these things, but I alone was the smartest. This belief defined me, allowing me to cope with the vicissitudes of my life.

Soon, I had a feeling of superiority about being smart. Sadly, that only compounded my problems.

During indoor recess due to heavy rains, the teacher coordinated a sort of Secret Santa game, without gifts, to both pass the time and to reinforce a lesson on adjectives. She rearranged the seats in a circle so that she and each of the forty-five classmates could see one another. Each of us pulled a name from a hat and wrote three adjectives that described the person. Once finished, we placed the list of adjectives, without the name, back in the hat.

"Now, pull a paper out of the hat and read the three adjectives," the teacher said. "Then look around the room and try to guess which of your classmates the adjectives are describing."

At first, it was funny because most people guessed wrong and laughter ensued. Soon it was my turn. The adjectives on the piece of paper I pulled read "smart, intelligent, and pretty." It is true that nobody before had ever said I was pretty, so I should have known better. But I focused on the words "smart" and "intelligent" on the paper I held. I briefly looked around the room, judging the intellectual capability of my classmates. As I had held the top rank for the previous two years, I quickly determined that nobody else would come even close to my achievement. Wrapped up with myself, I could not conceive of who could be described as "smart" and "intelligent" besides me.

For a second, I chuckled inside, thinking it was a funny coincidence that I had pulled my own name out of the hat.

"So what do you have, Isabelle?" the teacher asked when it was my turn.

"Smart, intelligent, pretty," I read out loud while holding the paper with the three words scribbled on it.

"Who do you think it is?"

The answer to this question, I thought, was ridiculously obvious.

"Me, naturally," I responded.

There was a collective sigh from the other forty-four students. My teacher looked down and shook her head. I felt puzzled for a moment by their reaction. Who else could it be but me?

It took no time for the answer to become clear. "It isn't you!" said one of the boys loudly, standing up from his desk. "Pretty?" scoffed another boy. "You are not pretty!" He was offended that his adjectives did not immediately identify the object of his affection.

He held his finger towards the prettiest girl in the class, Fabiana. She had blondish, straight, shiny, and perfectly coiffed hair. She had a button nose, straight, luminous teeth, and decent grades. "It's her!" he said loudly.

The entire class laughed.

Unnerved by the jeering, I abruptly left the room and ran towards the bathroom. Nobody followed me. I stayed in there until the bell rang, indicating it was time for the next class. I did not want to suffer further humiliation by seeing my classmates again. With a bowed head, I walked quietly to my seat in the front row and tried to pay attention to the class, but I could not focus as my eyes welled with tears. I kept my head low for the rest of the school day so that nobody would pay attention to me. Following my blatant lack of social grace, any attention was most unwelcome.

Chapter 18

A PRISON BUT IN NAME

*N*othing good could come out of having an absentee parent. With my father gone, there was no one to whom Lauro and my mother had to be accountable. Not surprisingly, life swiftly changed once my father departed to Los Angeles.

First, my mother ceased speaking to us in French, which she had done, even when Lauro was nearby, so that we could learn the language she once loved.

"It is rude," she said when I remarked that she no longer addressed us in French.

"I don't think anyone cares that we speak French," I said. "It isn't as if we talk to our maid or to Dad in French," I said, meaning Lauro, whom I now called *Dad* as was expected of me.

"Well, it is rude, and that is that," she said. She spoke to us in Portuguese at all times, even when the only people in the room were my sisters and me.

While I do not recall whether we ever had previously attended a school field trip, they were certainly out of the question now. I wanted to go, especially upon hearing the excited chatter about the upcoming outing from my classmates. When my mother did not sign the permission slip, I tried to convince my mother to allow me go.

"Mom, there is a field trip to an amusement park."

"You are not going."

"But, Mom, school field trips are school activities. Everybody is going."

"We are not everybody," she responded.

"But why can't I go?" I insisted

"Carnival rides are a sin. There are tons of people with polluted auras. You are not going, and we are not discussing this further."

Whenever references to dark auras or energy came up, I knew that it was the end of the conversation. I stopped asking about outings to amusement parks or other outings perceived as frivolous. Instead, I focused on trips that had a more educational slant.

"Mom, there is a field trip to the museum."

"No, there is too much negative energy at the museum. It will pollute your aura."

"But, Mom, we are going to learn about things that will be in the school text," I lied. I thought if I linked missing a field trip to poor academic performance, she might be persuaded.

"The school should teach you what you need in class. Do you want to have a polluted aura?" she asked, showing me a picture of a person surrounded by a hazy light around his head, with that shade peppered by nebulous black figures, resembling ghosts in a fog.

"Is this what you want?" my mother repeated, shaking that picture in my face and running her hands across her arms as to remove the negativity that the thought inspired.

The image of the black figures surrounding an anguished face scared me. "No, that is not what I want," I reluctantly responded, with tears in my eyes.

I should have known better than to keep asking, and for the most part, I no longer asked about day trips. However, the most important event of my classmates' lives to that date was in the planning stages. The entire class was planning a weekend in Cabo Frio, a beach town a couple of hours north of Rio de Janeiro. It is all anybody talked about: what they would do; which parents would serve as chaperones; who was going to stay in the couple of vacation homes that some of my classmates owned. I had not been formally invited. Yet,

I thought I should try to attend by first seeking permission from my mother for this not-to-be-missed trip.

I explained to my mother how everybody in my class would go on this trip that would be chaperoned by various parents. I added that some teachers would join too—although I knew that was unlikely.

"Mom, please. I really want to go," I begged.

"No, you can't. I already told you that you can't go. Besides, you need a male chaperone with you."

That was a new argument I had not heard before.

"Well, if I had a boyfriend, could I go then?"

"Most definitely not. You are too young," she said.

"Some girls at the school have boyfriends."

"But you will not," she curtly stated, raising her voice.

"How old do I have to be then to have a boyfriend?" I insisted.

"Don't speak of it. Men are only after one thing," she said, slapping me on my mouth. I was wondering what exactly was the "thing" they were after, but she did not tell me. Either way, arguing about a boyfriend was not the point of this discussion. I returned to the main task of changing my mother's stance on social events.

"But, Mom, the teachers are going too," I continued begging.

"It does not matter. These people are not enlightened. Their aura is black. Do you want your aura to be black? They will end up in hell!"

I did not want my aura to be black. The pictures in the books were so realistic that I could imagine the change in my aura colors. Until then, I had not recognized as clearly that my inability to participate in any event, including school activities, was about preventing darkness from entering my life. Yet, I was feeling that there was not much light shining through as it was. I was feeling ostracized from my classmates, from life. Yet, at this time, I felt that maybe darkness was an acceptable price to pay—a little dark aura in exchange for a chance to participate in this trip.

My mother's final answer was no.

I spent the next few weeks on the periphery of school life, listening to others' plans. On the weekend itself, I wondered what my classmates were doing. After they returned, tanned, happy, and more closely bonded, I overhead the chatter about the fantastic time they all had together.

Not being allowed to join field trips was only the beginning of our woes. Once it was clear that no event was reason enough to leave the house, Lauro ensured that nobody would come into it either. Despite his short stature and hunched gait, we felt afraid of him—and not just my sisters and me, but also my relatives, neighbors, and one-time friends.

Lauro took every chance he could to criticize anyone that came in contact with us. It began with my Aunt Simone. "What is wrong with you that you can't find a man to love you?" he asked, simply to irritate and humiliate her. She did not answer. Instead, she no longer joined my grandparents to visit us for a long time.

Once she had left the house in tears, he turned to us and said, "Your aunt is a slut. That is why no man will want her." My unmarried aunt was nearing thirty-years-old. When she did marry a couple of years later, Lauro burned the invitation in front of my sisters and me. "You are not attending a slut's wedding," he said gleefully as my sisters and I recoiled, not knowing what to answer to that.

Next Uncle Sylvain, my mother's brother, became Lauro's target. He filled our minds with lies: "Sylvain is dangerous. He is epileptic, you know. And he hurts people if he were to have an epileptic attack in front of others. He cannot come here." Sylvain visited us in Shangrila once. He never returned either.

My mother did not defend her siblings. She agreed that Simone was a slut and, therefore, a bad influence. She also believed that her brother was dangerous; it was better to keep him away. Over time, Lauro's voice would come out of my mother's mouth, as she parroted everything he said, as she became increasingly fearful of anyone and of the world in general.

Soon after, it was not just family who were to be avoided. "You see that neighbor? He is a drug addict. He can't come here. You know that other neighbor? He beats his wife. You do not want to be involved in such a violent family."

On the rare occasion neighbors came to visit, both my mother and Lauro tried to convert them, asking them to join the religious meetings. When the neighbors did not join in, Lauro often "found out" something horrible about them, thus establishing their poor influence on us. Eventually, nobody came.

I thought that since people did not come to our house, I should seek invitations to theirs. When we first arrived in Shangrila, I remembered playdates with neighborhood families, especially those who vacationed in the area and had large homes with pools. The invitations to spend the afternoons with them, so common earlier on, stopped coming. Noticing this change, I asked my mother whether we could invite someone over.

"We don't have any money to go on a playdate," my mother would say.

"But it does not cost anything!" I responded, puzzled.

"Yes it does," she explained. "If you go to their house, then they have to come to our house, and we don't have money to invite them. We have nothing to offer."

I saw our pantry overflowing with groceries. "Well, can we invite them right after Pappy sends us money every month?"

"No. We can't. Your father does not send us enough money. Do you know that he has not given us a cent more, even though he is now traveling the world? Do you know that he refuses to send money in weekly payments because he does not want to pay the transfer fee? He is the one keeping us this miserable," she said, raising her voice as her sentences progressed, to emphasize my father's role in preventing us from having playdates. She wished me to blame him, rather than the tyrannical rules of my household. When I tried to argue that we did not need money and that it was not my father's fault, she defaulted to people's dark energy, which did not usually allow for any argument.

We did not leave home. Nobody came to visit. We were all alone.

Chapter 19

WINDOWS TO THE WORLD

t never occurred to me to criticize or resent my father for having abandoned us. I had not understood that my father made an active choice to see us only one day per year, when he had at least three weeks of vacation. All I saw in him was the adventurer.

His life—or what little I knew of it—seemed infinitely more interesting than what my mother had chosen. Every so often, we received a postcard from some far-flung place my father visited during his global travels. While he did not speak much during our visits, he did tell us that he petted kangaroos in Australia, purchased silk blouses for Carroll in Hong Kong, and ate a baguette while gazing at the Tour Eiffel in France. My curiosity about these places peaked, but my father only described them broadly, without much attention to specifics. I, however, wanted to learn details about Australia, Hong Kong, and Paris. I became fascinated with tidbits that indicated internationals did not live like Brazilians, that they ate different foods and did not even know how to samba. Yet, without much choice, I had to accept my father's general reticence about his travels. I had to settle for learning about these remote places from postcards.

This changed when my father purchased a package of European stamps on a whim from a newspaper stand at the airport in France. They were mostly used stamps, given they carried the marks of having once been attached to an envelope. Technically, these stamps had no value, but to me, they were a found treasure. They were windows to a world I longed to know. The French stamps bore a figure of Marianne, the French symbol, in multiple colors. Stamps from the Netherlands had a windmill. The stamp from England confused me because it did not have the country's name emblazoned on it, but rather only the effigy of its monarch. I figured out its origins because it bore the Tower of London. There were some countries I had never heard of before, such as Yugoslavia and Hungary. I looked at a world map to learn where they were.

My father, noting my interest in the little pieces of colored paper, brought me stamps on every subsequent visit, and sometimes he sent them by mail. I carefully rearranged my stamp collection by the country's alphabetical order. I saved the stamps from my father's postcards before my mother burned them.

That is how I came to learn that there were geishas in Japan, bald eagles in America, and temples in Thailand. I learned about countries named Oman, Brunei, and Yemen. I studied these little windows to the world with intense curiosity about the stories they told. I learned about Olympic Games, World Cups, and World Expos. I spent entire afternoons looking at pictures of far-flung places, longing to be there among colorful trees, marine animals, and tall mountains.

Through organizing my growing stamp collection, I realized the world was large and full of beauty, not evil and danger. I saw there were events that drew people in and these occurred all the time—without me. This realization sparked a feeling of resentfulness. There was so much to the world outside of Shangrila and the small town of Petropolis. I also recognized that, given how we lived, I would never be a part of this world. I could not even go to a museum in Petropolis on a field trip. How would I ever go anywhere else?

The limitations of my own life became stark and clear to me. For the first time, I realized that some people had a better life than mine. Somebody clearly participated in the activities shown on the stamps. Somebody must have taken the hot-air balloon in Turkey, seen Icelandic volcanoes, or attended the Olympic Games in Russia. I did not know what to do differently. How could I go to the places and participate in the events on the stamps? I remember realizing that I would never be the one to travel, as long as I lived in my house and belonged to my family.

I spent hours wondering what I could do so that one day I too could see the world. All paths pointed to my father as the one person who could help me. That he had abandoned me and hardly helped at all did not deter me. My father lived the life I thought I wanted to live. Although he was awkward and shy around people, as was I, he still boarded airplanes as often and easily as Brazilians boarded buses. He freely explored the world. He must have been wealthy enough to afford all these trips too. At a minimum, I concluded, he must be an important and influential person for his job to send him on global jaunts. I placed my father on a pedestal. His stature grew larger with every visit and every little packet of stamps that he brought to me.

I only saw the possibilities he embodied, never his faults. I admired my father and wished fervently that one day I would be just like him.

Chapter 20

MONEY

$\mathcal{M}$y mother complained from the day we set foot in Shangrila about how little my father provided for us in the form of alimony when he was clearly better off than he let on.

It turns out, it was not just my family who complained. The Brazil of my childhood was a country that struggled economically. As such, my mother's complaints turned into rants as the country plunged into a major economic crisis.

The possibility that anyone in my household could hold a job was never discussed. My mother claimed to be too ill to seek employment. Lauro felt that work was beneath him, thus never earned a day's keep in his entire life, preferring to let my father provide for us instead.

The alimony agreement established that each of my sisters and my mother received 10 percent of my father's salary, for a total of 40 percent. My mother insisted on receiving a percentage of my father's salary so that as my father's salary increased with the promotions that would surely occur, then the monthly payments would increase as well.

Unfortunately for us, the Brazilian court's jurisdiction over my father's income ended when he moved to the United States. My mother threatened to take him to court. Yet, he knew that she did not know how and would not. He ignored her threats, taunting her to take him to court, indeed, if she wanted to.

While my father never missed a single alimony payment, the frequent promotions he eagerly shared did not translate into a better lifestyle for us—quite the opposite. As time wore on, our financial situation worsened. I knew this, not because I fully understood how much money my father sent, but because we began to eat differently.

We did not need much. Fruits mostly came from within Shangrila, with its easy, year-round abundance of bananas, mangoes, avocados, pineapples, and papayas that bulged from the trees throughout the property. The neighboring farm delivered raw, fresh milk each morning to our door step. Rice and beans, the staples of every Brazilian's diet, were always plentiful. What became scarce were vegetables and meat.

There was a lot of talk of hyperinflation and Brazil's debt to the International Monetary Fund, a worldwide agency that had loaned money to the country but now wanted it back. The country of Brazil had spent beyond its means. The Fund wanted its debt paid, and Brazil, unable to do so, printed money so quickly that it led to a rampant inflation rate. The consequences for all Brazilians, who felt a bit bewildered by what their government was doing, was that the prices of everything changed daily.

Practically speaking, that meant we purchased what we needed immediately. The prices would be higher tomorrow, perhaps even by that afternoon. At its worse point, prices increased about 700 percent per year. We mostly guessed what prices we would find once we got to a store. As expected, Brazil's legendary, widespread poverty became worse. Streets became less safe as the poorest would steal anything they could to trade for something to eat.

Those who could, adapted. Most salaries were paid weekly so that wages increased along with prices. Thus, those who held jobs trailed price increases by one week.

For my family, there was no adjustment. When the worst of the hyperinflation hit, my mother asked my father to send us the alimony payments weekly so that we could keep up with the price increases.

However, without a phone, we had to negotiate through my grandparents. My mother not only asked for weekly alimony payments, but also that he increase the amount he sent. It was the only way, she stated, that we could keep up with price increases as the exchange rate changed daily too.

My father refused. He asked my grandparents to relay the message that my mother should learn how to budget better to make the money last through the month.

He had no inclination to help my mother, plus he did not want to pay transaction fees weekly for wiring us money more frequently. Even if my father was trying to make a point, he just did not understand. It had nothing to do with budgeting. Nobody who was not experiencing these daily price increases could understand what it was like. Prices rose so quickly that an item costing one dollar on the first day of the month could cost sixty at the end of it.

My grandparents, weary of my mother and Lauro ensconced in Shangrila, were not sufficiently aggressive in explaining the consequences of not having an inflation-adjusted salary.

Therefore we, as everybody else, just found a strategy to cope.

The alimony payment arrived on the tenth of each month. That day, Lauro departed the house in a flurry of activity to pay school fees, utilities, and all other monthly bills as this debt also adjusted daily. Immediately after, we dashed to the supermarket.

Until then, Petropolis was a haven for smaller businesses, a place where people knew the baker, the butcher, and the auto mechanic. These merchants knew what we liked and often cut the type of meat or prepared a crunchy, white baguette, without us having to say a word.

But we, and most Brazilians, no longer had time to go from store to store when the afternoon price was higher than the morning price. We rushed to the large supermarket that had recently opened in town to accommodate this new economic reality. With a horde mentality, residents bought as much as they could in one shopping trip. Many of the smaller shops ceased to exist.

At the supermarket, we grabbed two shopping carts. One cart was for all non-perishables: soaps, toilet papers, crackers, as well as rice and beans. Lauro calculated how much that would cost and then told us how much money we had left for the fresh produce aisle where we bought as much as our budget allowed.

Freezing food, or buying it already frozen, was not something any of us considered. A frozen food section of readily prepared meals did not even exist. Microwaves were mostly unheard of, and our freezer was so small it held only a couple of ice cream cartons, at best. Besides, in Brazil, the maids cooked fresh food daily. And despite our shortage of funds to buy food, we had enough to keep a maid at our house.

During the first week following our shopping trip, we ate heartily. As the month ended, however, we mostly foraged. During that period, we subsisted on vegetables from our garden and plucked fruits from our trees. We gathered eggs from the chicken coop. While there, we caught the chicken or duck and twisted its neck, removed its feathers, and ate it later that evening. The only perishable we purchased was milk, every few days, until the next alimony payment arrived again on the tenth of the next month.

Discretionary expenditures were out of the question. We purchased clothes twice a year. In late December, right before the school year started, we bought a new set of school uniforms. This included shoes that were a size bigger than what I needed to allow enough space for my feet to grow throughout the year. The second time we bought clothes was the week before my father came to visit so that we could show him how well taken care of we were in new, pressed clothes.

My mother, resentful that food became scarce as the month wore on—while my father continued sending postcards of exotic trips—redoubled her efforts to increase the alimony payments. She complained more loudly, asked my grandparents to talk to him again, and even wrote letters.

My father still refused, claiming that he sent what he owed and that my mother was wrong to ask for raises when he had not received a salary increase, nor the promotions she claimed he had. There was no way to know if my father spoke the truth, but my mother discredited these claims. She pointedly noted that besides the postcards showing the evidence of his large living, my father continued to bring us a trunk full of gifts at his annual visit.

No matter what she did or how much she complained, my mother was ineffectual in changing our living situation. Yet, my sisters and I incessantly heard about the horrible person we had for a father. He abandoned his children to go live with a mistress and was starving us while showering Carroll with Swiss chocolates and silk blouses.

I may have suggested more than once that Lauro could go work, as did the fathers of all my classmates.

"That's ridiculous. Your dad's job is to clean the world of bad energy," she said, and then redoubled her complaints about my father.

Wanting to collect data on my father, my mother relied on my sisters and me to probe about his job status and financial situation.

"I wish I had gotten a raise," or "I did not receive a promotion yet; I do have more responsibility, but my salary is the same," my father told us when we dutifully asked about his salary and assumed promotions.

Eventually realizing we were pawns of my mother to draw information from him, my father stopped the little sharing he did of anything that might indicate his station in life. He no longer described his house or vacations. He stopped talking about work, except describing the long hours he put in. And with this reticence to speak with us so that he would not betray his financial situation, my sisters and I lost further opportunities to connect with him. There were so many topics that were off limits between my father and me that we spent most of his visits in silence or in making superficial commentary about the here and now. Our conversations focused on the weather, how polluted the river that crossed Petropolis was, or the traffic we encountered on the highway. We did not talk about his life. We did not talk about ours either.

Upon returning home, my mother immediately inquired about what we learned during the day.

"His salary did not change, Mom," I said wearily.

"He lies. Did he travel anywhere?" she asked.

"I think so. He said he had gone to Japan . . . and to Switzerland." Seeing her puzzled look, I quickly added, "For work."

"How come Pierre manages to travel the world, yet gives us no more money?"

Then she would start again, about how irresponsible of a father he was, giving us postage stamps instead of what we needed, which was food on the table.

The following year, I stayed quiet about the little my father shared with me. By not telling my mother anything, I perpetuated our culture of silence.

Although my father held firm about not sending us more money or sending the payments more frequently, he must have taken notice of our tattered appearance the year when we did not have extra money to buy a new outfit for his visit.

The following year, his rental car trunk was bulging with even more gifts than usual. The loot usually included puzzles and books, often an electronic game or two, the requisite bubble gum, and a packet full of stamps from whichever countries my father had visited the previous year. The bubble gums made the entire set of gifts smell sugary. However, among our gifts on that visit, there were now clothes: T-shirts, dresses, and sweaters, which we had no use for in the typically warm weather.

My sisters and I squealed in delight, donning our new clothes right there in the parking lot. They were generally oversized and not necessarily in line with Petropolis' fashion sense. But they were from America, and in my little town, that carried a heavier weight than being fashionable. The T-shirts were stamped with a loud drawing of something American, such as a guitar with big labels such as "rock and roll" or stars and stripes colored in white, blue, and red. Keeping up with the equality tendencies of my mother, my sisters and I each got the same item of clothing. At least my father or Carroll, if she was the one who shopped for him, had the sense to vary the colors so that we did not look like triplets of different heights.

Although these clothes were not what we would have chosen for ourselves, we prized them. My sisters and I stretched our sparse clothing by treating all that we received interchangeably, giving the appearance that we owned more clothes than we actually did. It worked well for me because I always received Nathalie's hand me downs, and Catherine's clothes were always a larger size than she needed, but perfectly sized for me.

It was not as if we needed many clothes, however. I looked for any opportunity to show off my new wardrobe to my classmates who felt I did not belong in their midst. But there was hardly ever a chance. We wore uniforms at school. We never traveled, nor attended playdates, birthday parties, after school events, or school field trips. We did not go to relatives' homes, parties, or weddings. So we wore our American clothes at home, and soon they became muddy and tattered—just like the rest of our wardrobe, just like our lives.

Chapter 21

POSTMAN

The following year, my father called my grandparents to announce the date of his next visit. My father never consulted us about our schedule because he knew and assumed we were always available. He must have also thought there was nothing more important for us than to see him and that his visits would be our priority. That July, though, an event I can't remember overlapped with my father's planned visit. And my mother, who never let us go anywhere, agreed to let us go, this one time, that one Saturday.

"Mom, we need to write to Pappy to tell him to come a different day," I begged my mother upon hearing that the event and the visit day overlapped.

"He will just have to come and find the door closed," she responded, without looking away from the book she was reading.

"But, Mom!"

"No buts. It is not my responsibility to organize your father's travel schedule," she said, closing the book abruptly. "He will figure out he picked the wrong date when he finds the door locked on him," she said, smirking.

I envisioned my father showing up to pick us up for the day, his car trunk full of gifts, ringing the bell, only to find nobody home. He would be crushed, I imagined. Then it would be an entire year until we saw him again. I decided I must not let this happen.

But how could I prevent this tragedy? I did not know how to communicate with my father. We did not have a phone. We did not have friends, either, whose phones we could use. It was astronomically expensive to call the United States, so I assumed most people would hesitate to help me. My mom forbade us to write to my father. Even if I had written, I had no way of mailing him a letter as the nearest post office was an hour away in Petropolis. And in Brazil, nobody left the mail for the postman to pick it up.

I needed a plan. I walked around the grounds of Shangrila, incessantly thinking about how to change my father's travel dates. I found holes in all possible scenarios.

A few days later, my grandparents came to visit. And then I thought of a solution. I would ask them to warn my father.

Yet, I could not ask them directly. During their visits, either my mother or Lauro always hovered around, never leaving them alone with my sisters or me. Regardless, even if I found myself alone with them, I would be terrified to ask for their help directly. Surely they would tell my mother; surely there would be consequences. My grandparents and I simply did not have the kind of relationship where I could openly ask for help. What if they did not believe me? What if they refused? Or worse, what if they began asking questions? I did not have the fortitude to answer them. Chances were, I would start crying as soon as the questioning began, afraid that my parents would overhear me and I would be caught sharing the family secrets. Besides, I had been trained to tell lies. How could I tell them what was truly going on in our lives? No. It had to be stealthy; I could not ask them outright.

I excused myself from the gathering and rummaged through my school bag to retrieve a piece of paper. I wrote a short letter to my dad: "Pappy, don't come visit us in June. Come after July 15."

Making sure everybody was still gathered in the living room, I opened the door to my mom's room to find my father's address. My mother typically opened the letters my father sent before she gave them to us. We read them quickly, and she took them away to burn in the fireplace in front of my sisters and me. But she had not yet had time to destroy the latest letter that my grandparents had brought along on this trip. I got the envelope out of her room and moved back to mine. It was the first letter I ever wrote and addressed, to anyone.

I examined the envelope. The left hand corner had what appeared to be the correct address. Yet, I felt doubtful because I noticed that the address did not have "Los Angeles" in it; instead, it had a city I never remembered him mentioning before called "Canoga Park." What if that was not the right place? My father never spoke of Canoga Park; he always said he lived in Los Angeles. And I had to ensure the letter made it to the right place.

I copied the address carefully and hid the letter under my shirt. Just as I was about to leave the room, I returned to my desk and examined the address again. Just to be sure, I added LOS ANGELES and UNITED STATES OF AMERICA in big, underlined letters, as if that would make the postman sure of where to route that important missive.

While the family was still chatting in the living room, I hid the letter under my shirt and walked out of the house, saying that I wanted to play outside. Nobody stopped me.

I walked towards Grandfather Isidore's car, which was parked at the gates, well hidden from view of the living room windows by the massive trees that surrounded the small, grassy area between the house and the parking lot. I reached for the car door, and it opened. My grandparents left the car door unlocked, given that they were inside the tall walls that sheltered Shangrila from view of the highway.

The first part of my plan worked! I thought, feeling relieved.

I looked around to ensure that nobody could see me and entered the car, closing the door silently behind me. I crouched so that anyone looking from the outside would not realize that there was a child inside the car. I opened the also unlocked glove compartment and slipped my letter in. My heart was beating loudly as I closed the glove compartment, raised my head slightly to confirm that nobody had seen me, and closed the car door silently. Within a few of minutes, I was back in the living room with my family, and I joined them at the table for lunch. My heart beat as loudly as a drum; the palms of my hands were covered in sweat. If anyone noticed how flustered I was, they would have attributed it to the fact that I may have been running outside.

Once in the house, I hardly said anything, feeling my stomach churn with nervousness. I was generally not talkative in front of adults, so it was not out of the ordinary for me to be quiet. Still, I felt that I had to tell someone about the letter. Or at the very least, I needed to go back and remove the letter from the glove compartment. Doubt permeated my thinking.

Yet, as I began chewing on green beans at lunch, I thought that everything had happened too fast. I had not thought this through. Now, I considered how unwise my plan was and decided to go back and remove the letter from the glove compartment. But we were not allowed to leave the table until everybody had finished the meal. I got fidgety.

However, as soon as the meal was over, Grandfather Isidore got up to leave. There was simply no way I could return to my grandparents' car unnoticed. I couldn't speak directly with my grandparents as the family hovered around them. I was too nervous to do so anyway. I accompanied my grandparents to their car, hoping to garner the courage to tell them what I did. Instead, I saw them leave without uttering a word, without giving them any instructions about what to do if they found my letter.

There were a lot of "if's" to my plan. They needed to open their glove compartment, find the letter, know that I meant for it to be mailed, and then mail it in time for my father to change his travel plans. I worried. What if they did not open their glove compartment at all? What would they do with the letter if they found it? What if they did not know what to do with the letter? What if they trashed it? Would they have laughed about it and thrown it in the garbage? Would they be puzzled by it and not know that I meant for them to have it mailed? And horrors, what if they told my mother and Lauro about it?

I felt conflicted. If I did not warn my father, I would be betraying him—and disappointing myself because I wanted to see him again. But by writing the letter, I betrayed my mother and Lauro, along with their explicit instructions never to write to my father. This moral conundrum ate at me. I played with my hair obsessively and pulled strands of it out. I bit my nails and fidgeted constantly.

I knew the moment of reckoning was coming. About four weeks later, I realized that I must own my actions. My grandparents were returning for their monthly visit, and I was sure they would either ask me about the letter—or worse, talk to my mother about it.

I had two options: say nothing and wait to see what would happen or preempt the problem by telling my mother the truth. I could not deal with the uncertainty of the first option. A few hours before my grandparents were to arrive, I approached my mother.

"Mom, I need to tell you something."

"Tell me," she said

"Not here," I pleaded. My eyes welled up as I looked at my sisters sprawled on the couch in the living room.

She walked with me to the adjacent temple room and closed the door behind us. Rather than talk to her next to the door that led to the living room, I kept walking towards the windows.

"What is it?" she asked when I stopped to face her.

I tried to speak, but felt a mixture of fear, panic, and shame. I began sobbing instead. As the tears fell to the floor, my ability to control my emotions decreased. My arms and legs shook. My mother towered over me, but at the sight of her eleven-year-old daughter falling apart, and without Lauro or my sisters around, she did something that was rare in our household. She opened her arms wide and engulfed me in a hug. She held me tightly until my frantic sobbing decreased.

"What could you have possibly done?" she whispered as she caressed my unruly, curly hair. Her hug displaced my thick glasses. I distanced myself a bit from her as I got the courage to reveal the secret. I wanted to place myself far enough away so that it would not be easy for her to slap me.

"I wrote a letter to Pappy."

She looked at me without saying anything.

"I put it in Grandpa's car," I continued, now with tears welling up on my eyes, "in the glove compartment".

"What did the letter say?"

"I asked Pappy to change his travel dates."

She came towards me. I recoiled by taking a step back, anticipating a beating. Instead, she hugged me tightly for a few seconds. I did not know exactly what to do or how to feel. Should I hug her back? Before I could act on my thinking, she got up and left the room, saying nothing, leaving me there, not knowing whether she would forgive me or whether she would return with a harsh punishment. After she did not come back for about fifteen minutes, I managed to stop crying and entered the house again.

My mother behaved as if nothing happened as she continued speaking with my sisters about some banality in our lives. She never mentioned that moment again.

A couple of hours later, my grandparents arrived. I braced myself for having to explain and defend my action.

But there was no need to. Everybody behaved as if there was nothing special about this particular visit—as if there were no secrets kept, no messages delivered, and no hidden truths about our lives.

"Pierre called us!" Grandmother Mathilda said to the family gathered in the living room, almost as an afterthought. I looked at her in panic when she uttered my father's name. She kept talking without looking at me.

"He is changing his travel dates because he had a commitment at work and cannot come the day he originally said. You know Pierre; he takes airplanes as easily as we take a bus!" she said with a nervous laughter, revealing the admiration she held for my father. "By the way, he is coming about two weeks later; he just asked me to tell you that."

I felt flabbergasted. I couldn't believe that I confessed my "betrayal" to my mother when my father changed his travel schedule without any help from me. I felt frustrated. I did not have to send that letter. All that lying and stress had been for nothing! Then it occurred to me that maybe my grandparents had never found the letter and I still had time to remove it from the glove compartment.

I tried the same ruse as the time before, but this time, the car door was locked. As nobody mentioned the letter, I did not bring it up.

At his next visit a couple of months later, once we were comfortably buckled in his rental car, my father looked directly at me, smiling. Nathalie was sitting in the front seat and Catherine next to me.

"Isa, thank you for your letter," he said.

"What letter?" my sisters asked, surprised.

I had not told them about the letter because I feared that they would talk to my mother about it too.

My father had repeatedly asked for us to write to him. He sent us postcards from his travels around the world, so he thought we should write back from time to time. We did not tell him we were not allowed, that our letters would never be mailed, even if we had written them. We nodded our heads, agreeing that we would write as he suggested. We would, however, eventually have to give some half-hearted excuse about having too much homework when he questioned why we hadn't written.

"The letter where you asked me to change the travel dates," he responded, not noticing the surprise in my sister's voices. "Had you not warned me, I would not have been able to see you!" he continued. Then he turned to look directly at me sitting in the back seat. "You should write more!"

While I felt elated at having pleased my father, part of me felt mortified that my sisters now knew about the letter. Since I had believed my grandparents when they said my father had changed the travel date on his own, without my help, I did not want my sisters to know that I had sent a letter, against my mother's expressly stated wishes.

"Grandma Mathilda said you came now because you had to travel for work two weeks ago," I noted, both to verify my grandmother's version of the story and avoid any follow-up questions from my sisters on the letter.

"No. It was not work. If it was not for your letter, I would not have been able to see you," he repeated. He turned back towards the wheel and turned the key to the car's ignition.

The sound of the motor broke the conversation. I looked out the window, immersed in thought, processing this new information. My grandparents had come through for me after all! Yet, that did not make me feel happy; it made me feel betrayed. It turns out, they lied too. They never mentioned that they had found and mailed the letter. They never questioned why I hadn't asked them directly. They knew. They knew the life we lived. And they also hid and omitted information. They lied. Everybody lied about everything.

I wished I had the fortitude to tell my father the emotional investment it cost to send him that letter. But I said nothing, as I did not want to have this conversation with my sisters present. Despite his request, there would not be another letter. I wanted to tell him why. But again, I said nothing, letting that opportunity pass. It was a chance to raise my father's awareness of the imprisonment his absence allowed in our lives, but instead, I looked away towards the window. I didn't want anybody to see the tears falling down my young face. These tears betrayed the disappointment I felt at the adults in my life.

We meandered through the mountain road towards Petropolis. I remained quiet. Nathalie broke the silence.

"Pierre," she said, addressing my father.

My father slammed on the brakes.

"What did you call me?"

"Pierre," she said again, but this time more softly, with her own set of tears welling in her eyes.

My mother had told us that our father was Lauro and he was the one we should address as *Dad*. Our true father should be called by his proper name, as someone who abandoned his children for a mistress and then failed to support them properly did not deserve to be called Father. "A father," she said, "would not abandon his children to go follow a lover. A father who truly loved his children would support them."

My mother not only tried to ensure that we did not respect our biological father, she also did what she could to embellish Lauro's efforts to raise us. She went on about Lauro taking us to school and protecting us from evil—all the while putting down my father. Often she asked, "Who do you love more? Your dad (referring to Lauro) or Pierre?" She asked us to state publicly whether our allegiances were to our biological father or our impostor dad.

"Lauro, of course!" Nathalie and Catherine quickly responded to please my mother. "Lauro is our real father."

While I did call Lauro *Dad* at my mother's bidding, I never embraced the idea that Lauro was my father. My sisters, however, realized that acknowledging Lauro as such was the fastest way for that line of questioning to go away. I knew what my mother wanted to hear, yet I could never make myself betray my father so publicly like that.

"I love them the same," I answered whenever this question came up, even if that was not the truth. I loved my father more, always, but I hoped this middle ground would clear me of any trouble.

Once the car was stopped on the shoulder of the precipitous mountain highway, my father stared at Nathalie, who by now was recoiling in fear.

"I am your father!" he exclaimed in an unnaturally raised voice. "And you will call me *Dad*," he continued, while looking at his three daughters.

Now it was Nathalie's turn to look towards the window so that nobody would see her tears falling silently on her pretty face.

The air felt heavy in the now silent car. As we made our way to our typical first stop at Park Cremerie, the prettiest park of the city of Petropolis, my thoughts were swirling about this strange day.

For the first time, I put the pieces together.

My father was unaware of Lauro's existence. He never once asked about my mother, nor us, or about our living situation. I suppose if he had asked, we would have lied anyway. But the truth was that nobody ever asked about our lives—not my father, nor my grandparents. My mother—especially my mother—turned a blind eye to the discomfort of our situation, thinking that having a man in the house who pretended to be our father was for our well-being. All my relatives, my grandparents, Aunt Simone, Uncle Sylvain, and their kids, kept my mother's secret. My father had no way of discovering Lauro's existence when so many people were focused on keeping that information from him.

I realized, at that moment, that there were no adults to turn to. I looked away from the window and stared at my sisters, as if I was seeing them for the first time. Nathalie was now sobbing because she had attempted to do what my mother asked of her. She was the older sister, but she was too obedient, docile, and fearful to change her situation, and by association, mine. Catherine was too young. She was a bit oblivious, it seemed, to what was happening in our lives. And I did not have any friends.

There was no one to help me.

I broke my stare from my sisters and gazed at the scenery, making a note to myself: if I wanted to change something in my life, I would have to do it on my own.

Chapter 22

ESCAPING FROM MY LIFE

*I*n Brazil, the social classes were well defined. Either the matriarch hired a full time maid, or she was a maid. Maids worked six days a week for a minimum-wage salary, cleaning the house, cooking meals, and taking care of the boss' kids, while her own lingered away.

We did have a maid. Even during the worst days of the hyperinflation period, we kept a maid at our small round house who cooked and cleaned for us, my mother claiming to be too ill to maintain a cramped, two-bedroom house. On the maid's day off, my mother expected my sisters and me to maintain the house and cook for the family. Since microwaves were not available in Brazil, at the time, food was always cooked fresh. There was no such thing as leftovers, since we ate every crumb of what was available. And we made just enough for every meal. That meant we cooked at least twice a day.

Having a maid, a symbol of being above the poverty line, did not in any way put my family on the same socioeconomic level as my classmates who lived in colonial houses with manicured gardens on the streets that flanked our school. Their homes had statues lining their large verandas and flanking their pools.

Our little round house was the size of a gazebo on these properties. My classmates' homes had tall walls with broken glass on top, and the well-off had security guards. Kidnappings of children in Brazil's wealthiest families was a relatively common occurrence. So, those who could opted to keep the riffraff away. We were somewhere in between poverty and wealth: a cut above the riffraff, or so I hoped, but most definitely not in the same echelon as those who sat next to me in class. At first, my classmates were curious about me.

"You live in the round house?"

Everybody knew about the round house. It was an unmistakable point of reference on the highway that linked Petropolis to Rio de Janeiro, with its prominent and protruding tower.

"Yes!" I said, excited that someone was actually asking me a question. My excitement quickly deflated at this follow-up statement.

"I always thought it was a sort of a temple."

Well, it was a temple, but I did not want to admit that to anyone. I felt deeply embarrassed that my family presided over religious meetings. I was not worldly, but I knew having a cult in one's house was not normal, just as it was not normal to have divorced parents, to have a stepfather, and not to be allowed to participate in any extracurricular school activities.

"It is my house," I said, not wanting to give away that they were, indeed, correct, that my house was technically considered a temple by many. So instead, I chuckled along with them.

I never corrected anyone when they referred to Lauro as my father. Classmates would say, "Your father always picks you up. Do you even have a mother?" They were puzzled that a man would concern himself with picking up and dropping off children at school; they were so used to having mothers be the responsible party while fathers worked or engaged in pursuits other than child rearing. Many thought my mother had died.

"Yes, of course, I have a mother," I said, correcting them. I did not offer that my mother was always sick and unavailable—or that she never left the house, for any reason, ever, or that Lauro did not work, or that he was not my real father. I did not disclose that my real father did work and paid for our expenses. It was too difficult to hold a conversation with anyone when I had so much I wanted to hide.

I learned to stay quiet. People quickly grew bored of me, since I shared nothing, experienced nothing, and contributed nothing.

As a result, even while at school, I did not partake in the few opportunities for social mingling. School commenced at 7:10 a.m. so that all students could be dismissed by lunchtime and go home for a meal. The drive to school took an hour, so most days we arrived to class just in time. There was a twenty minute recess at ten o'clock, a time when most students ran around the school grounds, played a game of soccer, or hung in circles, gossiping about fashion, music, and other people. I sat on a bench, typically alone, reading or watching others play.

I felt so uncomfortable among my classmates that I actively avoided them. I sat in the front row, in the seat closest to the door, so as to avoid having to cross other students on my way in to class. My class was large, with forty-five students. The teachers were frazzled, moving from grade to grade to teach their subjects. Nobody paid attention to me. None of the teachers or the nuns who walked the school grounds during recess questioned why I sat alone.

It was just the way it was. It was not as if the teachers asked about the other students' welfare either. For the most part, the nuns and the teachers did not engage with students. They taught; we listened. Nobody asked questions, even about the subjects we were learning. Talking, including questioning the teacher, was a sign of either insolence or ignorance. It was highly discouraged—either through criticism, scolding, or surprise from the other classmates.

Yet, I enjoyed and even looked forward to attending school—primarily because I would rather be anywhere other than at home. I was a good student, quiet and never causing any trouble. In essence, I was mostly invisible.

One day, however, my classmates noticed me. The unnatural nature of my life in my house spilled over at school. I had become arrogant about my perceived superiority because I maintained my perch at the top of the academic rankings, despite my inability to fit in socially.

As I waited for Lauro to come pick us up after classes were dismissed, I mentioned to Ana Paula, a student who repeated a grade the previous year due to her poor academic performance—a fact that made me feel utter disrespect for her—that I played the piano.

"You? You don't play!" she retorted, with a clearly disdainful tone.

We did have an upright piano in our house, a gift from my grandfather, more because of lack of space in his tiny apartment in Rio than a reflection of how much he wanted us to learn to play a musical instrument.

"I do!" I insisted. I did attempt to play the piano by reading through the simple scales and music sheets, slowly upgrading to more complex music, teaching myself along the way.

"You don't!" she responded, taunting me and laughing.

Clearly she did not believe me. I don't recall why proving her wrong was so important. Rather than walk away from someone I felt was clearly not smart enough to discourse with me, I pushed her, and she fell to the floor.

She got up, pushed me back, and pulled my long hair with such force that I screamed. Feeling I had no choice, I retaliated by pulling her hair, and we stayed that way for a few seconds, locking horns, screaming, but not letting go of one another. Within a couple of minutes, she had broken my glasses. A small crowd surrounded us, and the principal nun came marching through, separating the two of us by our shoulders.

While I tried to stare Ana Paula down, I caught the sight of my sister Catherine watching the fight. My bravado evaporated. The nun's stern admonition that there was not to be any more hair pulling going forward hardly registered.

I let go of Ana Paula, agreed to whatever the nun said, including showing up the next day so that she could give me a proper punishment. I would agree to anything so that I could catch my sister before it was too late.

"Don't tell Lauro!" I whispered to Catherine.

Catherine shrugged her shoulders with a smile, knowing full well that she could leverage my desire to keep the fight hidden into a gain. She let a smirk spread over her face, but she did not answer the question. Meanwhile, I saw Lauro coming through the gate, ready to take us home.

"Come on, tell me that you will not tell him," I begged, holding Catherine by her skirt.

"Let go of me," she said while continuing to walk away. I turned back to dry my tears and whispered to my sister one more time: "Don't tell!"

She did smirk, but she did not tell. My sisters and I knew that we covered for each other. The nuns did not talk to Lauro about the incident, much to my surprise. It had been a playground scuffle, nothing more. So insignificant was I, this public fight did not warrant the principal asking me what happened—or even reprimanding me. She forgot to punish me the next day. It was as if it never happened.

Except that it did happen, and the fight made the gossip circuit among my classmates. Ana Paula was not exactly a trouble-free child. She had failed academically; that was why she was repeating a year. But no one besides me seemed to hold that against her. She was friends with my classmates, whereas I was not. My entire class moved to protect one of their own, standing against the arrogant, smart girl.

I was called names about being aggressive and violent for the next few days. As if it were even possible, I was further ostracized. I made a point not to care. Books kept me company. I tried to be as invisible as I could be.

Catherine once told me she felt embarrassed to see me always hanging out alone on the bench during recess. "You look like an abandoned orphan," she said. "How come you don't have any friends?"

It wasn't as if I wanted to look like an orphan—although that aptly described how I felt most of the time—or that I did not want to have friends. I just did not know how to do it.

Yet, despite these outward signs that I may have been slightly troubled, nobody ever came forward to ask me about my life. Besides all the adults in my immediate and extended family who actively protected my mother's secret, all other adults were also guilty of ignoring the obvious signs of a troubled child. None of my teachers, or the nuns who ran the school, once asked me about my life. Not once did anyone offer to help me become more socially connected. They thought all was well. I had good grades and was quiet, thus the ideal student. Truly, nobody cared.

So when it came time to seek help, I had nobody to turn to.

CALL FOR HELP

I want to run away," Nathalie told me while we were in our bedroom playing with our toys.

"Where would you go?" I asked curiously.

"To grandpa's apartment in Rio de Janeiro."

"That will not do you any good," I said. "I am sure they would send you right back."

I had not told Nathalie about the hidden letter I placed in the glove compartment of Grandfather Isidore's car. I don't know why I told Nathalie that our grandfather would not help. He had mailed the letter after all, as I had intended him to do. Perhaps it was because I felt he also was part of the problem, because he never uttered a word about the letter to me or about Lauro to my father.

"And when they send you back," I continued, "your life will be infinitely worse than it already is." I was thinking logically and speaking sensibly.

"I don't think it can get any worse," she said.

I did not understand what she meant.

I would soon find out.

Chapter 24

COMING OF THE NEW MESSIAH

*H*aving assumed the mantle of the cult leader, Lauro felt all powerful. He firmly believed that he was going to father the next Jesus and constantly reminded us of this glorious destiny. "It is my destiny to have a boy," he often said. My mother repeated it often as well. "Lauro needs to have a boy; it is his destiny."

I found this confusing. He had had an opportunity, by fathering my sister Catherine, yet she was clearly a girl.

"How come Catherine is a girl then?" I asked more than once. Pointing out this obvious evidence of an unfulfilled destiny earned me a smack on my mouth every time. I learned not to question it again. Whenever the topic came up, I just remained silent. One day this topic surfaced again, as the five of us were sitting in the living room. Lauro turned to me and asked, "Isa, wouldn't you want to be the mother of Jesus?"

For a moment, I imagined myself pregnant and the mother of Jesus. I nodded my head and responded yes with a smile. After all, Jesus was so adored in Catholic Brazil, I thought it would indeed be great if my eventual son had the power to transform the world like that.

I was thirteen years old then and had never had a discussion about sex, so I did not quite understand what getting pregnant entailed. My mother was in

113

the room during this conservation. She just smiled, nodding her head too, as if giving implicit consent for this idea. My sisters were also present. Nobody thought the statement was weird or fully understood what it meant. We all took it at face value and thought little of it. Besides, it was clear to me that if Lauro was meant to be Jesus' father, then it would be my mother who would bear the son.

A few days later, I was in the bathroom washing some clothes in the large laundry sink that was common in Brazilian homes where washing machines were a rarity. Lauro entered the bathroom and closed the door behind him.

He placed himself behind me. I felt this action was weird, given that he had enough clearance to go past me in case he wanted to use the toilet, even though we did not have the habit of using the toilet in front of one another.

I heard some movement which I ignored as I kept washing the clothes. Suddenly, however, Lauro placed his hands on my hips and lowered my shorts. He placed his flaccid penis against my back as he was too tall, relative to me, to place it lower.

"Stay quiet," he ordered.

It was so unexpected and slightly disgusting that I did not know what to do. Resisting Lauro was typically a bad idea and would result in a beating. I remained frozen in place and pretended nothing out of the ordinary was happening.

I could not think of what to do to make it stop. We lived in a small house. People were always around, and we did not have clear boundaries about closed doors in general. Yet this time, the door had been closed. Lauro stayed behind me, rubbing himself against my backside for a few minutes, until a noise in the nearby kitchen made it apparent that someone was about to enter the bathroom.

He quickly put his own pants back on.

"Put your shorts back on," he barked at me as he left the bathroom.

I did not know what to think, but I stopped washing the clothes, deeming them clean enough, and left the bathroom as soon as I could.

I avoided eye contact with Lauro after that, but he kept hovering around where I was. Noting that I stayed glued to where my sisters were, he later ordered me, in a whisper, to "stay in the house when I tell your sisters to go play."

Not used to defying orders, I nodded my head.

"Make an excuse why you have to stay here," he demanded, holding my arm forcefully.

As we did most afternoons, my mother retreated to her bedroom to take a nap, and my sisters made their way to the yard. I desperately wanted to follow them, but I knew that Lauro would hit me if I did not obey him.

"I will stay here to do my homework," I told my sisters when they asked me to come along to play with them. They left, and I found myself alone with a man I was scared of.

So he took me to my bedroom, next door to where my mom was napping, and removed my bra.

I felt a surge of anger. Not because he was fondling my breasts, but because it was the first day of my life I had worn a bra, a hand-me-down from Nathalie that I begged her to give me. I had noticed that all the popular girls at school wore a bra, so I wanted to be like them and wear one too. I had felt so excited about wearing my new, hand-me-down bra to school earlier that day, feeling so grown up. Now, here was this monster destroying that moment for me. He played with my breasts and kissed them. I was disgusted and frozen in place, unable to move elsewhere, although I desperately wished to be anywhere but here.

Miraculously perhaps, there was a stirring of noise. Nathalie returned to the house to pick up something she had forgotten. Upon hearing my sister, Lauro stopped touching me and left the room. I wanted to thank my sister and tell her what just happened, but I could not articulate what was happening. I felt a mixture of shame and shock, so I said nothing.

The next day Lauro cornered me before we got in the car to go to school. "Did you like what we did yesterday?"

I felt the now familiar sensation of feeling frozen in place. I said nothing but nodded as I lowered my head.

He closed the distance between us and whispered, "We can do it again later." He began slowly driving the car forward, but before he drove even a few feet, he stepped on the brakes abruptly. He wanted to remind me of what was at stake if I dared tell anyone what had happened: "If you tell anyone, your mother will die!"

I widened my eyes while I looked at him, but said nothing. "Do you want your mother to die?"

I shook my head.

"Do you?" he spoke louder, expecting an answer.

"No," I said quietly.

"Then you know what to do," he said, driving away.

I shed silent tears at the thought of my mother dying and the horror of having the responsibility for killing her if I dared tell the truth. And if she died, then I would be all alone in the world with this horrible person.

Lauro tried again a few times to convince me to stay behind in the house while my sisters left to play in the afternoons. When I could, I outsmarted him. I would say loudly, ensuring that either my mother or sisters heard, that I wanted to go play outside. Lauro then could not ask me to stay behind without arousing suspicion or providing a reason why.

Unlike previously, I now locked the bathroom door whenever I used it. I sought to spend most of the afternoons, while my mother napped, outside in the large yard, playing with the dogs, riding my bike, and doing my homework. When in the house because of hot weather or the frequent thunderstorms that fell in the afternoon, I stayed glued to one of my sisters—either in the living room or in our bedroom, doing homework or playing games.

Given how unsuccessful Lauro was in accessing me during the day without arising suspicion, he tried at night.

We went to sleep early because of our typical, half past five wake-up to arrive at school on time. That meant Lauro was wide awake when my sisters and I retired to bed at around half past eight.

Again, unlike we did before, I now locked the door to the room I shared with my two sisters. I placed our new dog Luna, a cocker spaniel we got to replace Dobby (who had remained Lauro's dog), on my bed so that she would make noises if anybody tried to come into the room. I hoped she would wake up my sisters and alert my mother in the room next door.

For a couple of nights, I saw from the top of my bunk bed his attempt to open the knob of the locked door, and I heard the swearing that accompanied his failed effort. I felt smug in my cleverness to have locked the door. After two nights of this, Lauro took the key and threw it away. He tossed it out the window, in front of all of us, swearing loudly. I sought the room key in the yard below, but the dense vegetation thwarted my efforts.

Now that he had eliminated barriers, the next night Lauro returned to our room and began fondling me on the top bunk. He told Luna to be quiet, and my two sisters apparently did not wake up. Nathalie slept in a single bed perpendicular to the bunk bed I shared with Catherine.

He asked me to join him in the living room, but I pretended to be asleep so that I would not have to accompany him. He spoke a little more loudly, demanding I join him and shaking me a little bit, but he incurred the risk of waking up my sisters if he raised his voice. So again, after a few minutes, he left.

With the key gone, I had to device another plan to prevent these middle of the night visits. The solution came in the form of my shoes. I had the rather flimsy, rubber flip-flops that were commonly worn by Brazilians everywhere. I took the worn-out, yellow shoe and jammed it in the door so that it worked as a door stopper. Lauro tried that night to come in again. Although he tried, he could not open the door more than a few inches without making a lot of noise. Once again, I heard the profanities. The next day, Lauro removed my shoe from the bottom stop of the door and threw it away. He also gave me a beating that he did not try to hide from anyone. Nobody asked him why he hit me. It was not the first time he had hit me for no apparent reason. This time there was a reason, yet I did not protest.

Lauro may have thought he was clever to throw the shoe away, but that approach backfired. I had exactly two pairs of shoes: the black leather shoes I wore for school and the yellow flip-flops that I used around the farm. Given that one flip-flop was missing, I walked around barefoot while indoors but wore my school shoes to go outside to play. That guaranteed that my good shoes got dirty and muddy, which upset my mother.

"How many times do I have to tell you not to wear your school shoes to play outside? Where are your flip-flops?" my mother asked, seeing me wear my soiled school shoes.

If I told my mother that Lauro had thrown the shoe away, she would ask why. Then I would need to tell her the reason. And if I told her, she would die.

"I lost one of them in the mud," I lied. Lauro was in the same room with us.

"Go back to the mud to fetch it," she said, upset about how careless I was with my belongings.

"I cannot find it," I said tearing up.

"Get her new shoes!" she told Lauro, feeling frustrated with me.

She addressed me again: "And you make sure you take better care of your belongings. God knows that your father does not send us enough money to keep buying you shoes!"

Lauro could not argue. He stalled for a few days, assuming that would give him a few days of an unblocked door to have access to me. In the meantime, though, I took my sisters' flip-flops to use as door stoppers. It would be too suspicious if my sisters also "lost" their shoes. Within days, I had new, pink flip-flops, which I immediately used to jam the door.

Lauro tried less often, but one night he successfully opened the jammed door. Rather than walk towards my bed, he walked towards my sister Nathalie's bed. There, he whispered, increasingly using louder tones of voice, betraying his frustration, for her to join him in the living room.

For a moment, I felt relieved Lauro's attention was directed at my sister, rather than at me. Yet, as I heard his insistence, I knew my sister was obviously resisting his advances and must be distressed that he was bothering her. I felt I had to do something, but it was pitch dark.

I spoke loudly, meaning it to sound as if I had just woken up. "Hi, Dad!" I said cheerily, piercing the cloak of the night and foiling Lauro's plans once more.

He cursed under his breath, but left us all alone that night.

Chapter 25

FIRST DOMINO FALLING

*U*ntil Lauro started molesting me, I almost felt a mixture of love, admiration, and fear towards him—the way children love their parents even when they do not deserve that love. Lauro had been a father figure of sorts. Outwardly, he did appear to care for us while my mother languished at home, isolated from the world, feeling sorry for herself. He drove us to school and did the grocery shopping and bill paying.

But now, I felt mostly disgust towards him, and that stronger emotion pushed away any tenderness I may have felt previously. These negative feelings then expanded to everything related to Lauro. I questioned the purpose of the religious meetings and whether they were meant for our salvation. I questioned whether I should fear dark auras, when those with the cleanest auras—my mother and stepfather—seemed to be the ones who caused me the most problems. Although I did not clearly understand and still feared the dark forces that would engulf me if we disobeyed, I recognized that obeying created its own set of problems. Whatever ill would befall me from questioning the meetings could not be worse than the current ills of my life.

I had been a dutiful daughter. I did what my parents told me to do and never questioned it. But what had that given me? I felt alone, scared, and increasingly resentful. The words Lauro spoke in the meetings—about love, tolerance, salvation, and helping thy neighbor—were inconsistent with his predatory ways. His violence when we disobeyed him, even if unintentionally, and how he and my mother fought with everyone who came in contact with us made me question the sincerity of his mission.

Lauro had made himself large and important at home, but in public, he was small and hunched. I felt increasingly embarrassed when he came to school: embarrassed of his gait, his clothing, his mannerisms, of his being. I no longer wanted to associate with him.

Slowly, though, I found a path.

I remember it was a Thursday, and I felt unusually happy because that meant that there was still a full week until the next religious meeting the following Wednesday. I dreaded Wednesdays. For the past seven years, I had not missed one meeting. My mother or Lauro did not excuse us, even when I came down with mumps. I attended the meeting with swollen lymph nodes—whether I was contagious or not did not matter to them.

I had long ago stopped inventing visions during meditation. My sisters and the other attendees let their imagination grow over time about what they saw. Years earlier, I tried to create visions for a few weeks after "seeing" the blue light. I had seen red and green lights the subsequent weeks. When that failed to impress, I saw a rainbow. Eventually, I fabricated something so extraordinary that everybody rolled his or her eyes, knowing it was a blatant lie. When I failed to benefit from "seeing" anything, I stopped making visions up. I reverted back to my standard answer when it was time to share our visions: "nothing."

At the following week's meeting, I stared at Lauro while he spoke to the small crowd. For the first time that I recall, I felt a spark of hate igniting inside as I realized his hypocrisy.

I do not want to be here, I thought. And by *here*, I did not simply mean being at the meeting that day. It was that I did not want to have the life I led. I longed to fit in at school. I longed to have friends. And most of all, I longed never to see Lauro again.

At that moment, I think the desire to be normal became a stronger force than the fear of punishment. The images of the dark ghosts and the anguished and contorted faces that my mom showed me whenever she felt the stirrings of rebellion within me were not as paralyzing now, and they simply became drawings in a book. I decided I would much rather have dark ghosts around me than have this particular life.

I had reached the tipping point.

The following Wednesday, I did not enter the room as the meeting was about to start, choosing to remain in my bedroom. My sisters and the other guests had already entered the temple and found their seats, waiting expectantly for Lauro to rise up and address them. My mother, noticing my absence, came to fetch me.

"I am not going today," I said calmly.

"Of course you are. Come!" my mother gestured towards the door impatiently.

"No, I am not," I said, staring at her.

My mother was livid, but not enough to scream at me, lest she create a scene where those in the house would witness how she and Lauro typically treated us. She let it go for the moment. I stayed behind in my room, feeling a mixture of triumph and fear.

I worried about what Lauro or my mother would do to me once the meeting was over. Despite my bravado, I also worried about dark forces and contorted souls hovering around my aura now that I so openly defied my mother. I had been taught to believe in the power of the occult and in the wrath of God. I felt certain I would pay for my insolence.

When the meeting adjourned, nobody came to check on me. I do not even think anybody besides my family noticed my absence. Perhaps they were indifferent, but I believe they ignored me mostly because I truly was not one of them. My visions were nothing special. I stayed in my bedroom, reading in the darkened room, feeling the pulse of my heart pounding with a mixture of fear, anxiety, and elation. I became terrified of the potential consequences. I had escaped this time, but how long would that last? I had witnessed people getting possessed and had heard the warnings. Getting a beating from my mother or my stepfather was child's play compared to what I was expecting from God and his spiritual acolytes. But I was readying myself for a beating first. I would worry about karma and bad aura later.

Eventually when everybody else left, my sisters and mother entered my bedroom. "How come you did not join us tonight, Isa?" my mother asked.

"I was not feeling well," I said.

Surprisingly, that seemed enough of an answer. Lauro did not come at all to ask why I missed the meeting.

Despite this surprising outcome, I felt afraid of what the night would bring. I feared that Lauro would try to enter my room. I feared what punishment the universe had in store for me. I fell asleep eventually, drenched in sweat, shivering in fear. Yet, I slept soundly. There were no disturbances that night.

The morning eventually came. I woke up as I always did, along with the symphony of birds that chirped around our windows, serving as an alarm clock. I looked around the room, and I felt a wave of relief. Nothing out of the ordinary appeared to have happened. My sisters woke up gloomily. As the sun rose, we followed the morning routine to ready ourselves for school. The spirits must have taken pity on me and decided they had better people to scare. We left at half past five, as usual, to catch the van to school. At school, nothing seemed different either. I was my ever-lonely self, and the day went by as any other, with my longing to belong, with my inability to do so. Upon my return home, I resumed my routine, helping around the house after lunch, doing my homework, reading a bit of the *Rational Immunization* book in front of my mother, and then spending the rest of the afternoon playing in the mud. Amazingly, there was no mention of my behavior until the following Tuesday evening.

"Isa, I expect to see you at the meeting tomorrow," my mother stated in a tone that indicated that there would be no discussion about it.

I knew this moment would come. I puffed my chest to show a level of confidence that I certainly did not feel. In actuality, I trembled inside for the wrath of God that would surely follow my defiance to my mother and to the spirits.

"Mom, I am not going."

My mother and Lauro were in the kitchen; both stopped what they were doing.

"Isa, you are."

"No, I am not."

Lauro grabbed my arm and shook me.

"I will see you there tomorrow. No discussion."

"No, you will not," I said defiantly.

He hit my mouth. But rather than cower and just agree, I stared at him and said, "I am not scared of you."

He let go of my arm. My mother placed herself between Lauro and me and tried a softer tactic.

"But, Isa, you are finally opening up," she said, referencing the visions I once reported having. "All you have to do is try a little harder. Remember when you had visions? They mean you are opening your spiritual side," she tried to say soothingly. Even so, I could hear the frustration in her voice.

"No, I am not opening up," I continued defiantly. "I never saw anything. I made it all up!" Somehow, I said all this while looking directly into my mother's eyes in a show of budding teenage defiance. I wanted to ensure that she understood my point.

Surprisingly, she diverted her eyes away from my stare and sighed with great disappointment.

Lauro cursed. "You little snake," he said condescendingly. "You will pay the price. You will see what the spirits have in store for you!"

Yet, they both walked away, leaving me standing in the middle of our small, pie-shaped living room, uncertain of what to do next, surrounded by my sisters whose eyes were even wider with disbelief than mine.

OLYMPICS

*I*t was during that time that I decided to focus my efforts on improving my athletic performance so that I too could become popular and have friends in my life.

I found every excuse to go outdoors to play in our yard. This was partly because I did not want to be in the house within Lauro's reach in the afternoons, but also because I had decided that I wanted to be chosen first, at least once, for the school's handball team, whereas I was usually always chosen last.

My sisters played with me a little, but they did not have any interest in throwing the ball around for hours. So when they stopped, I hit the ball towards the wall of the landlord's house, in an area where there were no windows. If I did not catch the ball when it ricocheted from the wall, then it would roll down towards the wooded, grassy area behind me, which was on a slight slope. To avoid chasing the ball down the incline, I became increasingly more agile and able to catch the ball with every play.

I became quicker on my feet and developed faster reflexes so that I could grab the ball, seemingly from anywhere. My endurance increased too as it was rare the day that I did not spend at least an hour, often two or three, kicking the ball around. I threw the ball to the wall for hours, for days that turned into weeks that turned into months. I placed all my anger, disappointment, and

124

rage on that ball for having a monster for a stepfather. I vented my angst at having a father who was unreachable, a mother who was sick, and classmates who ostracized me.

The wall became what a boxing bag would have been if I had access to one: a way to escape, to release my frustration, to tire myself so that I could escape from my reality—even for a few minutes each day.

Yet, despite all this effort, my team standing did not improve; my performance during school games was not better. I became aggressive, yet all that accomplished was that I was made to sit out whenever there was an odd number of players. After months of practicing, the captains still selected me last for the sports team. I added this injustice to my list of grievances.

One morning I woke up feeling miserable after having coughed all night. I may have had a fever. I certainly had a runny nose and swollen eyes. Despite my mother's suggestion that I stay home, I went to school. I dreaded the thought of staying home alone while my sisters were at school. I now had to stay near one or the other at all times to avoid Lauro. So I lied that I was feeling better, and off to school I went.

Once at school, though, my head throbbed with pain. So I had asked the P.E. teacher to let me sit out the game that day.

He did not let me.

The regular goalie was out because she too was sick. I had tried to play goalie a year or so earlier, but had done poorly because I removed my glasses before the game, fearing that they would be broken, as they had been before. Plus I liked to run and feel active, to break away from the constant limitations of my life; therefore, I had no motivation to play the goalie position.

That morning, however, I felt so sick that I agreed to stand in front of the goal, and I felt so miserable that I even kept my glasses on.

I heard my classmates snickering as they saw me walk towards the goal. My team groaned, saying that they had already lost the game with me at that position. The opponents cheered, agreeing that they had already won.

I felt anger within me. I was tired of being the worst player in the class. I was tired of trying and longing to make friends, yet never succeeding in doing so. I no longer wanted to hear the jokes and snickering. This anger pushed away my desire to while the hour away. I stood tall in front of the goal, readying myself as if for battle.

I may have let a goal or two get by early on, but I moved so fast from one corner of the goal to the next to catch the ball that there simply was not a sliver of space where the ball could slip through. I had learned to anticipate where the ball would come from my endless practices against the wall in Shangrila. I sensed where it would be, and I placed myself in front of it. My actions were instinctual.

My team won by a landslide.

At the end of the game, I felt stunned. And apparently so did everyone else. My classmates looked at me as if they saw me for the first time.

"How did you do that?" they asked.

"I don't know," I responded, stunned.

My feat as goalie made the gossip circuit, but it did little to change my social standing among the class. I, so used to being shunned, did not try to reach out to anyone. Plus, I felt that blocking the ball so consistently was a bit of a fluke. I had not understood why my performance would be that different from when I tried to be the goalie before, except for keeping my glasses on. Nevertheless, the following week I made sure to keep wearing them.

This time, the P.E. teacher placed me on the goal, without me having to ask, even though the regular goalie was back. As I had the previous week, I blocked all balls, and my team won the game. I felt more confident about my skills, and apparently, so did others. After two weeks, I was picked third in the lineup. I felt utterly content with this outcome. Third? That was seven spots away from my typical spot as last pick.

That week, for the first time in my life, the team captain held her arm around my shoulder as she whispered a winning strategy for our team.

"I will make all players move to the offense and block the strikers on the other team. If the fastest players are all marked, they will throw less. You can block the balls from the weakest players without our help anyway." Ana Cristina said.

I liked that vote of confidence, and even more, the hug she gave me.

"It's on you, Isabelle," Ana Cristina said.

"OK," I responded.

I did not disappoint. The bulk of my team moved towards offense, and the defense strategy was that I blocked goals. And I did it. My team won again, for the third consecutive week. That was a first. My teams generally lost.

When the day came for the captains to select the teams for the Olympic Games, I knew that I would no longer be chosen last. I felt assured that I would have a place on a team. I even dared think that I would be placed on a potential winning team and win a medal for the first time. Both my sisters had won medals at the Olympic Games in previous years, a fact they made sure I did not forget.

The Olympics were such a big deal that the entire school talked about it incessantly. During this week-long competition, the entire school occupied Petropolis' only sports center, a large stadium with indoor handball, volleyball, and soccer courts. My seventh-grade class had won top honors in the opening parade two years in a row now, and discussions of the uniforms we would wear, the flags the more talented moms of our classmates would sew, and what floats we would construct filled the days. These discussions started long before the teams were selected. Team selection day was so important that we all whispered about team configurations and speculated about who would partner with whom. I did not participate in these discussions, but people talked so much about the topic that I overhead most of the important points. Thus, I felt excitement about team selection that one, muggy Tuesday morning.

I had expected that the best two offensive players, Isabela and Flavia, would be two of the three team captains. It was only fair, I felt, because otherwise, they could be placed on the same team and would be invincible together. To my surprise, only Flavia was a team captain. I don't know why the P.E. teacher selected Ana Cristina, a strong but not stellar player as captain of the second team, and another girl, equally ordinary, to head the third team. I wondered if somehow Flavia and Isabela arranged this on purpose so that they could be on the same team. I prayed that, at a minimum, Flavia would not be chosen to pick first so that the other two teams would have a chance.

Ana Cristina chose first. I felt relieved because I was sure she would pick Isabela, and then the teams would even out and be more equitable.

It was perfectly silent as Ana Cristina moved to select her first player.

"I want Isabelle," she said, pointing at me.

I was sure she had misspoken. The other girls, anxious to be selected into a strong team, thought so too, gauging by the loud murmur that pierced the silence once Ana Cristina had spoken my name. Everyone thought the same thing—that it was madness Flavia and Isabela would now certainly be on the same team.

It did not make sense, so I assumed she did not say it right, even though she pointed at me. But we were all bunched up together, so I reasoned she meant Isabela with an "a" —in my opinion the best athlete and the prettiest and most popular girl in our class—and not me, Isabelle with an "e."

I did not budge.

"You heard her, Isabelle," said the P.E. coach, placing his hand on my shoulder, urging me to go join my captain's side so that the team selection could continue.

Instead of walking towards Ana Cristina, I said, in a whisper, "Don't do it." I was slightly panic stricken, quite aware that all eyes were trained on me. "Pick Isabela first!" I said.

She looked at me, puzzled.

"Why?" she asked

"Get the next strongest player. Don't let them be on the same team. Worry about the goalkeeper later!"

Ana Cristina frowned. The coach shook his head. All the other girls simply stared, not quite sure what to make of what was happening. I could not tell whether their puzzlement was because Ana Cristina picked me or because I told her she shouldn't, or because they also calculated that the other team was the one they would be lucky to join.

"Isabelle, just come over here!" Ana Cristina gestured to me, more as an order than as a request. I left my place among the other girls and crossed the chasm to join my team captain's side.

Sure enough, as I had expected, the next name I heard called was "Isabela." Flavia had done what I and everyone else expected. *Now our fate is sealed,* I thought.

"What did you do?" I asked Ana Cristina. "Now Isabela and Flavia are together!" I almost had tears in my eyes.

Ana Cristina then spoke loudly enough so that everybody who had the same doubts as me would hear. "Isabelle, if I do not choose you, then Flavia will. And then my team will not have even the smallest chance. Nobody can score when you are defending that goal. You are the most important player here, and the one I want on my team."

I felt stunned, but said nothing. The murmurs from the other girls got louder. Most felt torn about whether they wanted to join Ana Cristina's or Flavia's team.

I watched attentively as Ana Cristina picked subsequent members to join our team. I needed to have a glimmer of hope that our team could come out on top. Once we had the teams selected, I still felt uneasy that the top players were not on our team, but then again, I felt that, overall, our team was strong. And maybe I could live up to Ana Cristina's opinion of me.

It was then that it dawned on me what had just happened. Suddenly, it no longer mattered who was part of my team. Ana Cristina, who had the pick of the field, including the strongest offensive player, instead chose me. Then I remembered an earlier dream, that one day I would be chosen first. I had given up on the dream when all the practice I did to become a better offensive player did not yield results. I was astonished that it happened at all. But most importantly, I had never imagined that the dream would become true on the most important day of team selection of the entire school year, for the most important of all events.

My eyes widened. I felt my chest puff up with a sense of wonder and elation I had never experienced before. I wanted to laugh. I wanted to cry. I did a little of both.

I had been chosen first! I was picked over the best and most popular girls at school—for the Olympics! I just couldn't contain my happiness, and I smiled for the rest of the school day. When I went home that day, all I could say to Lauro, to my sisters, to my mother, or to anyone who would hear was that I had been chosen first.

FATHER

J had been so overtly excited to share the news about the order of the Olympic team selection that I neglected to anticipate that the situation provided Lauro the perfect weapon to hurt me.

"You will not play," he said definitively as I kept talking to my mother and sisters about my morning and how I could not believe that I had been selected first.

Silence fell in the room.

"I have to play; I was selected first!" I exclaimed.

My mother and my sisters were gathered in the living room. My sisters' eyes widened too, and they let out a sigh of frustration. They realized that if I was not allowed to play, they would not be allowed to either.

I turned to my mother.

"Mom, please. I have to play."

"Your father said you will not; he must have a reason."

"What reason?" I asked, frustrated.

Lauro, who normally did not bother providing reasons for his decisions that concerned me proceeded to state how my sisters and I did not deserve to play because we had not been cooperating at home. He could not overtly say that I had not cooperated with his attempts to isolate me within my own home, but I knew the source of his frustration.

"You will not play. End of discussion!" Lauro said, with a tone of finality that we knew too well. There was no pleading that would change his stance.

At that moment, the smirk on Lauro's face betrayed just how pleased he was with himself for inflicting pain on me. This realization led me to a new feeling towards him, one stronger and more potent than the fear I usually felt. This emotion tensed my entire body and made me clench my teeth. It was a feeling of hate.

How could he spoil this moment for me? I had dreamt of this moment. I had plotted and practiced and worked so hard to be chosen first, to belong, to make friends. How could my stepfather so eagerly rob this from me? Why did my sisters just stand there and do nothing and let me beg all alone? Why did I have to fight to do things that everybody else was allowed to do? Why did we have to be different?

"Mom, please," I begged, turning to my mother, pleading with tears falling freely over my distressed face.

My sisters stood closer to the wall, knowing that my mother would not reverse Lauro's decision. There he stood in the middle of the room, with his arms crossed and a smirk of triumph on his thin lips. And I knew that nothing I said or did would change that decision.

Unlike other times, though, I did not feel resigned to my fate. This time I had something bigger to lose. And as my fear turned to hate, it grew, heavy and black in my heart, pushing away any other emotion that I may have harbored towards the sadistic person who stood in front of me.

I dreaded the moment I knew was coming at school. I held out for as long as I could, and I even considered not sharing the news at all, pretending that I had not been forbidden from playing. Yet, I felt I had to tell my schoolmates because Lauro and my mother made sure that I withdrew from the Olympics at the first opportunity.

As my team gathered for our first training session, I sought Ana Cristina, hoping to catch her alone. However, since she was the team captain in the midst of the Olympics season, she was never alone. I placed myself as close to her as I could, trying to block the others by giving them my back.

"I am not playing," I whispered to Ana Cristina as we were readying for a training session.

"What?" she asked loudly. She was dumbfounded, as I had expected. Raising her shoulders and reducing the personal space between us, she sought to overpower me physically so that I could feel her disbelief and anger. All my teammates turned towards us, robbing me of the chance to share this disaster privately.

"My parents told me I can't play."

"I am certainly not surprised!" she shouted, turning her back to me, speaking in a loud enough voice that drew in my other team members, making my shame and despair public and deep.

"I chose you because the team needs you. You have to play," Ana Cristina said.

"I can't," I said, now crying. "My parents won't let me."

She was fuming and refused to engage any more "Don't bother training with us at all then," she said.

She meant it. She told the P.E. teacher: "Isabelle is sitting out. She isn't willing to help the team."

The P.E. teacher, who never let a player out because of illness, decided not to intervene this time. I stood on the sidelines while Ana Cristina selected another player to fill the goalie position. My team captain had meager choices. Thinking that I would block all goals, she had only chosen offensive players. That may have been a good strategy when she had a good goalie on the team, but it proved disastrous now that I was sitting out. My team was decimated during the practice game that day—and every subsequent day. With every loss, Ana Cristina's anger was visible in her face; she barely addressed me. But she forced me to sit on the bench and watch the team lose at every practice. And then she and my other teammates made me feel guilty about it.

After the game, a couple of my teammates came to talk to me.

"We will lose if you are not the goalie."

"I am sure somebody else can train to become a strong goalie," I responded unconvincingly.

"Even if we pick another player to be goalie, we are still down a good offense player."

"Sorry," was all I could say. "I really asked my parents to play this time."

"How come your parents don't let you play?"

"I don't know," I responded.

"Do you ever go anywhere after school?"

"Not really."

"Why is your house round?"

How could I tell them the complexities of my life? I had always done what my parents had asked me to. It had never occurred to me to disobey them; lack of obedience was swiftly followed with a harsh punishment. But once my teammates questioned my parents' choices, it made me realize that perhaps I should start questioning them too. Was there a worse punishment than having my dream shattered? I would take a blow any day over the crushing defeat I felt sitting on the bench, watching my team struggle and blame me for their poor performance during practices.

During these demoralizing practices, I observed them and their frustration and felt bad along with them. Yet, I realized that once the game was over, none of my classmates had the limitations I had in their lives. Why were there so many limitations imposed on me? These students did not seem any more likely to have a dark aura than I did. They were doing all that my mother forbade me to do so that my soul would not be corrupted, yet they were significantly happier than me. Thus, I decided that it was vastly preferable to have a dark aura and go to hell than continue to miss out on this life.

I felt the unfairness and injustice of my situation. I also felt strongly that I did not deserve it. I felt angry at the world. What was the point of being the best goalie if I was not allowed to play? What was the point of rising in the ranks academically if all I accomplished was to feel even lonelier and more abandoned at school and at home?

There was no point at all, I realized.

Somewhere along the way, my frustration pushed away my earlier fears of Lauro and of punishment. No amount of screaming, hitting, or hair pulling would be worse than the misery I felt sitting alone on that bench, seeing life unfold in front of me, unable to be a part of it.

I renewed my efforts and begged my mother and Lauro every single day to allow me to play at the Olympics. I ensured that whenever I spoke with Lauro about this topic, I was never alone with him. Therefore, not only my parents, but also my sisters heard the incessant begging.

Yet Lauro carried that dreadful smirk on his face throughout the following weeks, deeply enjoying the power he felt over denying me what I wanted.

Despite the constant refusal of my pleas, I talked about nothing else when at home. Even my sisters eventually felt frustrated at my persistence.

"Isa, stop! We already heard it a million times!" my sisters said. "You know Dad will not allow it, so just stop."

My sisters felt frustrated too. Given that everything was equitable in the house, they were also banned from playing. And Nathalie and Catherine blamed me.

"If you hadn't been so cocky about being chosen first, then Dad would not have thought the Olympics was so important! So, stop talking about it," they pleaded.

"Don't you want to go to the Olympics too?" I asked, desperately trying to garner support for my ineffective persuasion tactics.

"You know we are not going," they responded, resigned to their fate.

"I will not stop. This is not right. We should play. We have always played!" I said, noting that we had participated in the Olympic Games the previous two years.

They shrugged their shoulders in frustration and stayed mostly quiet when I resumed my barrage of pleading. My sisters did not join me in the begging, even though they would benefit from a reversed decision as well. They stayed quiet. I, in the meantime, was hit and shaken for my insistence, yet I would not stop. It did not matter how many times I heard no or how often I would be punished. Nothing else mattered to me besides having permission to play.

This impasse continued for seven, long weeks. Week after week, I saw my team's defeat during practice. Even though nobody talked to me directly, the chatter about the Olympics reached a feverish pitch at school, with talks about the parade and which team was likely to win and all the fanfare that surrounded the big competition. I felt my heart tear when I saw my team line up to measure their waists and hips for the custom-made uniform, a body suit with a diagonal stripe of green and a miniskirt that resembled those worn by female tennis players.

Once the team received their custom uniform order, I realized in frustration that I should stop hoping. Now, there was no way I could play at all, even with a last minute miracle, because I did not have the uniform that identified me as part of the team.

I felt entirely dejected.

With a week to go before the Olympic Games opening ceremony, rather than launch into begging when I got home, I just slouched on the couch and took a book out of my bag to read, although we did not have assigned homework for the next two weeks because of the games.

My mother entered the room with a wide smile on her face.

"Nathalie, Isabelle, Catherine!" She always repeated our names to ensure that she did not miss any of her daughters. "I talked with your father!" she said, looking at Lauro, who entered the room right behind her.

We looked at her unenthusiastically. What could she possibly discuss with Lauro that would be beneficial for us?

She paused for dramatic effect. "You can play at the Olympics!" she said excitedly.

My sisters immediately squealed in delight and, as expected, jumped from the couch excitedly. They both rushed to hug and kiss Lauro, thanking him profusely for the privilege he was granting us.

"Thank you, Dad!" my sisters exclaimed while they hugged him.

Lauro stood in the middle of the living room with that constant smirk, making himself look like a good man for granting his daughters a privilege that he shouldn't have taken away in the first place.

I, however, did not feel elation. I felt a surge of profound hatred. It was one week before the games. I had not practiced. I did not have the uniform. I suffered the humiliation from having to sit on the bench for seven weeks while I was harangued for letting the team down. This gesture simply came too late.

I did not budge from where I sat. I looked at my sisters with contempt for their hypocrisy, hugging the man who created the problem in the first place. I had begged and stooped—and been punished for it. Along the way, I realized I should not have had to beg and stoop. None of my classmates had to beg to play. Their parents just let them. So now, I had no intention to show a fake display of gratitude when all I felt was anger, when all the damage of his actions had already been done.

Once my sisters' squeals died down, all four of them noticed that I had stayed seated on the couch, holding my book.

"Go thank your father for allowing you to go the games," my mother prompted.

I stayed seated and silent.

The big smile vanished from my mother's face. Silence reigned in the room where a few seconds earlier there was the thrill of excitement. Both my mother and my sisters looked at me in horror at my insolence and in pity at the inevitable consequences that would follow.

To me, suddenly, everything became clear. Even though my mother wore the façade of the strict parent, it was Lauro who controlled all of us, as if we were puppets in his plan. This arrangement amounted to nothing more than a coward with a false sense of power, controlling those who couldn't defend themselves. He was the true reason why we couldn't do anything. For the most part, we went along, feeling powerless against this tyranny. But as it is true in most power struggles, there is a moment when things just go too far.

This was my moment.

I had worked for over a year to obtain a spot in the team. I had practiced, and I had prayed, and unexpectedly, my dream had come to pass. Yet, Lauro denied me my dream and destroyed the joy that accompanied it. It was the ultimate injustice. I felt the seeds of hatred and disgust take root in me.

"No, I will not." I answered, not moving from where I was, not breaking my stare.

"Don't be insolent!" my mother replied quickly. "Go thank your father. And do it now!"

I still did not move.

My sisters intervened, worried that their chance to go to the Olympics would fade along with my insolence. "Please, Isa, just do it!" they pleaded, with quivering voices and tears in their eyes.

I felt the increasingly familiar feeling of anger rising up within me.

"No," I said. "My father would not have prevented me from going in the first place."

I broke so many rules with that one statement. I had defied my parents, talked back, refused to obey an order, and not shown respect—all at once. Any one of these infractions would have earned me a big slap on the face. Yet, for a moment, Lauro, my mother, and my sisters just stood with their eyes widened and their mouths open. Realizing that I had taken them by surprise and feeling emboldened, I continued.

"And Lauro," I said, emphasizing his name, spoken for the first time since we moved to Shangrila seven years earlier, "is not my father!"

Lauro's smirk evaporated from his face. My sisters stood still, flanking him. My mother did not know how to react. It was as if time stopped while everyone was taking stock of what had just happened. I had openly rejected the typical mores where parents pontificated and daughters scurried to please and obey.

"Isa, please thank him," Catherine pleaded with her eyes full of tears, fearing the consequences of my disobedience. I ignored her pleas. I ignored my mother's stare. I ignored what anybody had to say. I held my stare, full of hatred, towards Lauro.

Eventually, he broke the stare first. He could see in my eyes that he had gone too far.

He said nothing, turned around, and left the room.

Chapter 28

WAY OUT

The next morning, I ran to find my team captain, Ana Cristina, who made a point for the past two months to keep me seated on the school bench while the team trained another goalie.

"I will play!"

"Isabelle, I don't have time for this."

"No, truly, my parents told me I can play."

"What? Is this a joke? Now? A week before the Olympics?"

"Not, it isn't a joke," I pleaded. "My mother let me, for real!"

"Did she have to leave it until the last minute?" Ana Cristina responded, frustrated.

I shrugged my shoulders. How could I possibly tell her the whole story behind my parents' behavior?

"You don't have a uniform," she noted.

I felt a small pain in the pit of my stomach. I knew this was an issue. The team uniforms were custom made especially for the parade; not having a uniform a week before the event was a difficult spot to be in.

"I know," I said hesitantly. I hoped to convince Ana Cristina that since I was the goalie, I could wear a different uniform, even if that would prevent me from walking in the opening parade. I was considering how to explain this to her when she interrupted me.

"Tell your father to take you to the store where we special ordered our uniforms—today," she stated quickly, rushing to help me solve the problem. "Maybe they can fast track an order for you. Or sometimes they have extras," she said, referring to the discard pile resulting when the staff at the store made measurement errors. "Now you can also practice with the team," she added.

I smiled broadly.

"But why did you have to wait until the last minute? It messes up my whole team strategy!" she said.

I could feel Ana Cristina's frustration, but if she only knew what I went through to be allowed to play at all, she would be less harsh. I had longed to practice with the team for all of the previous weeks. She had forbidden me to do so.

Yet, that is not the point I wanted to make as I interrupted her. I needed to start correcting some important facts about my life and choices.

"My father lives in the United States!" I blurted out, completely changing the subject.

Ana Cristina stared, as if there was something wrong with me, her glare communicating a mixture of frustration and concern.

My statement was improbable to Ana Cristina—and to anyone who knew me. Everybody assumed that Lauro was my father. After all, I called him Dad. He was the one who attended school functions where a parent's attendance was mandatory. Whenever he came, he grudgingly sat on the last row of seats, irrespective of whether there were plenty of seats available, making himself as small and hunched as possible, as if he wanted to remain invisible. My mother never once set foot at school.

Ana Cristina burst out laughing.

"OK, Isabelle," she said without wanting to engage.

"It is true!" I continued, "Lauro is my stepfather."

Having a stepfather was so rare in a country where only a handful of people ever divorced that she assumed I made up that tale. Yet, despite all the doubts, disbelief, and snickering I experienced, I went about setting the record straight. From that day forward, I told whomever would listen that my real father lived in the United States.

"You? You have an American father?" Ana Cristina asked suspiciously.

My classmates assumed, as did I, that an American father must mean a wealthy one. And I had never shown any vestige of wealth through my clothes or backpacks. Our cloistered life proved we didn't have impressive financial means.

"But you call your dad, *Dad*," one of my teammates said, confused.

"I know, my mother asked me to," I said.

"How come your American father is never here?" she asked.

"Because he is in the United States," I responded, as if this was not already patently obvious. I quickly added, "He visits once a year."

"Does your father truly just come once a year?" most would ask incredulously, either horrified at how little I saw my dad or wistfully wishing they would see theirs so seldom.

"That's why you bring all those toys, then?" the more observant classmates asked, connecting the one time a year I came to school loaded down with the new toys my father brought during his annual visits—the same toys that the nuns confiscated after two days of class disruption and that nobody would ever see again.

I obtained a team uniform that was an ill fit because it was not quite my size, but it had been discarded by a teammate as too small.

As I did not quite fit in with the other girls, I carried the school flag during the parade, typically an honor in so many situations. In this case, however, it was so that I would not walk next to my team and distract from their unity in sock, hair style, and ribbon color as they all had their hair coiffed together that morning.

My class won the top prize for the parade.

It was the first victory of the week and surely a sign, I thought, that there would be more wins to come.

It turns out, it was the only victory.

Having sat on the bench for seven weeks, I had not practiced enough to be the goalie I had shown I could be during the weeks leading to the team selection. In the meantime, the other teams had practiced together for two months, and they knew what they were doing. This lack of practice showed during our first game. I blocked plenty of goals, but the offense of the best two players in my class on the opposing team was impossible to beat. The combination of Flavia and Isabela, as I had feared, was too potent. We lost the first game and then the next. We lost the tournament, coming in last place.

The school held an awards ceremony for those who won gold and silver medals. As my team sat on the sidelines, Ana Cristina grew cold towards me again, blaming the team's loss partly on my lack of training, which she felt could be blamed on unnecessary family drama.

It had not been my fault. It was Ana Cristina's fault for not letting me practice and Lauro's fault for refusing to let me play. I felt the whole situation was unfair. Yet, rather than feel upset at Ana Cristina, I redirected my anger and frustration towards the person who caused this failure. Had I not been forbidden to practice with my team, we would have had a real shot at winning. But Lauro took the championship away from me.

I was so tired of my life. I felt so full of hatred. I determined I would find a way never to have my dream stolen from me again.

BREAKING AWAY

tore a piece of paper from my notebook and wrote my father a note: "I want to come to the United States and live with you."

I did not explain why. I placed the letter in the glove compartment of my grandfather's car next time he visited, as I had done three years before. This time, I felt more confident that it would be mailed. My father, not in the habit of probing and without a chance to talk to me, did not question my motives. Upon receiving my letter, he began the lengthy process to obtain a Green Card, a document which would allow me to study in the United States.

My mother found out about the visa application because the United States Immigration Office mailed a packet of information to Shangrila.

Although the envelope was addressed to me, my mother ignored the addressee and opened it—as she did with all correspondence. She walked into my bedroom, interrupting a Monopoly game I was playing with my sisters.

"What is this?" she asked, brandishing the document in my face.

"This was addressed to me!" I protested. "You can't just open it."

"What is this?" she repeated while opening the thick, official-looking envelope.

"I believe it is my visa application to go to the United States."

My sisters' eyes opened wide, perhaps at my daring or perhaps because the thought had not occurred to them that they could do the same thing.

My mother became furious. "How dare Pierre send you an application for a visa?" She raised her arms, as well as her voice, in frustration.

My mother's raised voice brought Lauro into the room too, as he was always hovering, wanting to know what we discussed.

"I asked him to."

My mother stopped pacing and stared at me. So did my sisters. So did Lauro.

"Why?" she asked, genuinely puzzled.

"I want to live with him."

"This is your home. Your home is here, not in the United States. You will not go anywhere!" she said, screaming.

The air grew stiff in our tiny, crowded, triangle-shaped bedroom. Lauro, hearing the commotion, entered the room, but he stayed by the door—that is, blocking my exit. My sisters remained stiff as statues, realizing that their best strategy was to be out of the way.

"I want to move," I responded.

My mother launched her usual vitriol about how my father had abandoned us to go live with his mistress Carroll and how they did not care at all about me and my well-being. She insisted that I most certainly did not want to go live with them.

Once my mother started her monologue, there was no point in interrupting her. When she finished a few minutes later, she stomped out of the room, but not before saying, "You are not going anywhere!"

The winds of change, however, had arrived in Shangrila.

Lauro turned pale during this discussion. He must have wondered what else I may have told my father, besides asking to move. It had to be a shock that I communicated with Pierre in the first place, not having access to a phone, nor a post office.

Suddenly, he must have feared that his presence and his actions might be discovered. He had to know that his unwelcome sexual advances and forbidding my participation in the Olympics had something to do with the current situation. He must have recognized the risk these actions brought to him. If my father asked questions, then his current way of life, living off my father's largesse, could change.

Since we moved to Shangrila, my mother had been powerless. She allowed Lauro to run the household unchecked, avoiding any confrontation with him. If she had to choose sides between Lauro or her daughters, there was no question she would side with Lauro. In a way, she realized that if she let him manage all of us, then she would not have to do it herself. Because of her laziness, Lauro did what he wanted with impunity. My mother believed so deeply that my father abandoned us, she figured he had no interest—not now, not ever—in having his daughters live with him. She felt convinced that Carroll would never want to parent the children of her husband, as Carroll had previously stated that she had no interest in having kids.

The possibility that we would ever live with my father seemed so far-fetched to her, it was not an option my mother had ever considered.

Both my mother and Lauro had a vested interest in keeping me by their side as the alimony payment would be reduced by a quarter if I left, as each of my sisters, as well as my mother, claimed 10 percent of my father's salary. Now she sensed she could lose me. And not only because I wanted to move, but also because the regular punishments—spanking, the strict nature of our lives, the fear mongering about a dark aura—were no longer effective. I talked back. I denied Lauro in front of everybody. I no longer attended the Wednesday meetings. Neither my mother nor Lauro quite knew how to control me anymore.

Yet, she said nothing more about the visa application process. I did not bring it up either. Noting no further activity, my mother must have thought that her statement about Shangrila being my home was enough to discourage me from continuing with the process.

Quite the contrary. It further encouraged me.

The topic did not come up anymore because I did not need her help. I knew where my mother kept important documents, such as our birth certificates and school records, as well as a stash of rolled cash notes in a drawer in her bedroom. I availed myself of the money needed for pictures and photocopies. I forged my mother's signature when required and mailed the needed documents to my father through my grandparents. This went unnoticed as the application process was lengthy and slow.

It is hard to say what Lauro thought about this situation. But he must have figured that keeping me close was safer for him than if I moved away. Although I was always still on alert about Lauro's whereabouts, I eventually noticed that Lauro had curtailed his attempts to molest me. After a few days, I found it peculiar that he actively left me alone and almost tried to avoid me. Yet, I continued to jam the bedroom door with shoes every night, stayed glued to one sister or the other while he was near, and ensured I spent most afternoons around Shangrila's grounds, reading schools books, playing with the various animals, and riding my bicycle in circles around the small parking area by the main gate. Although I talked back more frequently and insolently, the frequency of sudden slaps that usually followed defiance also decreased. Maybe these improvements were because I felt gutsier in opposing my parents.

But it also was because, around the same time, a bigger crisis took their focus away from me.

Their temple was in trouble.

A couple of months after I refused to attend the religious meetings two years earlier, my sisters followed. They noticed I had not been punished—neither by my parents, nor by all the dark energy and bad karma my mother had claimed would engulf me by refusing to attend the meetings.

It turns out, my sisters and I were not the only ones to turn our backs on these meetings. Over time, fewer people came.

My parents had not thought much about it, so used they were to burning bridges with anybody who crossed our paths; besides, a core remnant of a dozen people still faithfully attended every week. Having no interest in what happened around the meetings, I hardly noticed, nor inquired, about the trickle of people who now attended the Wednesday meetings, so it was hard to say what actually happened. The newspaper headlines, however, reported a cult fraud in the area around Rio de Janeiro, which included Petropolis. I recognized the names of some of the regular attendees listed in the article, who were reportedly in prison for embezzling funds from trustworthy worshippers for their own personal fortunes.

Even in Brazil, the preying of the powerful over the weak and poor was frowned upon. Within weeks of the scandal breaking in the newspapers, nobody came on Wednesdays. For two or three weeks, Lauro and my mother still held a ceremonial meeting just for the two of them. Not seeing the point of the formality, they stopped the pretense that it meant anything.

Thus, Wednesday nights became as uneventful as any other night in Shangrila.

Chapter 30
WRONG SIDE OF HISTORY

My father, Pierre, was a quiet, self-effacing man. He never spoke about his past. He rarely mentioned his parents. He hardly talked much at all. All I knew about him was what my mother told me, all cast in a negative light. It seemed that family bonds were unimportant to him.

Laja Gurfinkiel, my Polish grandmother, lived in abject misery with her parents Nusen-David and Perla in the Jewish Quarter in Warsaw, Poland. It was either the general misery or the stress of providing for eleven children that proved too much for Perla. She died when she was forty years-old, of unknown causes, but likely of tuberculosis. Her husband died a few months later of a broken heart, so goes the family folklore. As there was not any one person who would keep the entire family together, the children disbanded and were taken in by various relatives. Laja, her sister Sophie, and an older brother went to live with an aunt in the countryside. Laja was three years old. She never saw the remaining eight siblings again.

Grandmother Laja began working at a factory when she was eleven years old, as was common among poor families at the time, and not surprising, given her orphan status. She was, after all, expected to help with her keep. Her older brother, who was involved in communist ideas in Poland in the 1920s, picked Laja up at the end of her shift every day. He noticed that she always left the factory later than the scheduled time.

147

"Laja, why are you always late?" he asked.

"I leave as soon as the bell rings!" Laja responded.

The bell rang when the clock reached six o'clock, announcing to the factory workers it was time to change shifts. Laja's frequent delays arose suspicion in her brother, who once entered the factory and noticed that the clocks within did not match the watch on his wrist. The first time this happened, he adjusted his watch. When it happened again, he realized that it wasn't his watch that needed adjustment. It turns out the factory chief tampered with the clocks to extract a few more minutes out of his workforce each day. Laja's brother gave his sister a watch, with the time aligned to his own watch. Instead of waiting for the bell to ring at the end of her shift, Laja referred to her new watch to determine the right time to walk out of work.

"Where do you think you are going?" her boss asked when Laja left her station before the bell rang.

"My shift is over," she said, "so I am leaving."

"No, it is not over!" her boss said, fuming. "Look at the clock. There are a few minutes left."

"My clock says a different time," she said.

"You will stay here until the bell rings."

"My brother is waiting for me outside, so I will leave," Laja responded.

"If you leave, you are not to come back."

Laja did not have a job to return to the next day.

Discouraged by her limited employment prospects, given her tender age, experience, and new reputation for being difficult, Laja joined her older sister Sophie who had moved to Brussels, Belgium, to get married. In Brussels, Laja found work in a clothes sweatshop.

It isn't clear what transpired at this new job, but in Belgium, as in Warsaw, Laja also found issues with the conditions of her factory job. Recalling how her brother fought for her, she sought to fix the poor working conditions and long hours at the factory. Her bosses quickly realized that Laja was a rabble-rouser and that the trouble she caused was not worth the output she produced. Her bosses accused her of stealing. She was imprisoned briefly and subsequently deported to neighboring France. She settled in Paris, where she was as far away as possible from any family she ever had. Finding herself alone, she sought a community where she felt belonging. Thus, she joined a group of young Jews who congregated regularly as they fled the wave of anti-Semitism that swept over Poland and was making its way even to France. Within this group, Laja met Rachmiel.

My grandfather, Rachmiel Giecyls, was born in Vilnius, Lithuania. His family was of modest means. Daniel, his father, was an accountant while his wife, Chana Liba, stayed at home to take care of their three children. From an early age, Rachmiel had an innate talent for drawing and painting. He daydreamed of attending the Ecole D'Art in Vilnius. However, he had two obstacles to realizing his dream. The first was the family's inability to pay the private school tuition. Most relevant, though, irrespective of his family's financial abilities, was the certainty that he would not be admitted because he was a Jew. No Jews were allowed to cross the stately doors to the Ecole D'Art.

Determined not to let his heritage stop him, Rachmiel decided to try his luck elsewhere. He set his sights on the more prestigious Ecole de Beaux Arts in Warsaw, Poland. His parents begged him to reconsider. Why would Poland be any different than Lithuania? News was hard to come by, but they knew that life in Poland would not be any easier than it was in Vilnius. Rachmiel did not think the possibility of new obstacles should prevent him from realizing his dream. When Rachmiel did not waver, Daniel and Chana Liba withdrew any monetary support of their son. "If you continue in this foolish adventure, you are on your own!" my great-grandparents emphatically told Rachmiel.

Defying his parents, set on living his dream, Rachmiel departed for Warsaw. He reportedly walked most of the five hundred kilometer journey, during a time when cars were not prevalent, and the concept of giving rides to destitute youth would not occur to those who could drive a car or a carriage. Despite this valiant effort, as his parents predicted, once he arrived in Warsaw, Rachmiel found that the anti-Jewish sentiments were even stronger than they had been in Lithuania. The doors to the Ecole de Beaux Arts were closed to him too.

Dejected, he quickly realized that there was nothing for him in Warsaw either. Given his parents' lack of support, Rachmiel decided against returning home to Lithuania. He continued his journey westward. Having heard of the throngs of artists who indulged in their craft on the streets of Paris, Rachmiel set out to reach the art capital of the world.

It was a long journey. Once he arrived in Paris, he was as penniless as when he started this journey months earlier. He needed to find a job quickly. Without much of an education and realizing that painting on the street would not put food on the table, he put his artistic skills to use in a more practical way. He could not yet become the artist he dreamed off, but he could paint walls. The walls of homes, that is, in one monotone color after another. He indulged in more sophisticated drawings, of landscapes and portraits, on his own, late into the night.

Away from his family, he sought belonging. Shortly after his arrival, Rachmiel joined the same community of young Jews that Laja frequented.

They married in 1938.

A couple of years later, in 1940, history knocked on the doorstep of their small apartment situated in the 10th arrondissement of Paris. Hitler declared war on France. All Jews in France were required to have new identity papers stamped with the words "JUIF" in bold, red letters.

Perhaps not realizing the hatred that would be directed towards the Jews as the war progressed or out of a desire to contribute to changing the tide of history, Rachmiel joined the French Army, as did many Jewish immigrants. He was quickly deployed into battle. Within weeks, his battalion fell, and he became a prisoner of war in Germany.

Rachmiel spoke multiple languages: French, Russian, Polish, German, and Yiddish. These polyglot skills became useful in raising his status within the prison. He became an interpreter between the German guards and the prisoners of war from various countries. While still a prisoner, he attended the meetings where the German guards made decisions about prison life, work assignments within the prison, and most importantly, the outcomes about who would stay and who would go away. He often heard whispers of opportunities he knew had a short shelf life within the prison walls.

This way, Rachmiel learned that the French government wanted to make a deal with the Germans. France claimed that the imprisonment of large numbers of French citizens robbed the country of enough peasants to work the agricultural fields. The French claimed that if the Germans and their army wanted to be fed, they needed to release prisoners to grow food for them. Thus, France negotiated that fifty prisoners were to be freed from Rachmiel's prison and sent to plow the fields. It was unclear what the Germans would receive in return, but once Rachmiel heard this news, he saw an opportunity for himself. He acted quickly. There was one obvious problem, however: he had never touched a plow. He was a painter, not a peasant. However, the manual labor he did while in prison had callused his previously fine hands; thus, he figured he could pass himself off as a field peasant. He spoke loudly about his agrarian past before joining the army and quickly rounded up another forty-nine men. The fifty of them marched to the prison guards, offering to be the ones to be sent off to work on remote lands to grow food for the Germans. Not caring about one set of prisoners over another, the German guards consented and so granted Rachmiel's band of fifty men passage out of prison. They were loaded into a truck and carried back to France.

Rachmiel never once touched a plow. He separated from his group during transport, and rather than finding a field, he made his way back to Paris. Not wanting to risk being discovered again, he made the journey back on foot, as he had years earlier when he first arrived in Paris. This caution and the resulting delay in his return to Paris served him well. While in transit, he missed the strictest registration requirements of the time for Jews living in France.

On September 21st, 1940—while Rachmiel was walking back to Paris—a German ordinance demanded all Jews in the occupied French zone register at a police station or in the sub-prefectures of Paris and elsewhere in France. Not understanding the foolishness of fulfilling this request, nearly one hundred and fifty thousand Jews, including Grandmother Laja, registered at the Department of the Seine, encompassing Paris and its immediate suburbs. There, as others, Laja gave her name and address to the French police. These files were subsequently transferred to the German Gestapo. Rachmiel's whereabouts were unknown at the time of registration. My grandmother, unaware of whether Rachmiel was even alive, did not register him. Consequently, in the official records of Jews, Rachmiel did not exist.

Upon Rachmiel's return from prison a few weeks later, Laja got pregnant. Their son, Pierre Gecils, my father, was born on New Year's Eve, December 31, 1941, in the middle of World War II.

The birth of his son made it clear to Rachmiel that painting homes—especially during war when homes were bombed rather than painted—would be insufficient to support his growing family. Laja stopped working to stay home with my father, as was customary at the time. Rachmiel's need for a new job came at the time when several professions, especially the better paying ones, became forbidden to Jews. Lists of forbidden jobs were published, and those caught hiring Jewish workers faced fines and prison time. Nobody would hire a man that had the bold, red letters of the Jewish stamp on his identity papers.

Rachmiel quietly found a solution. Closely examining the red letters printed on his identity papers, he tried to lift the stamp. When it did not work, he used his artistic talent to paint, painstakingly, over the stamp. After hours of detailed work, he and Laja had newly forged identity papers that erased the Jewish designation from their lives. He attentively observed their new documents, recognizing his work was flawless. The ultimate test, however, was if others thought so as well. Rachmiel considered showing the documents to his neighbors as a test. However, he astutely determined that he did not want anyone aware of his forgery, lest one day his acts would be given away. Instead, he removed the jacket that bore the yellow Star of David that he, and all Jews, were required to wear and tested the quality of his forgery at different check points throughout Paris. He felt immense pride when others unflinchingly accepted his documents. Once convinced he could pass for a non-Jew, he searched for a job that was forbidden to Jewish people. Those jobs paid more, and it would be another way he could hide his Jewish identity. He found a job at SNCF, La Societe Nationale des Chemins de Fers, the French railroad system. The vocation was as far as possible from painting, but it was steady employment where he could ride out the war.

In the spring of 1942, the Germans issued a proclamation that was carried out by the French police. All Jews aged from sixteen to fifty were to report to the Velodrome D'Hiver, a stadium previously used for indoor bicycling competition. The list further said that the police knew who should come because they had a list of registered Jews from the previous year.

This notice said that the roundup was an effort to provide jobs to Jews who were forbidden from holding them. That is, France and Germany were recruiting able-bodied people to work in camps during this time of war. The proclamation said nothing about these work camps or the gas chambers within them, the true destination for those who answered the registration calls.

The true purpose of "Operation Spring Breeze," a name which was later given to the Vel d'Hiv Roundup (a Nazi-decreed raid and mass arrest by the French police in July of 1942), was to exterminate as many Jews as the Germans could. The Germans knew that the French population was not so anti-Semitic that they would accept their extermination plan at face value, so they disguised the mass arrest of Jews as a work opportunity. Thus, the proclamation stated that the elderly or women "in advanced state of pregnancy," who were breast-feeding, or who had children under two-years-old were exempt. Although these exceptions were established on paper, the proclamation also stated that all Jews—whether old, pregnant, or mothers of young children—had to report to the designated assembly center. Only there could their age and pregnancy status be established. But once in the velodrome, it was hard to know whether kids or elderly were included in the crowd.

The offer of jobs was an irresistible message among the Jewish population, most of whom could no longer obtain dignified work. Not knowing they were marching to their deaths, thousands of Jews reported to the velodrome that fateful July 16th, beginning at four o'clock in the morning, eager to work at the promised jobs. That day, more than thirteen thousand Jews were arrested, according to records of the French Prefecture de Police. Despite the disclaimers, 44 percent of those arrested were women, almost one-third were children. Once they checked in the velodrome, they were only allowed to leave on board trains destined to Auschwitz.

The evening before the roundup, as my grandparents were packing their bags, they heard a knock on their door. A French policewoman stood on the other side of the door. She swiftly entered their apartment before receiving an invitation to come in.

"Do not go to the Velodrome d'Hiver tomorrow," she whispered, closing the door behind her.

"Why not?" Grandmother Laja asked suspiciously, doubting that the police would do much to help Jews. "Everyone is expected to be there."

"It is a death sentence," the policewoman responded. "This is a cover up. The Germans want to kill all Jews."

"What about the jobs they promised?" Rachmiel asked.

"It is a ruse. How else do you think they could lure people to come to the velodrome?" she said.

My grandmother, who was rocking my father, then seven months old, to calm him down, stared suspiciously at the woman standing at her front door.

"I am exempt," Grandmother Laja said, holding my father by his waist to show the policewoman her baby.

"You can forget about exemptions," the policewoman said. "The gendarmes will look for anyone who does not report to the velodrome—whether or not she has a baby. And I assure you that once you arrive at the velodrome, the only way out is on trains that will take you to places you do not want to go."

"Why are you helping us?" Rachmiel asked suspiciously.

This policewoman risked her job, and perhaps her life, to warn my grandparents. Those who interfered with the affairs of the German police found themselves with a short life. She felt saving a few lives was worth the risk. She belonged to the French Resistance, a loose coalition of people who saw it as their role to resist the war, the occupation of France, and the extermination of Jews.

"I have committed to warn as many people as possible. I want to help. You must believe me," she said as she left to knock on other doors, aiming to warn as many Jews as she could that night.

While my family felt suspicious of the policewoman's intentions, they thought it foolish not to heed the woman's warning. Grandmother Laja learned to mistrust authority long ago, during her youth working at the factories in Warsaw and Brussels. This time, though, she did not know which authorities to mistrust. Not knowing whom to believe in, my grandparents hatched a plan that night.

My Grandfather Rachmiel's name was not on the proclamation list, as he missed the registration while in prison in Germany. Nobody would likely look for him. He planned to hide in the large sewer pipes that ran underneath their apartment, just in case. Laja had unfortunately registered, and as such, she was expected to report to the velodrome. Yet, she had a baby now, and the proclamation clearly noted that mothers of young children were exempt. When the police came to check on her, she would show them her baby and then ask to stay behind.

As expected, that fateful morning of July 16th, the French police went from home to home in my grandparents' neighborhood, and in other Jewish neighborhoods, looking for those, like Laja, who defied the proclamation orders.

Laja answered the door, holding my father in her arms.

"You did not report to the velodrome. You must come!" the uniformed gendarme told her.

"I have a baby!" Laja said, thrusting my father towards the gendarme, who grimaced at the sight of a baby. "I am exempt," Laja continued, showing the proclamation flyer she held in her hands.

"We will determine who is exempt at the velodrome, Madame, and not here on your doorstep," the gendarme replied cursorily.

"I have a baby. I am exempt. I do not need to go," Laja repeated raising her voice as she stood on the threshold of her door so that any passerby would hear her, hoping that the gendarme would want to avoid a scene. Indeed, some curious people stopped to witness the commotion at the front of my grandmother's apartment. My father, sensing the mounting tension and hearing my grandmother's shout, cried. My grandfather, hearing from the sewer pipe my grandmother's loud voice and my father's screams, sensed that Laja would be imminently arrested. He came out of hiding. In a show of heroics, he placed himself between Laja and the gendarme. "Take me instead!" he said.

"Who are you?" the gendarme asked.

"I am her husband!" Rachmiel said defiantly.

"Give me your papers!" the gendarme demanded before letting Rachmiel utter another word.

Rachmiel handed his forged identity papers to the gendarme who examined it closely. However, Rachmiel had done such a detailed job of removing and painting over the JEW stamp that the gendarme thought his claim to be the husband was a ruse. The identify papers did not bear the stamp classifying Rachmiel as a Jew. The gendarme sought my grandfather's name on the registration list. Rachmiel's name was not on it.

"This isn't a joke!" the gendarme said. "Now get out of the way!" he said, giving him back the papers and closing in on my grandmother, grabbing her arm, pushing her towards the door. "And do not be so stupid as to be involved with a Jew!" the gendarme continued.

There were punishments for gendarmes who rounded up the wrong people. Thus, despite how upset the gendarme was with what he perceived to be a joke, Rachmiel stayed behind, seeing his screaming wife and baby son disappear as they turned the corner on their street. There was nothing he could do. He wondered in despair whether he would ever see his wife and child again.

My father wailed all the way to the police station. Once there, Laja screamed, begged, and pleaded. She repeated, "We are exempt! I have a baby!" as if that were not evidently clear from my father's piercing screams. Whether it was because it had been a long day or that the police workers couldn't handle the screaming baby or that they were concerned about the public uproar Laja caused, the French police told Laja to leave. So she did. She left the police department with my father Pierre in her arms, holding him tight, not believing that she managed to escape. She felt grateful for having a screaming baby who had just saved her life.

On her way back to her apartment, Laja witnessed the flood of Jewish people, her people, her neighbors, her friends, walking in the other direction, towards their death at Auschwitz and Dachau. She did not utter a word. She did not make eye contact. All she wanted to do was to join Rachmiel and promptly disappear.

Having narrowly escaped death at the concentration camps, my grandparents knew they could no longer remain who and where they were. They had to move. They had to erase any vestiges of their Jewishness. They had to change their name. *Giecyls* sounded too Jewish, too foreign, too eastern European. The family needed a French-sounding name. So Rachmiel changed the family name to the more French-sounding *Gecils*. He once more forged his and Laja's identity papers, now bearing the newly created Gecils name.

Rachmiel also quit his job at SNCF. They took their meager savings and moved to a non-Jewish neighborhood where they could start a new life with a new name and a new home, among total strangers. He found employment with a construction company.

My grandparents kept a low profile and suffered with the masses the deprivations and shortages of war and the drone of constant bombings in Paris. Feeling more secure, or perhaps out of sheer foolishness, my grandmother got pregnant again. Their daughter, Paule, was born in June 1943.

One year later, in the fall of 1944, Rachmiel returned from work to find the word JEW painted on their apartment door. Their cover was blown. Afraid of entering his apartment, even to retrieve his belongings in case they were being spied on, Rachmiel took his wife and children to see his boss instead.

"We cannot go home," my grandfather Rachmiel said rather desperately.

"I will help you," his boss said.

His boss requested that one of his architects, Jacques Prevost, help my family. Jacques and his wife Gisele had two small children and lived in a modest apartment. Despite the dangers, the Prevosts agreed to house my family, making a small room available for the four of them. They all knew this was a temporary plan until another solution could be found.

When their apartment proved too small for four adults and four children, the Prevosts asked that my grandparents find another place for their children.

It was harder to place my father because his circumcision identified him as a Jew. The Gestapo and other authorities often asked boy children, whom they believed to be Jews, to remove their pants so that they could tell by their penises whether they were only passing as a gentile.

Despite the risks and fear, a family eventually agreed to care for my father. Another family cared for my aunt. My grandparents said goodbye to their children and had no idea when they would see them again.

In the meantime, Paris suffered constant bombings. Thus, Gisele Prevost moved away with their children to the countryside. Now, only my grandparents and Jacques Prevost lived in the small apartment. There they stayed for more than a year. They did not work, did not see their children, nor hardly ever ventured out, lest they be reported by curious neighbors.

This way, my family survived the war that killed their neighbors and their family and changed their life.

Once World War II was officially over in 1945, my grandparents reunited with their children, my father and my aunt. They settled in a small apartment in a non-Jewish neighborhood of Paris. My grandfather, no longer interested in putting his artistic dreams on hold, opened a painting business where he decorated windows, doors, and plaques in beautiful lettering, so common among the French restaurants and other businesses. His business achieved some success. His work was sought after, and he traveled all over France to paint the façades of businesses and to display his works at various art conferences.

My family, now that the war was over, petitioned to have their new name, Gecils, officially recognized. France formally accepted the Gecils family name in its registries in 1948.

My family lived modestly. On Sundays, my grandparents hosted afternoon tea for a few other friends who had survived the war. During these gatherings, they spoke about the friends who disappeared, wondering what had become of them. They talked about those they knew who had perished in the concentration camps. They talked about my great aunt, Aunt Sophie, Laja's sister, who had remained in Belgium. Her husband, although not Jewish, died in the war at the Drancy camp, accused of protecting a Jew by marrying her. Aunt Sophie, heartbroken for the loss of her husband, decided to flee Europe, to leave behind the memories of the war atrocities. She sought to go as far as she could. She found the distance she longed for in Rio de Janeiro, Brazil.

My family vowed that once they rebuilt their life, they would never be caught in the web of history again.

This wish was not to be granted.

My father turned eighteen-years-old in 1960, right when a war in Algeria, a small African nation colonized by France, was waging their war for independence. The Algerian War had started six years earlier in 1954. France did what it could to hold on to its colony through dirty, dusty guerrilla warfare, terrorism against civilians, the use of torture, and other horrible and predictable evils of war. By the time my father was of age for military service, all new recruits were sent to

Algeria so that France, which was losing the fight, could make a last, desperate dash to hold on to the colony in an increasingly brutal and senseless war.

Grandmother Laja felt strongly that she would never willingly send her only son to fight in a war she did not care about. "We did not survive the horrors of World War II to have my only son perish in some other ridiculous war!" my grandmother Laja said indignantly. "We are French, yes, but Algeria means nothing to us."

My family, so adept at finding ways out of mandatory requests, found a loophole. French students who lived abroad could ask for a postponement of their mandatory service. Wanting to ride out the Algerian War, my grandmother sent my father to live with her sister, Sophie, in Rio de Janeiro.

My father, always more of an observer than a participant in conversation and social circles, did in Rio as his parents had done before him. Once in a foreign country, he sought belonging. So he joined the Alliance Française, a place where French people gathered to have some ties to their home. There, he met a woman with a coquettish style and sparkling, translucent green eyes. When my father wrote home to my grandparents to give them news, he gushed about his experiences in Rio. In one of these letters, he told his family he met the woman he would marry.

Chapter 31

FAREWELL

J told those I could at school that my departure to America was imminent. "You? How can you go live in the United States?"

It seemed they had forgotten what I told them about my American father.

"I have a father who lives there, remember?"

"Really? We all thought you were lying."

"I didn't lie."

"Well, you can't blame us. Nobody knew you had an American father. When are you leaving anyway?"

"I don't know yet."

They groaned as my reticent answers confirmed that I must have concocted this coveted story. "Yeah, right!" most answered, rolling their eyes and shrugging their shoulders.

"You will see. One day soon I will be coming here and telling you all goodbye," I responded.

That day never came.

My father called my grandparents to tell me the visa had been approved. Yet, before it could be issued, my mother needed to sign a custody release—in person, in court, in front of a judge—before the Brazilian government would issue me a passport. So he asked to speak with my mother. Not able to tell my father that my mother knew nothing about the visa process, my grandparents spoke directly with her about my father's request.

"What are you talking about?" she asked my grandfather while looking at me, surprised.

Needless to say, the rest of that conversation was a disaster.

She refused to go to court and refused to sign the form.

This was a signature I could not forge.

"I will not let you live in the United States with a father who abandoned you and a witch for a mother," she screamed. "Your home is here! And you will stay here."

"Mom, you have to sign . . . Everything is approved. Everything is ready," I pleaded.

It was so close. Yet, here I was, again, having my plans thwarted by my mother. I resorted to tactics that had worked before during the Olympics debacle. I screamed, cried, begged, pleaded, pouted, and relentlessly requested that she appear in court to release her custody of me. This time, however, she did not relent.

"You will not go!"

"But I told Pappy I would."

"Now tell him you will not."

"You only want to keep me here because you want my father's money!" I said bitterly.

My mother did not take the bait. "You can believe whatever you want. You will stay here. And I do not want to hear about it . . . ever again."

My mother missed the court appointment. And the window of opportunity for me to leave Shangrila closed along with it.

For the first time in my life, I was glad we did not have a telephone. I could not bear the thought of telling my father directly that my mother refused to sign the papers. He had believed all along that she had supported my decision. Yet, I needed to communicate that I was not coming after all. I wrote a letter—one that my mother read and to which she added caustic language—telling my father that I had reconsidered my request and chose to stay in Brazil after all.

My father's response was swift and hurtful.

"Isa, you told me your mother had agreed that you would move here," my father wrote in a letter. It is possible that I may have hinted that she approved. I had not needed her to prepare any of the US-related documents. I had not expected that she would need to appear in court to release my custody.

"You lied to me!" he wrote caustically. "And I know you are better than that."

My father had not realized that it was possible that my mother did not know about my plans to leave, did not realize that I lived in a family where we did not speak truthfully and candidly to each other. His letter expounded on deceit, the cost he bore in application fees, and how disappointed he felt in me. That letter left me so distraught that I offered to burn it myself.

Worse than reading his letter was having to face my father when he arrived for his annual visit a couple of months later, on the day we had previously agreed he would accompany me to Los Angeles.

While I typically longed for my dad's annual visit, anticipating the gifts and the day away from Shangrila, this time, I dreaded his arrival.

At first, the day moved along as it normally did. My father did not bring up the topic, leading me to the false belief that perhaps all he wanted to tell me about the incident was included in the letter.

Once we arrived at the Park Cremerie, however, he told my sisters that I would meet them at the pool later.

"I want to go swimming too," I said, not wanting to be alone with my father.

"We need to talk."

I stayed behind, seeing my sisters disappear through the changing rooms.

"Isa, what happened?"

I could no longer avoid this conversation. I felt myself stiffen with anxiety and fear.

"Mom did not want to sign the passport application," I responded.

"You told me you had her permission to come."

"You know how mom is," I trailed.

"Isa, do you know how much it cost me to obtain your visa?" he asked sternly.

I lowered my eyes so that he would not see my tears and shook my head.

"Did you even want to go?"

I had told everyone at school that I would go. I knew I would face ridicule once I admitted to my classmates that I would not move after all. They would call me a liar too. I wanted to move away from Shangrila, to be away from Lauro. I wanted to play sports. I hated my life. But did I truly want to live in the United States? Could I live with a father I saw but a handful of times in the past five years? Did I want to live with Carroll, who had said she did not want children in her life? The truth was, I did not wish to live in the United States. What I *had* wished for was to flee my current life. I could not find the words to articulate all these thoughts to my father. I chose the quicker, if less truthful, answer.

"Yes, I did," I lied, amid tears.

My tears did not discourage my typically quiet father from talking. He felt he had to teach me a lesson. He lectured me about how irresponsible I had been, about how much it all cost him in terms of time, money, and disappointment. My father only stopped the lecture once my tears became sobs. Seeing how miserable I felt, he softened his stance.

"The hardest part was that I wanted you to come," he said. "Now I will have to wait four more years. But I want you to come live with me, OK?"

I am unsure whether this last statement made me feel better or worse, but it dried up my tears. So the doors to the United States, and my father's heart, had not closed altogether, I realized. Four years seemed a long time, but that meant I could try again, once I no longer needed my mother's permission to leave.

My father allowed me to join my sisters in the swimming pool, and we ended the visit as we always did, with a nice meal, a movie, and a whole lot of silence.

At school, I avoided the subject. I had not spoken of a firm departure date and given how little people talked to me, the topic did not surface. I was not about to volunteer the information that would confirm what everybody believed to be the truth: my big move to the United States and my American father were nothing more than a figment of my imagination.

The school year was rapidly coming to a close, and I thought maybe it would go unnoticed that I had not yet left. Yet, towards year-end, as my classmates talked about their plans for the graduation ceremony and the dinner party to follow, the party organizer asked for a count of those who would attend the graduation dinner.

"There is no need to find a spot for Isabelle. She is leaving soon for the United States. Or so she says!" a classmate said, snickering.

Indeed, I would not attend the dinner. Not because I would be in the United States, but because I knew my mother and Lauro would not allow me. Yet, rather than say that I would not join due to my parents' restriction, I said instead, "I will not move to the United States after all."

"Of course you won't!" she said, causing a ripple of laughter. "It is obvious that you will never go anywhere. You are such a liar!"

THE MOVE

$\mathcal{E}$ ighth grade graduation was, apparently, a lavish affair where all the girls wore nice gowns to a white-tablecloth dinner, followed by a prom-like party. I did not go. Aunt Simone, learning of this party as she joined my family at the graduation ceremony held in Petropolis' cavernous cathedral, insisted that I go. She said I would regret it if I did not.

I did not have a formal dress, but even if I had, and even if my aunt's insistence convinced my mother to allow me to join the party, I still would have chosen not to attend. I had no friends at the San Jose Institute, nor created one happy memory during the four years I attended the school.

Graduation brought along a feeling of immense relief that this part of my life was over. I vowed never to set foot in the school again. I wanted to go to a high school where none of my classmates would follow.

Nathalie attended Santa Isabel, a Catholic, all-girls high school Lauro selected for her, to ensure that she would stay away from boys. All her Institute classmates went en masse to San Vincent High School. The poshest of all the private high schools in Petropolis, San Vincent perched high on one of the city's tallest hills, affording a superb view of the city and the mountain ranges that cascaded down to Rio de Janeiro. Nathalie had begged to follow her friends to San Vincent, but the more she cried, the more resolute Lauro became about forbidding her to join her friends.

I had no intention of joining Nathalie at her school. I also had no intention of attending San Vincent as it was the top choice of my current classmates, those who labeled me weird and a liar.

Nathalie, sensing a battle of school choices was brewing between myself and Lauro, offered to become my ally.

"I will support your request to go to San Vincent," she said.

"I don't want to go to San Vincent," I responded.

"It is the best school there is!" she exclaimed.

"Not for me, it isn't," I said.

I wanted a new set of classmates, people who did not have preconceived ideas of who I was or what I could be. Nathalie cried with frustration. That she cried meant nothing to me. I would have even chosen Santa Isabel rather than go to the same school as my former classmates.

Lauro, as always, initially turned a deaf ear to my request, telling me that I would register at Santa Isabel and that was the end of the discussion. As the registration period was fast approaching, I knew I had to act fast to change my fate.

I searched for a strong motive for avoiding Santa Isabel. As luck would have it, I found it. At the time, a scandal involving the school made the headlines of the local newspapers.

I showed the newspaper clipping to my mother.

"Mom, look at this!" I said, handing my mother a folded newspaper article. "Santa Isabel is a terrible place. The math teacher got his student pregnant."

A smiling picture of a statuesque sixteen-year-old, with beautiful, long, blond hair next to a forty-something, bald, heavy, slovenly man was plastered on the front page. The couple had married, a solution that often was employed by couples when pregnancy was involved.

"How could the nuns have let this happen?" my mother asked, shocked.

"Well, seems like they don't really keep an eye on their students," I said innocently.

And so my mother agreed with me that the school's morals were questionable and that my sisters and I would be better off attending school elsewhere.

"I will ask your father," she said, referring to Lauro, "to find a different school for you."

"There is no need. I already have found a school," I said.

I could hardly count on Lauro to look out for me. I knew I needed an alternative to Santa Isabel once I convinced my mother to send me elsewhere. I also knew I needed to prevent Lauro's input on school choices. I researched on my own, asking the nuns at the San Jose Institute about all the school options in Petropolis. I discovered EPA, one of the few non-religious private schools in the city. It had the added benefit that tuition was cheaper than at Santa Isabel's.

My mother did not care about one school over another, as long as it was private so that my grandfather would not carry through with his threat to reveal my stepfather's existence to my father. That EPA was even cheaper was another advantage. My mother did not ask whether the lower price meant it was an inferior school. I had convinced her that this was the best choice.

Lauro, realizing he had lost control of our schooling, tried to reverse the decision. But his arguments held no weight; clearly, an all-girls school did not really keep students away from boys as he had asserted.

Once I was safely registered in high school, I pursued the next step of my plan.

Now the three of us would attend different schools. Nathalie and I would be at EPA, at one end of town, while Catherine would stay at the Institute on the other. Despite how compact Petropolis was, the logistical burden of getting us all to school increased. We already woke up at half past five to prepare for school. Now, with two drop-off points, we would have to rise even earlier.

My mother, again, was indifferent about early starts and long drives as she left all the burden of the logistics for Lauro to sort out. Lauro complained loudly about the early start because our new school was out of the way compared with Santa Isabel. This complaint was yet another way he tried to reverse my mother's decision.

I used his complaining to my advantage.

"It really is difficult to wake up early," I said, agreeing with Lauro. "So I think we should move to Petropolis; that way, we will be closer to school," I suggested slyly during dinner as we sat around our cramped kitchen dining table.

My sisters almost choked, as they anticipated a swift punishment for my bold suggestion. It was not the first time this topic came up. My grandparents had frequently suggested it, but these discussions ended in heated arguments about the dangers of living in a city, even one as bucolic and small as Petropolis.

Petropolis had two main roads in the downtown area, housing all the businesses and main schools. The suburbs where people lived were spread out from the center of town for many miles, extending the city over the many hills and mountains that surrounded downtown. Petropolis was about sixty miles from Rio de Janeiro, nestled deep in the mountains, with a mild climate and, for the most part, uninteresting people. But it was a big stepping stone from where we were.

But this time, no scene followed my suggestion.

Now, the calculus was different. I had almost left for the United States. Nobody attended the religious meetings anymore. Our few neighbors detested my family. They shunned my parents to avoid their relentless attempts to recruit new worshipers or to avoid their hurtful comments about the dark auras and ominous futures awaiting those who lived around us.

We were teenagers now. That meant we were capable of taking the bus so that Lauro would not have to chauffer us everywhere—if we lived in the city. My mother assumed this change would make Lauro more likely to spend time with her. Also, if we did not wake up as early, the incessant complaining about leaving the house in the darkness would cease. It turns out, there was not a single factor tipping the scale in favor of staying in Shangrila.

My mother mumbled something to respond to my suggestion. It was not quite yes, but she also did not say no.

Sensing an opening, I did what I knew to do: I started the relentless and persistent tactic of incessantly talking about the same subject until I got what I wanted. At any occasion, I interjected a reason why we should move. We could get to school on time if we lived closer. We could take the bus and lift the burden off of Lauro to drive us to school every single day. Our pie-shaped bedroom was too small for three teenagers. Having one bathroom for the five of us made us late for school. We did homework on top of each other in the round house.

If we were tardy coming back from school or swamped with homework—or even any other unrelated reason—I would seize the chance to say, "Well, if we lived in Petropolis we could (fill in the blank)."

It was unclear whether my mother worried at all about our tardiness to classes, how frazzled Lauro would be dropping off and picking us up in multiple places, or the fact we had to wake up before the sun rose to prepare for school. However, after a few weeks of this, either because she agreed with me, or just wanted to shut me up, she relented.

"We are moving," she said one day.

"Where to?"

"To Petropolis, of course."

My sisters and I smiled broadly.

"When?"

"Soon. Your dad found us a new house."

RETIRO

L eaving Shangrila was uneventful.

Within a few days, we packed our meager possessions. My sisters and I did not know what to expect of this new home Lauro found. He had a tarnished track record with his choice of a round house on a farm in the middle of nowhere. The eight miserable years we spent in Shangrila tempered our hopes.

"What is the new house like?" I asked.

"You will see once you arrive," Lauro responded in his typically curt manner.

Nobody shed a tear. There was no one to say goodbye to, and there were no send-offs the day we left Shangrila. None of us looked back once the car left the driveway. There was nothing to miss about a place where none of us built one happy memory. We simply put our belongings in the car, leaving the farm and all its furniture behind, as if we were simply embarking on another trip up the curvy, mountain road towards Petropolis to attend school or go to the supermarket—except that this time, we would not return.

We reached Petropolis' small, colonial downtown at which point we veered onto one of the streets that led to the suburbs. We meandered through a tree-flanked, river-lined road. My sisters and I widened our eyes as the landscape changed from the simple, dilapidated apartments and large crowds in the downtown to the more sparse, stately homes of farther away neighborhoods. We finally stopped in front of an iron gate that blocked a long driveway up a little hill, flanked by trees and blooming flowers.

"It this our home?" Nathalie asked, not believing that this house could be where we would live.

"This is our new home!" Lauro said, beaming.

"How is this possible?" I asked, not reconciling how we could have left dilapidated, cramped Shangrila for the stately, two-story, whitewashed house, with blue windowpanes and ivy-covered walls that appeared at the top of the driveway. The lawn was manicured, and flower beds spilled over the path leading towards the home.

My mother was beaming too. We all squealed with delight and hugged Lauro. Our new home was large, luxurious, and rectangular. It came furnished with tasteful furniture and decorated with pleasing colors. It had four bedrooms, which meant we all got our own rooms for the first time.

My sisters and I ran upstairs, squealing and laying claim to our bedrooms, not quite believing that we would no longer need to share a room. While part of me felt excited that I would have my own space, I also panicked momentarily, thinking that now I could not guarantee having at least one of my sisters next to me at all times. Thus, immediately upon choosing my room, I removed the key from the door lock and placed it in the oak commode in the corner of the room. I planned to find a better hiding place later. For now, I needed to ensure that Lauro would not grab the key before I did and throw it away as he had done with our bedroom key in Shangrila.

"How can we afford to live in a place like this?" I asked my mother and Lauro once I returned downstairs.

My mother looked at Lauro adoringly.

"Your dad made it happen for us," she answered.

At first, I was unsure which dad she was talking about. Was it my biological father and his money that allowed us to live here, or was Lauro inexplicably contributing to the rent?

I learned later that one of the religious meeting attendees allowed my family to rent this house at a discounted price, as their way of thanking my mother and Lauro for all the enlightenment they had received over the years.

172 | LEAVING SHANGRILA

Not used to living in such a cavernous space, we congregated in the sunroom veranda, despite the house's multiple bedrooms and large dining and living rooms. We ate, completed our homework, played, and talked in the veranda, leaving most of the rest of the house unoccupied. We continued living as if we had a limited space, either because we were so used to cramped quarters or, perhaps, because I was not the only one in my family who felt that there was safety in numbers.

Our neighborhood, Retiro, was as its name implied: remote and calm. For the most part, nothing noteworthy happened in the leafy, residential neighborhood. After Shangrila, however, Retiro seemed to me to be bustling with life and activity. Neighbors walked to the local pharmacy and bakery, something unthinkable when we lived along the busy highway between Rio and Petropolis. The bus stopped on the corner of our street, and we would see people pass by, going about the business of their lives.

My father, not used to communicating with us, did not avail himself of the fact we now had a phone, except for a brief call on each of our birthdays.

At the time, international phone calls were astronomically expensive, so we never initiated one either. My father, not quite the conversationalist and always budget conscious, preferred to send postcards from his travels.

The year we moved, however, rather than coordinate his annual visit through my grandparents, my father called us directly to communicate the date and time of his plane's touchdown in Rio de Janeiro for his annual trip.

While we excitedly told him about our new house, my father would never see it as he would hereafter meet us in Rio. While it is true we were teenagers, too old for Park Cremerie and the limited entertainment Petropolis held, our venue was changed primarily because of my mother's insistence. She felt concerned that my father would, upon seeing our large house and stately yard, reduce the alimony payments. So, she told him that he was not welcome in Petropolis. Instead, my mother orchestrated with my grandparents that we should meet and spend a full weekend in Rio de Janeiro that year.

My sisters and I were excited about the prospect of two full days with our father, plus visiting Rio de Janeiro, our birthplace, for the first time since we moved from there years earlier.

Meeting in Rio de Janeiro was not without its complications. Lauro drove us to my grandparents' apartment in Rio and was careful to leave hours before my father was supposed to arrive. My grandparents had previously refused to meet Carroll, out of respect to my mother, who asked them to spare her the pain and betrayal of having them meet my stepmother. She wanted my grandparents to join her in overt disapproval that my father left us for a mistress, even one to whom he was now married.

But Carroll accompanied my father for the visit. Given that she was not welcome at my grandfather's apartment, my father came alone to fetch us so that we could meet Carroll at their hotel, located on the oceanfront of Copacabana beach, a block away from my grandparents' postage-stamp-sized apartment.

This was the first time I experienced anything I could remember about the city where I had been born. I felt surprised by the simplest of experiences. I marveled at the blast of cold air that instantly chilled away the humidity and sweat once we walked into the Hotel Le Meridien, the luxury hotel where my father and Carroll were staying. It was my first time walking on marble floors and seeing the fashionable tourists and businessmen crowding the lobby. I watched my father hand over a wad of US dollars to the hotel staff who magically turned it into Brazilian currency. I puffed my chest a little with the pride of having such a wealthy, worldly man for a father.

At first, we were all undecided about where to go. My father asked us what we wanted to do that day, but my sisters and I knew nothing about what Rio de Janeiro had to offer. My father was somewhat at a loss because now he had to come up with a new plan, rather than rely on the routine schedule of past visits. He did not know us at all and pondered what teenage girls might like to do.

Carroll filled the vacuum with her own ideas of what we should do that day. Realizing we knew nothing about the city, Carroll suggested we behave like the tourists that we were. We visited the botanical gardens and boarded the gondola to the Pao-de-Acucar, the postcard mountain with incredible views of Rio's beaches and bays. When we descended from the mountain, my father asked where we wanted to have lunch. The only restaurant we had ever visited was the churrascaria in Petropolis, so we did not know.

Carroll, appalled that we had never eaten a hamburger in our lives, suggested we go to McDonald's so that we could experience some proper American fare.

It was indeed an experience.

"You can order whatever you want!" Carroll said when we were making trade-offs between ordering a hamburger or a milkshake, so used to always rationing what we ate.

We took her offer literally. I ordered all I could eat: a huge hamburger, fries, soda, milkshake, and an apple pie. My sisters did the same. We behaved as if we had just won the food lottery. My father paid for this abundance of food without blinking an eye, without complaining about the cost of the bill, without telling us that we should do without. This perceived abundance confirmed what I believed to be true: my father was wealthy and worldly.

We devoured our food. My stomach distended at the consumption of so much food, and it hurt. Yet, I felt happy and thought that my first day in Rio de Janeiro had been the best of my life.

The next day, my father must have thought we needed a different kind of experience from eating hamburgers at McDonald's. He invited us all to lunch at the five-star Hotel Le Meridien.

My grandparents, who had for years refused to meet Carroll, let the offer of a white-tablecloth meal override their scruples of offending my mother and agreed to join us at the top-notch restaurant, where they would otherwise never be able go.

It was my first time at a luxury restaurant. As I sat down, I felt dazed by the array of silverware and glasses in front of me. There were three forks, multiple spoons and plates, and several waiters wearing tuxedos, fussing over our table. I did not know what to do, and rather than wait and watch what others did first, I proceeded to do what I knew. With a big show of theatrics, I took the starched napkin from my plate, flung it to unfold it and hung it on my shirt, as I had seen Lauro do once before on the rare occasion that we had company.

Not a second after I had done so, one of the waiters promptly came over and removed the napkin off my collar and placed it on my lap instead. Feeling embarrassed that I had done something incorrectly in front of my worldly father, I focused instead on the multiple forks flanking my dish.

"What is this for?" I asked my father, holding the skinny fork, which had only two teeth.

"For the fish," he said.

It felt overwhelming. I had only ever consumed fish with a regular fork. *Why was a special fork needed?* I thought but did not say. When I opened the menu the waiter handed to me, I could not comprehend that the names used on the menu were meant to describe food.

As the waiter took orders, my dad asked me to order first.

"Isa, what do you want?" my father asked in a calm voice, as if choosing a dish from that confusing menu was the most natural thing in the world. I did not know what any of the dishes were, but I did not want to admit it to my father, so afraid I was of appearing ignorant.

"What are you getting?" I asked him instead, to deflect the question.

He said something I did not understand.

"I want to have the same food as you," I said, feeling proud that I dodged the question of what to eat with aplomb.

Being French, my father had chosen escargots for an appetizer. I had heard my mother talk of them, but when I saw the green-sauced dish, I asked my father what they were. "Snails," he said.

"Yuck!" I said loudly.

"They are delicious! Have you not eaten them before?" my father asked, giving away his ignorance that we never ate much else besides rice and beans. Not wanting to display my ignorance of worldly ways, I told him that I, in fact, had eaten escargots, but it had been a long time ago.

I looked to what my father was doing so that I could imitate his actions. In the process, some of the snail shells splashed in the sauce, which spilled on the pristine table cloth and on my shirt. I felt flustered and thought that if the waiter had not removed the napkin from my collar, I would not have the spot on my shirt. The tuxedoed waiters were quick to pat the spot where the sauce landed to clean it up.

The next course was fish with their bones. I now understood why there were extra forks and extra knifes and all the utensils that I did not know how to use. As the meal progressed, so did my fluster and embarrassment. Again, I tried to be discreet in imitating my father, but all I managed was to drop the fish fork and almost gag on a bone. The waiter rushed over and asked whether he could debone the fish for me. He did not even wait for an answer and proceeded to do just that. For the first time in my life, I felt grateful that we knew how to pretend that there were no problems in our midst.

Despite how delicious everything tasted, lunch could not end fast enough. I felt relieved when we all got up to leave. I felt so embarrassed that I said nothing as we left the cooled restaurant and made our way to the humid sidewalks to stroll along the beach. Carroll returned to her room. My grandparents returned to their apartment. My father, my sisters, and I left the restaurant and arrived at a bakery, where I immediately pointed at a batch of cookies filled with condensed milk and covered with a sugary coat, a cross of cream puffs and profiteroles with a Brazilian twist. I pointed at them and turned to my father. "Can we buy some of these cookies?" I asked.

He proceeded to order them.

As I raised my arms to hold the bag of cookies the baker placed in front of him, he grabbed it first. "These are not for you. We will bring them to Carroll."

My eyes filled with tears, with the disappointment of not being given a cookie by my own father.

"Can I have one too?" I asked.

"You just had lunch, Isa. You cannot possibly be hungry."

We left the bakery as he held a bag full of cookies that I wanted to eat, intended for Carroll instead.

I stayed quiet as we met up again with Carroll and boarded the air-conditioned tourist bus that traveled along the Copacabana shoreline; it cost five times more than the regular bus. Only tourists and those who could afford the fare took the tourist bus, and we went to do a free tour of H. Stern, a famed jeweler who used Brazil's colored, precious stones. The five of us were facing each other as the bus got more crowded, and some people stood in the space between our two seats. This should have been a short, uneventful ride—except for the giddiness I felt for experiencing a cooled, air-conditioned bus for the first time in my life.

That happiness was short lived, however. A boy entered the bus, screaming and holding a bright, silver gun. He could not have been older than twelve, yet he kept screaming in Portuguese: "Give me what you have, or I will shoot." Those standing handed over their cameras, jewelry, and purses. We were towards the back of the bus, and I saw my father hide his camera behind his legs and remove his wedding ring.

I panicked at the sight of my father hiding his belongings. I felt terrified that the boy thief would come towards us and shoot my father upon his refusal to give his belongings. As he stole money, jewelry, and cameras, the thief made his way towards the back of the bus. Amazingly, the bus never stopped and kept rolling along the shoreline. The boy halted and pointed the gun towards a man who stood between our seats, affording me the perfect view of the gleaming gun. I felt a rush of fear as the boy turned to my father.

"Give me what you have!" the boy said nervously.

"I have nothing," my father responded calmly.

The boy, visibly upset and seemingly more nervous than those of us he robbed, left my father alone, moved on to collect the valuables of others, and left the bus soon after. The whole episode did not last more than ten minutes. Yet, as soon as the thief left, we did too. We exited the bus at the following stop and decided to take a cab back to our hotel instead.

While we all felt petrified, Nathalie's hands had seized into an unnatural position. She screamed, "I can't move my hands!"

Her hands were turned inwards, as a reaction to the stress and shock we all felt. My father took her hands in his and tried to loosen them up, but he could not. At that moment, I felt more afraid of Nathalie becoming disabled than I did of my father being killed by a thief.

I wished to return to Petropolis as soon as possible, where at least the threats we faced were predictable. I thought, perhaps, that my mother had been right all along, that my father had no interest in being a parent and did not understand me at all. And, it seemed that the world was, indeed, a dangerous place. Maybe we had been safer holed up on our farm. Right after that weekend, I thought that maybe my mother and Lauro had been right in their relentless attempt to protect us from experiencing what the world had to offer.

Chapter 34

AFTERNOONS

$\mathcal{T}$he story of the cookies I requested, which my father offered to Carroll, became an unwelcome addition to my mother's rant about everything that was wrong with my father. I never told her about my shame and embarrassment at eating at a five-star restaurant, but part of me believed that my mother was not altogether wrong about her opinion of my father. I stopped wishing to be like him. And I felt grateful that my mother had forbidden me from moving to the United States after all.

We tried to resume our life back in Petropolis. The bus robbery in Rio and Nathalie's reaction made my mother hesitate to allow us to take the bus on our own. So Lauro continued driving us to school when we first moved to Retiro.

Soon, though, with the multiple drop-offs and pick-ups, as well as different school schedules, Lauro was the one who said we should take the bus. There were numerous rules that came along with this relative autonomy. Nathalie and I must return on the 12:15 p.m. bus, which was the first one departing after school let out for day. While either my mother or Lauro accompanied us to the bus stop on the first few days, they soon preferred to sleep in rather than walk us there at half past six in the morning.

Moving to Petropolis had not changed the limitations on our schedule. We were still to return home immediately after school and were still forbidden to join school activities or study groups. I had not expected any different. I had been used to this restricted schedule and felt that, at least at first, there was nobody to visit anyway.

Lauro's role in our family, besides controlling our lives, was to pay all of the household's bills at the bank. In Brazil, nothing was easy or efficient. Paying bills required going to the bank in person and lining up in long queues. Different vendors required payment at different banks. The paying of households bills—electricity, water, phone, and schools—took at least a full day, often two. There was no wiring of money. Nobody trusted checks.

One afternoon my mother noted that Lauro forgot to pay the electricity bill. Lauro was out, and the note said our electricity would be disconnected if we did not pay that day. Not only would that be an inconvenience, but we would need to pay a penalty, and the price would continue to increase daily, along with inflation, until the bill was paid.

Seeing her distress, I offered to go to the bank to pay the bill.

My mother hesitated. I had never yet left the house on my own. Recognizing she had no choice if she wanted the bill paid that day—and after extensive instructions on where I should go, how long it should last, and which return bus I should take—she sent me on the errand. I boarded the bus towards downtown, on my own for the first time.

I followed my mother's instructions carefully, paid the bills, and returned home before the time she stipulated. With this show of responsibility, she soon asked me to go pay another bill. Within a couple of months, it fell to me to pay all of the household bills.

For at least two afternoons a month, I left the house alone to pay the household bills.

At first, I followed the rules. Soon, though, I added gallivanting around the city, admiring its colonial buildings, and twisting my nose at the foul odor emanating from the city's polluted river. I overstated the bus fare so that I would have pocket money to eat a slice of cake at the bakery. I explored every corner of that small city. I felt free, even though I did nothing more than walk the streets. Yet, for a few hours, I was completely on my own, feeling grown up and removed from my life. When my mother questioned why I arrived home increasingly later, I responded that the lines were particularly long that day.

Over time, my mother, in addition to the written checks for bills, also gave me some cash to buy sundries for the house. Soon, besides overstating the bus fare, I also overstated the prices of household items, which was easy to do in Brazil where prices changed daily.

My mother, ignorant of the cost of living, had no way to gauge whether I was being truthful, so she handed me what I asked for. When I felt that the money I collected through overstating prices was insufficient, I routinely entered her room to remove a couple of bills from her dresser drawer. I was careful not to overstate prices too much, nor to take too many bills at once; I wanted my misappropriation of funds to go unnoticed.

I used the stolen money primarily to buy cakes. Soon after, however, I also purchased hair products, as my mother previously refused to buy these for me, deeming it unnecessary and vain to try to tame my curly and frizzy hair. I carefully kept my hair product purchases hidden, removing them from the shower each time I used them.

I enjoyed immensely my afternoons outside of the house. But since we moved, I did not feel as compelled to leave the house for my safety. Life at home had improved noticeably. I fully recognized that Lauro no longer showed any interest in molesting me. Yet, every night I locked my bedroom door, just in case, and hid the key in the mornings before I left for school. I also used some of the stolen funds to make a back-up key, just to ensure I had an extra if Lauro ever got hold of my bedroom key and threw it away.

Chapter 35

HIGH SCHOOL

There were marginal improvements in my social standing at school. Rather than sit on the bench during recess, whenever a group of students congregated to talk, I stood on the edges, listening to the topics they chose to discuss. Nobody actively shunned me when I did that, so I became more comfortable lurking around. I mostly felt I had not much to contribute, or when I did think of something to say, the conversation swiftly moved to a different topic before I could articulate the response in my head. I felt frustrated most of the time, so one day I thought to interject, even if out of context, so I could contribute to the conversation.

My heart pounded in my chest as I waited for an opening. This waiting led me to feel increasingly nervous. I felt more afraid of letting that moment pass than of having heart arrhythmia; I could not face the let down if I did not say something. I eventually offered up a sentence completely out of context. The handful of people in the group stopped talking and looked at me, but not with the look of "What can you possibly have to say to us?" nor "Why are you interrupting?" Instead, they looked at me with genuine interest, having heard something they wanted to know more about. I had not planned a follow-up sentence or to carry on the conversation beyond that one line. I laughed nervously instead.

"It is OK, Isabelle," someone said. "What did you mean?"

"Nothing," I responded. So the conversation continued without any additional contribution from me. I did not mind. I felt so elated that I actually managed to speak and feel accepted that it seemed a small victory.

The next day I tried again, saying two sentences this time. Over time, I spoke a little more. Still, these group situations were so nerve-wracking that I much preferred to build my friendships one person at a time. And the person I most wanted to build a friendship with was Walter.

Walter sat in the opposite corner of the room from me, on the last seat on the last row—as far away as he could sit from the classroom door. I, on the other hand, sat in the front row as I could see the blackboard better this way. My seat was the closest to the entrance door, primarily to avoid having to visit with anyone as I came in and out of class.

Our seat choice was hardly the only difference between us. While my family rationed food as our resources dwindled at the end of each month, Walter's family owned the largest supermarket in Rio de Janeiro, the Carrefour. His family was one of the wealthiest in Petropolis.

Carrefour, with its large aisles, was a one-stop shopping megamall that had been revolutionary when it first opened. Until then, most Brazilians purchased their groceries one store at a time. The butcher sold meat. The baker sold bread. Milk was delivered to our door. Doctors made house visits. The idea of one-stop shopping was as foreign as the French mega-market's name. During the hyperinflation period when prices increased daily, the ability to buy everything at once, from rice to bicycles, held an immense appeal. Carrefour single handedly transformed a desolate area in the south of Rio into a must-go-to destination, which eventually became one of the poshest neighborhoods in the city. Despite it being on the outskirts of Rio de Janeiro, it was closer to Petropolis than it was to someone who lived in the upscale neighborhoods around the famed beaches of Rio's South Zone. The close distance to the store's location in Rio, the weather, and the relative safety, led Walter's family to choose to live in Petropolis. And they did not choose to live just anywhere in Petropolis. His mansion, as luck would have it, was the next street over, five houses down from mine.

And while his life was not as restricted as mine, he certainly was not free to wander as he pleased. A chauffer drove Walter to school in a car with darkened windows. He had a bodyguard who walked him to the school door and picked him up. This, it turns out, was a necessity for the children of Brazil's wealthy. They were often victims of kidnappers who traded them back to their anxious parents for large ransoms.

Given their success, it was not surprising that Walter's parents expected their son to be a high achiever. Walter, however, was a mediocre student. Wanting at all costs to avoid disappointing his parents, this relatively quiet, shy, and scrawny boy, with a bushy mane of auburn hair and freckles, came to rely on me.

Walter and I entered into a symbiotic relationship. I helped him complete his homework, and in exchange, he talked with me. And for me, who hardly ever had anybody to talk to, I loved feeling that I finally had a friend. Sitting at polar opposite sides of the classroom was a barrier to this blossoming friendship. Thus, I moved from the front row to the seat right in front of Walter, a move which required me to shed my self-imposed limitation of not crossing the room to reach my seat. There were at least four heads in between the blackboard and my seat, making it harder for me to see. Yet, it was worth it. Once I sat directly in front of Walter, speaking with him required a tap on my shoulder or a half turn of my head.

Walter benefited greatly as well. He could easily see my exam papers, especially those I purposely placed on the far right side of my desk after he asked whether I would not mind sitting to one side and having my exam paper on another so that he could have a clearer view—and that I should write in larger letters too. Enjoying the attention that Walter gave me, I acquiesced. I shifted my body towards the left of my seat and wrote on my test sheets on the right. I was no longer the first to complete exams, handing them over only after Walter handed his. Soon, Walter's grades improved.

Walter and I did not hang out during recess or at any time before or after school. Yet, I felt that I had a real friend in him. Either way, I felt that moving to the back row would help me shed my bookworm, nerdy reputation and help me in my ongoing efforts to have a friend.

Chapter 36

VISITOR

Although we now had a nice home and a phone, nobody visited and mostly nobody called. We may have changed homes, but we still had the same parents who still believed that anybody but us had a dark soul and that we would always be better off as isolated as possible. We lived like this for so long that it had never occurred to me to invite anyone over. I had no expectations to receive invitations either, especially because I still knew that I would need to decline them.

Thus, I had not even remotely considered that Walter would quite unexpectedly show up at my house's front gate. It was by chance that I saw him, from my bedroom window, standing at the gate, waving at me. At the sight of Walter, my heart leaped through my chest, as if the cavity in which it pulsed was not enough to contain it. Partly, it was due to the unexpected and pleasant surprise of his visit. Upon seeing him, though, I also felt a sense of full-fledged panic. I had not warned him about the dangers of showing up at my house unannounced. I had never told him about my family life at all. I feared what would happen if Lauro or my mother got to him before I could send him away.

I immediately dropped the book I was reading and bolted out the door, running as fast as I could without tripping down the stairs. *Please, don't ring the bell before I reach you*, I thought to myself as I scrambled down the stairs. However, the bell did ring while I was halfway through the living room.

It all happened too fast. By the time I reached the front door, I heard screams and saw a figure running past me at a fast clip. Lauro shouted obscenities as he walked fast down the driveway towards Walter.

"GET OUT OF HERE, YOU SCUM!" Lauro said, among other words in a rapid stream that neither Walter nor I understood. Lauro's face was contorted with fury, whereas Walter's face had turned white as his timid smile turned into a look of horror.

Walter had been protected from danger all his life. He had a bodyguard, who must not have known he was on an ill-fated attempt to see me. Walter, always coddled, always loved, had never been screamed at or faced a lunatic who threatened him. His timid smile evaporated from his face and turned into a flustered expression of panic. He looked past Lauro, towards me, with imploring eyes, half asking me to explain, half asking for help.

I was left full-on wishing that I could make this all go away. I wanted to do something, anything. Yet, I did not move; I was petrified by the scene that was developing in front of me. I felt the blood drain from my veins. What could I do? I did nothing. Walter realized I was not coming to the rescue. He felt scared of what would happen should Lauro reach him and was deeply humiliated by the small crowd of passersby witnessing the scene. My mother, sisters, the gardener, our maid, and their multitude of children stood around me. As people walked by our house, they congregated at our gate, curious about what all the noise was for.

As the crowds increased, Walter turned around and ran to his house—but not before I saw his flustered cheeks and teary eyes. Feeling guilty about the consternation I caused Walter, I snapped from my stupor and made my way towards the gate, wanting to run after him.

Lauro's short, stocky frame stood in my way. He had turned towards the house, satisfied that he taught my friend, and the rest of us, an unforgettable lesson. Noticing I was in the middle of the driveway, he stared at me with glee, already anticipating the humiliation I was about to feel as he shouted, "YOU STAY THERE!"

As Lauro walked towards me, with a smirk on his smug face, I felt an unbridled rage. How dare he treat Walter like a flea-infested dog? Rage over eight years of control, abuse, and extreme unfairness was welling up inside me.

Lauro had not noticed this shift within me and proceeded to turn his spitefulness towards me. He screamed and swore as he made his way back up the driveway.

"You are a whore!" he screamed loudly, ensuring that the small crowd witnessing this scene heard it. He picked up the pace as he walked up the long driveway, continuing with his stream of obscenities, raising his hand from hundreds of feet away, getting ready to strike me for the insolence of having a friend, a boy, come to visit me. Lauro was soon within inches of me, his hand raised and ready to strike.

Yet, the fear Lauro had previously instilled in me drained away, replaced by a bottomless pit of hate. He had destroyed every single good moment I might have enjoyed for the last eight years. He always had to be in the way. He always had to demolish what I built. That he crushed the one friend I ever had was unforgivable. His interference with my life had to stop. If I had the tools, I would have killed him.

I stood in the middle of the driveway. All the noise caused by Lauro's screams, my mother's pleas for me to turn back, and the murmur of the crowd ceased. I heard nothing, saw nothing. I did not move. I did not cower. I did not beg. I did not turn back. And I did not care if he hit me.

While Lauro was not a reasonable person, he was not altogether stupid. While I stood there, resolute, he was smart enough to look around. He noticed the crowds at the gate. He noticed my family and the gardener's family standing behind me, all anticipating what he would do next. He suddenly became aware that hitting me in public would, perhaps, be condemned. Lauro was used to abusing and controlling us in the shadows, when nobody was looking, but this event could show the world who he truly was.

He lowered his hand but continued to approach me with a stream of profanity coming out of his mouth.

I remained silent. I stood erect, hate and contempt spewing from my eyes and tense body.

Once he was in striking distance of me, he no longer knew what to do.

"Move!" he said loudly, as if my small frame could block the wide driveway where we both stood.

I did not move an inch.

"I told you to move, you little bitch," he continued.

I stared at him, staying in place.

All the murmur ceased. The audience around us was holding their breath, watching what would happen next. There was a deafening silence, a silence we all heard once Lauro stopped screaming.

Lauro stood in front of me for a few seconds. Realizing I would not budge and recognizing he could not push me in public, he went around me, whispering even more profanities. My family and the gardener's family blocked the door by their sheer number, but Lauro did not try to go through them. Instead, he walked towards the back of the house to enter it through the maid's door.

I stayed in the yard for a little while, breathing heavily and steaming with fury. My hate for Lauro knew no boundaries and oozed out of my pores. His hold on me ended that day as I grieved all he had taken from my childhood. He destroyed every moment that had been special to me. All the memories of the events he destroyed came rushing back: how he violated me the day I wore my first bra; how he shattered my happiness after I was selected at the Olympics; how the unreasonable restrictions and spankings came out of nowhere. But treating my one friend as if he was a vermin to be squashed was the tipping point. I had invested in Walter. I finally had a friend. I compromised my academic success so that I could have Walter in my life. And I knew, when I saw Walter's red, puffy face move away from the gate, that that friendship was over.

From that day forward, I would never again let Lauro rule my life. I decided he would never again get in my way.

The crowd at the gate dissipated, having no interest in watching a skinny teenager stand in the middle of the driveway.

"Isa, come inside," my mother joined me where I was and held me by my shoulder, attempting to hug and appease me.

"This is all your fault!" I spewed back at my stunned mother as I pushed her arms away from me. "It was you who brought this monster into our lives."

"Isa, do not talk like that about your father."

"I already told you. That vermin is not my father."

My mother mumbled some words that I had no interest in hearing. I pushed her aside and walked back into the house, locking the door behind me as I returned to my bedroom so that I could let the rage seethe a little longer, so that I could figure out how to fix the mess Lauro created.

First, I had to remove Lauro from my life permanently.

I did not consider running away. I knew that my mother would side with Lauro and that within minutes, we would all behave as if the events of the day had not happened.

My options were limited, yet I knew just what to do.

Despite the tension in our house, my mother and Lauro expected that we all sit together for dinner. Dinners were not lively affairs, but we did talk to one another and at least acknowledged what Lauro or my mother said. That evening, however, nothing went as expected. Not having had a chance to punish me yet, Lauro gleefully brought up the topic of chasing my friend away. I behaved as if nobody was talking, kept my head tall, and asked for my sister to pass the food dish.

"You look at me when I talk to you!" he screamed at me, frustrated and pounding his fists on the table.

I did not. I kept eating, again fully ignoring Lauro and his antics. My mother's and sisters' discomfort was visible. They sat silently, wishing, as I was, that our meal would end soon.

At the end of dinner, Lauro rose from the head of the table and walked to my side. I continued ignoring him. He pushed my dish away and placed his hands on my shoulder to shake me.

My mother screamed, "STOP!"

My sisters and I looked at her, stunned, trying to decipher whether she was defending Lauro or me.

"All of you, just stop!" she repeated. "Let's just eat in peace."

Lauro released my shoulders and left the room. My sisters and I finished our meal in silence.

The next day, I sought Walter at school. I found him on his seat with his head lowered.

"Hi," I timidly said.

He said nothing. He did not even raise his head.

"About yesterday—" I started.

Where would I even begin? Nobody in school knew how dysfunctional my life had been. All that everybody knew was that I was different, socially awkward, financially struggling (if my clothes were any indication), and just plain weird. They just did not know why all these circumstances seemed true, and frankly, they never bothered to find out. There was just too much to explain. How could I possibly justify how Walter got chased out of my house as if he had leprosy? Walter was not interested in listening, in any case. But even if he was, I simply did not have the courage and maturity to tell him. I had hidden my true life for so long. Where would I start?

He mumbled that he had come to my house so that I could help him with homework. "Can I help you now?" I offered. There was time, since class hadn't yet started.

"No," he said flatly.

The teacher walked in, and I turned back to pay attention to the lesson. I tried to talk to him again at recess. He did not answer.

Walter was used to pampering, adoration, and the protection offered by his family. He must have realized why his family was so protective of him and why he had reason to fear the world. He took a chance on the weird girl, and all he experienced with me was rejection. He got a glimpse of how dysfunctional my life was. It must have been hard to relate to it, especially when I tried so hard to keep it hidden, pretending to be a normal teenager. The sting of what he suffered with his visit and the difficulties of being a friend to someone who was never allowed to go anywhere or do anything proved to be too hard for him.

I tried to speak with him again the next day, but he did not answer. When recess came, he got up so quickly that I did not even have a chance to try. So I stayed at my desk. He had to pass by me on his way back to his seat. "Walter—" I said.

"Why are you still sitting here? Why don't you move to the front row?" he said curtly during my last attempt to talk to him. At hearing this, I turned back so that he would not see my tears. I did not have the maturity to see that he was lashing out at me as a retribution for the deep humiliation he experienced. I did not recognize Walter's need to process what had happened. I wanted immediate forgiveness, but saw no way to earn it from him. I felt my heart shrivel at Walter's rebuttal. I did not try to speak to him again.

The next day, I asked the nuns whether I could trade seats and return to the front row.

"Again, Isabelle?" they asked.

"I cannot see well from the back row," I said, pointing to my thick, bottom-of-the-bottle glasses as all the evidence I needed. The nuns could not argue with my appeal to eyesight hardship. They knew I was a top student and that my grades had deteriorated since I moved to the back row, in my effort to appear less academic to my classmates. The nun asked one of the students to give up his seat and told me that I could take my old place in the front row.

So I moved back to the top of the academic pecking order and the bottom of the social one. I never spoke with Walter again. But that was not all. The news of Walter's humiliation made the circles around the school. For the rest of the school year, all my attempts to make friends came up empty. I was no longer welcome to hover around groups at recess time. It seemed patently clear that high school would not be an improvement over the dreadful experiences I had in middle school.

Nobody spoke to me. And once more, I became resigned that this was the way it would remain.

Chapter 37

THE BUS

For the few days after, I continued ignoring Lauro whenever we were in the same room together. I never looked at him and did not wish him good morning or good night. If we dined together, I behaved as if his seat was empty. I never voluntarily entered a room if he was in it. Where I could, I left the room when he entered. He resented this new treatment deeply. He pushed me around a few times, screaming, "Look at me!" I averted my eyes just past him, denying his request. My mother, assuming my behavior was temporary, did not initially intervene. After a few days, though, she said, "Isa, that's enough."

"What is enough?" I asked, as if I had not understood what she was talking about.

"Say hello to your father when he walks in the room."

"My father isn't here," I responded.

"You know what I mean."

"Actually, I don't," I responded. "My father lives in the United States. And I would be living there too were it not for you."

When I mentioned the possibility of living with my father, she changed the subject from acknowledging Lauro to criticizing my father. I also learned to leave the room when my mother started her monologues.

My mother felt increasingly frustrated with me, and in many instances, my insolence brought her to tears. I cried too, alone in my bedroom or in the yard, out of frustration and hatred. During these times, I paced back and forth, thinking about what I could do to change my life. I often came up empty.

Not knowing what to do, I went about my days, feeling unhappy wherever I was. I wished classes would end as soon as possible so that I would not feel so ostracized by everybody. I wished I would not have to go home and face my family. The only times I felt happy were on the bus to and from school and during the afternoons when I walked the streets to pay bills.

The buses were crowded. In the morning, I stood up. On the return bus, I arrived early enough to claim a seat, but I typically avoided sitting next to anyone from school, even if that meant I had to stand up. One day as I sat by the window, Cristiane, one of my classmates, sat on the empty seat next to me.

Cristiane lived a few bus stops north from mine in Retiro. We had little interaction previously. I groaned silently, thinking I had been stupid to select a window seat. I wondered what we could possibly talk about during the twenty minute bus ride; alternately, I dreaded an uncomfortably silent journey.

Around that time, the first-ever international music festival was to be held in Rio, at a stadium next to Walter's Carrefour supermarket. The top rock bands of the time (U2, Bon Jovi, Michael Jackson, Madonna, and Tina Turner) were headlining the event. None of these artists had previously performed in Brazil; thus, anybody who could, vied for the hard-to-obtain tickets to this multi-day event. The concert, and who planned to go, was the talk of the school.

It was such a given I would not be allowed to go that I did not even ask. Attending an expensive rock concert, an hour away, among hundreds of thousands of people who would likely be drunk and drugged was not an option for my mother, who believed the only proper music was classical. I barely knew of the bands and their music—except for Michael Jackson and Madonna because my father had previously brought cassettes with their music.

"Will you go to Rock'n'Rio?" Cristiane asked me, initiating conversation on the bus.

"No," I said.

"I will not go either," she responded. "But it is so great that all these musicians are coming here. They will love singing for Brazilians. We love them. I love Bon Jovi," Cristiane went on. "They are my favorite!"

I did not know who Bon Jovi was. Not wanting to admit it, though, I responded that U2 and their song "Sunday Bloody Sunday" was my favorite.

Cristiane looked back at me with a wide, toothy smile and said, "I love U2, too!"

We talked music and who among our classmates was lucky enough to attend Rock'n'Rio.

From that day forward, we left school together and walked the fifteen minutes it took to catch the bus. It turns out, we had more in common than similar musical tastes.

Her parents were also divorced, still a rarity in Petropolis. Unlike me, though, she lived with her father and stepmother. Her mother lived on the other side of town, and it was not a convenient place, distance-wise, from school. Cristiane also had two sisters, one of which, her middle sister, was the beauty magnet in her family, like Nathalie was of mine. And so Cristiane made up for living in the shadow of her taller, gorgeous sister as I did, by becoming the best student in her family. For the first time in my life, I met my academic match. Sometimes Cristiane's grades even surpassed mine.

This, however, is where the similarities ended. I initially thought she also had strict parents, given that her father was a colonel in the army. Yet, I soon learned that Miguel allowed his daughters to have freedoms that I did not even know were possible. Cristiane moved about as she pleased. Her father drove them to nightclubs—suitable for teenagers—on the weekends and allowed her to samba away at Carnival. He let her watch TV and listen to any kind of music she chose.

So when exams loomed, she did not hesitate to invite me to join her at her house, a ten minute walk uphill from my house, to study together.

It had been years since I received an invitation to anyone's home. I felt elated—and also certain that my mother would not allow me to visit. Yet, with so many changes in our lives and my recent track record of getting my mother to agree to my ideas eventually, I thought, at a minimum, I should try.

"I have a big math test coming up," I told my mother. She looked at me surprised, since my education was not typically a topic of conversation.

"I am sure you will do well," she responded.

"I will do better if I study with Cristiane," I said. "She understands math."

"Who is Cristiane?"

I had not mentioned Cristiane before as my mother and Lauro so quickly criticized anybody with whom we came into contact. So I explained that Cristiane was a good student, who had better grades than me, sometimes. I went on to explain it was important that I study with her. I added that everybody in my class had a study buddy, though I made that part up.

My mother was weary: weary that I almost left her; weary that I openly ignored Lauro; weary of my insolence; weary hearing me incessantly repeat what I wanted until I got it. My mother, I was learning, felt it easier to acquiesce to what I asked for than to hear the same request until I wore her down.

Still, I preempted many questions I thought she might have. I told her Cristiane was a model student, who was polite, studious, and responsible. I told her she had a dad in the military and made it sound as if he was as strict as my mother was. I explained that her home was ten minutes away, so I could return home whenever she wanted.

"Why can't you just study here?" my mother asked.

"Do you remember what happened last time somebody came to the house?" I said maliciously.

"I meant, why can't you study here by yourself?"

"I already told you, Mom. Cristiane can explain difficult problems to me."

My mother considered all of this, and I suppose she thought that if I had a friend, maybe I would not be inclined to want to leave her again.

"You can go, but you must be back here not one minute after five o'clock," she stated emphatically.

"Thank you, Mom," I said, trying to hide my excitement.

It was already two o'clock. I picked up our phone and told Cristiane that I was on my way.

That first time, I wanted to show my mother that she could trust me and give me more freedom. I returned ten minutes before the five o'clock deadline. She looked at her watch when I returned.

"How was it?" she asked me.

"I studied a lot," I responded.

I did well on the test. I showed the report card to my mother, giving all the credit for my high grade to the single study session with Cristiane the week before.

"Look how well I did, Mom. Cristiane truly helped!"

My mother, who had not paid attention to my academic standing, could not tell whether this grade was an improvement or if I would have done as well on my own. Thus, seeing tangible proof of results, she allowed me to study at Cristiane's the following week and soon enough, every Tuesday.

We did study. But we also splashed in her pool, with me wearing a swimming suit Cristiane lent me as I did not own one. We played ping pong and spent a significant amount of time simply talking, among ourselves as well as with her sisters and neighbors who also attended our same school.

During these conversations, Cristiane described the Petropolitano, the only country club in Petropolis. Anybody who could afford it was a member. The club had the only Olympic-size pool in the entire city and had multiple tennis courts. The security of its fence, the palm-lined gardens, and its bar and restaurants attracted Petropolis' wealthy. Every Saturday, the club turned into a nightclub, and it was the most sought-after place to go during Carnival.

Cristiane and her sisters attended most of these events, chauffeured there by her own father.

"It is so fun, Isa!" she said, excitedly telling me about who they saw and which songs they danced to the previous week.

"You have to come with us!" she insisted.

I wanted to, so badly. But studying at Cristiane's house was one thing. Going to a nightclub was entirely another.

"I am sure my mother will not allow me," I said.

"But my dad will drive us. Your mother will know that you are safe."

"It is not about that. My mother just does not let me go anywhere."

"You need to try."

Upon returning home, I explained to my mother how Cristiane's dad allowed her to go dancing on Sundays.

"No!" my mother said, cutting me off, not letting me continue the discussion.

"But—" I said.

"No. Never," she said. Nightclubs horrified her. In the rare instances when the TV was on, whenever scenes of people dancing, kissing, or doing anything that remotely appeared fun, my mother would comment about how awful, in bad taste, and spiritually corrupting all those activities were. To my mother, allowing me to go to a nightclub was akin to sending us into mortal danger. This time, I knew that no matter how much I insisted and repeated my plea, she would not change her mind.

Every week, I heard how much fun Cristiane and the others had. She continued urging me, and I kept saying my mother would not let me go.

One Tuesday, Cristiane's father, Miguel, was in the room reading a book while we worked on program sets in our economics workbooks. He overhead us talk about plans for the following Sunday; the theme for the evening would be samba night. "It will be just like Carnival!" Cristiane said excitedly. "We will wear costumes too."

"Isa, are you coming with us?" Miguel asked.

I looked at him and shook my head. "My mom would not let me go."

"Why not?" he asked.

I explained again about how I was not allowed to do anything besides come to study at their home once a week and how my mother feared that horrible things would happen to us while at the nightclub.

"But nothing horrible happens at the club!" he responded, laughing. "They would have to deal with me if it did!" he stated, implying that the military would come marching in if anything untoward ever happened to one of his daughters.

I looked at him with tears in my eyes, thinking how unlucky I had been not to have a father like him.

Miguel, as a leader in the military, was used to having people do what he told them to do.

"That's nonsense," he said. "I will talk to your mother!"

Panic set in deep in my belly. The last time somebody visited me, they were chased out of my house. I couldn't bear to lose my friendship to Cristiane and the love of this family who was beginning to feel like my own. I tried to discourage Miguel.

"That's OK. You don't have to do that," I said.

"Do you want to go?" he asked, looking straight into my eyes.

His question was so direct and honest. I nodded my head.

"Then that is settled. I will call your mother."

He picked up the phone and called my house.

He introduced himself to my mother and explained he was an army colonel who took the safety of his children seriously and that he often chaperoned them to Som Petro for a little bit of fun that was completely harmless. He assured my mother that he would drive us there and then pick us up, that Cristiane had gone numerous times, and it was safe. He reminded her that he was a military man and would not ever lead his daughter to harm's way. Despite all of his assurances, at the end of their conversation, the answer was still no. Even so, I felt an upsurge of love and gratitude towards Miguel and Cristiane. Miguel was the first adult in my life who ever fought for me.

Once the welling up of gratitude subsided, the now familiar feeling of hatred welled up within me again. While that feeling had been directed towards Lauro in the past, it now spilled over to my mother. I thought with cynicism that my mother was a hypocrite. Here she was, forbidding me to go to a nightclub to protect me from danger, when the most dangerous person we could ever encounter lived with us.

Miguel's attempt to bring some normalcy to my life inspired me. I decided to take matters into my own hands.

"Do you think your Dad meant it when he said he would take me to Som Petro?" I asked Cristiane.

She smiled. "Yes, he did."

"I am not a member," I said.

"Don't worry about that. I can bring you as a guest."

NIGHT OWL

J had wanted to attend the teen-geared Som Petro on Sundays, but quickly gave up on the idea. It started at seven in the evening, too early for me to leave the house unnoticed. Instead, I focused on the next time Cristiane planned to attend the Saturday night themed balls where nobody who knew about social mores in Brazil would dare to arrive before eleven at night.

"Meet me at the front gate at exactly 10:15 p.m.," Cristiane said

"What happens if I am not there exactly at that time?" I asked, planning for the worst-case scenario.

"We will go without you."

"Don't worry. I will be there," I responded.

"What about your mother?"

"You make sure you are there on time. I have a plan so that I can meet you then," I said.

Lights were typically out before ten o'clock at my house. As the appointed time approached, I observed everybody's movements, with my heart beating fast at the possibility that this night, among all others, someone would linger later than usual and mess up my plan. I trounced around the house in my nightgown, an oversized, green and black plaid, long-sleeved shirt that almost touched my knees. I bought it with the money I stole from my mother and used it as my nightgown starting a couple of weeks earlier.

"That's funny that you are using that shirt to sleep. It is a day shirt," Catherine unhelpfully pointed out in front of the family a few days before. "Besides, aren't you feeling hot with those long sleeves?"

The long sleeves were out of place in the typically warm evenings, but I needed my choice in clothing to appear normal.

"Not at all. They are so comfortable!" I replied as I moved towards my sister. "Feel how light this fabric is."

She touched the thin sleeve and seemed satisfied enough with my answer. She did not ask about my clothes again.

The oversized shirt was, indeed, comfortable, but I did not wear it for the comfort. I wore it as a disguise. It was large enough to cover my real outfit for the night: a mini skirt and the dressiest shirt I could find among the slim pickings of my wardrobe, which had not been built up to allow me to look fashionable at a party.

"I will go to sleep," I said to the family while giving them the customary good night kisses, even though it was only half past nine.

"Already? It is so early; stay with us a little bit more," Nathalie said unhelpfully. My sisters did not know about my plan. I feared they could not hold to a secret, or worse, would complicate my plan by wanting to come along.

Although we now lived in a large, rectangular house, my family tended to congregate in the veranda, the room adjacent to the living room, flanked by endless windows that made it look like a greenhouse. The many windows allowed the coolness of the night air to aerate the house after the hot, humid summer days. The veranda had a direct view of the small gate to the house. It was a pleasant place for the humid nights, but it would be difficult to leave the house unnoticed if the family decided to linger in that room. The only window upstairs that had a view of the small gate was Nathalie's. I did not expect her to look out or to alert anyone if she happened to see me outside. Everybody else's rooms had a view of the side or the back of the house. The larger gate towards the left of the house was a poor alternative as it required walking the lengthy driveway under the moonlight. Plus, the maid and gardener's quarters had a direct view towards the gate. And Tom, our gardener, had the unfortunate habit of leaving his wife and children to cavort on the town most evenings, so he could be out and about. I had to ensure my family left the veranda.

"I am tired. I will read in my room before sleeping."

I went upstairs and closed the door, almost slamming it, to give the impression that I had retired for the night. I looked impatiently at my watch, waiting for the minutes to pass. Closer to ten, I heard the footsteps of my sisters, my mother, and Lauro as they made their way to their respective rooms. Soon enough, all lights were off.

I opened my door slowly and tiptoed downstairs. I crossed the veranda and unlocked one of the windows. I opened the door that led to the front yard and closed it quietly. I dashed down the stairs and across the short distance that led to the small gate. The air felt cool, and I could see the shapes of the trees in the yard. The concrete walls that surrounded the house were tall and covered with broken glass at the top, insurance against potential intruders. That made climbing the walls impossible. I tried to open the small gate through its handle, but as expected, it was locked. I had planned for that. The twists of the ornate gate served as steps, and it was relatively easy to climb over the gate, despite its height. The gate was conveniently obscured by the pergola, which was covered with lush leaves and flowers. I looked at my watch. I reached the street exactly at 10:14 p.m.

I had one minute to make it to the meeting time. Yet, as I looked back and forth over the street, it appeared desolate, empty, and dark. I felt an emptiness in the pit of my stomach, and I thought that Cristiane would not come. What was in it for her to help me after all? Maybe this was all a bad idea, and I still had time to turn back. But I stayed, frozen in place, hoping that no one would see me. She had to come quickly. Not only did I not want to raise the suspicion of those in my house, but also any neighbor passerby would certainly question what a fifteen-year-old wearing an oversized plaid shirt was doing outside a completely dark house.

At exactly 10:15 p.m., the bright lights of a car turned directly towards me and blinded me for a second.

They had come! I sighed heavily, suddenly noticing how unevenly I had been breathing.

The window of their Volkswagen bug was rolled down, and Cristiane gestured for me to walk away from the house so as to prevent anyone from hearing the noise from the car's motor. I walked down the hill a bit, towards the open car door.

"You made it!" she squealed.

Miguel was in the driver's seat.

He was an unlikely ally. Miguel served in the military and was strict with his four daughters. If it weren't for the pictures taken in his polished uniform, displayed throughout his house, and the medals hanging in a framed box in Cristiane's living room, it would be hard to tell he was a colonel. He was jovial and had an easy smile and a plump body. Cristiane told me, however, that she thought he was strict—not in forbidding her to go on outings, but in making sure he escorted her where she wanted to go. Cristiane and her sisters knew that he kept an eye on them. He had a simple philosophy which he shared with me, one that was confirmed as he saw me jumping the fence and deceiving my parents to go have a night out on the town. "Better that I know where my daughters are," he simply said when I asked him why he was helping me. "Besides, you owe me now," he said with a wink. "I am counting on you to keep Cristiane out of trouble."

As we drove the short distance to Petropolitano, I removed my oversized plaid shirt. Cristiane was ready with a bag full of makeup that she promptly put on me, asking her sisters whether it looked right.

"Yeah," they responded laughing, barely able to discern what I looked like in the faint glow of the car roof light. As we approached the club, I saw throngs of similarly aged teenagers walking towards the club. I was dressed, made up, and happy.

This was my first night out, ever. I felt elated to find myself about to enter the gates of the famed Petropolitano Club. My elation was abruptly tempered when I noticed a police car parked right outside the club. My palms began sweating. Were they there for me? I realized that if my mother found out that I was missing, she would most likely call the police. Yet, these policemen did not seem to be on the lookout for anyone; they were simply hanging out inside their car. I swallowed my fear and pretended that the sight of the police did not jar me.

I entered the nightclub and immediately forgot the police, my mother, and the risk associated with the plan. I marveled at the darkened room with the pulsing strobe lights and smoke that made people appear as if they were robots rather than humans. People were all around the club grounds, laughing, drinking, and talking to each other. A small crowd was inside the main room, dancing to the blaring songs.

Brazil, having more relaxed laws about underage drinking, openly sold alcoholic beverages to whomever was willing to pay for them. Careful not to push my luck, I focused on taking in every sensory experience that the night provided—but I did not drink, and I did not flirt. Mostly, I did not stop dancing until it was time to leave. At around five in the morning, Miguel's car was waiting for us in front of the club.

Upon exiting, I saw the police car again. My fear, so easily forgotten for the past few hours, returned, as did the sweaty palms. My heart beat fast again as it seemed that we had to walk past the police to reach the car. As in the beginning of the night, they did not seem to be making a move to catch me. Cristiane was oblivious to my fear. She walked past the police merrily. I looked straight to the ground and did not lift my eyes until we reached Miguel's car.

"Did you girls have fun?" Miguel asked while driving our sweaty and exhausted bodies back home. We laughed and told stories. He deposed me in front of the pergola-covered gate. I climbed the gate as quickly and silently as I could. The dawn of a new morning was making itself known by the lighting of the sky. The house, however, was as dark as when I left it a few hours earlier. I reversed my steps from earlier that evening, jumped through the gate, and opened the veranda door. The door had remained unlocked. I came inside, left my shoes at the front door, at the same spot where I had placed them the previous evening, not to arouse suspicion. I locked the window I had left open as a back-up plan in case someone decided to check whether all the doors of the house were locked. I tiptoed silently back to my bedroom. I entered the room, locked my door gently, and fell onto my bed. For a moment, I forgot that I did not believe in religion. I made the sign of the cross, saying, "Thank you, God, for this night." I closed my eyes. Within seconds, I fell asleep.

Despite feeling exhausted, I knew I shouldn't sleep much later than usual. The household woke up early, so used to our half-past-five departures to school from the days we lived in Shangrila. Despite how unusual it was for me to wake up around nine, nobody commented on the relatively late hour I joined them that day. I observed my family for any indication that my escapade had been noticed. My mother behaved naturally. Lauro paid me no heed. My sisters did not ask any questions.

It had worked!

"Cristiane, you are just the best. Imagine that nobody found out that I went to the club!" I told her excitedly next time we met.

"Great, because we will do it again!" she responded.

Chapter 39

MEMBERSHIP

J needed a membership to the Petropolitano Club.

I had used Cristiane's only guest pass on my first night out with them. Petropolitano was a member's only country club. The membership was expensive, as would be expected of the premier gathering place in Petropolis. I figured I could use Cristiane's guest pass once, but after that, I would need my own membership card.

I thought extensively about how to find a way.

Then I had an idea. Petropolitano, after all, was a tennis club, with tennis courts and courts for basketball, soccer, and volleyball. I was terrible at sports, but my mother did not fully know this. All she knew is that I was once chosen first for the Olympics. Nobody gets chosen first if they are not good, so she must have believed I was.

"I want to join the volleyball team," I told my mother, creating an entrée to what I wanted to do. Unfortunately, around the same time, a brand new, massive sports center was built within walking distance from my house. So my mother suggested that I go there instead. My mother still never left the house, so she was unaware of how the world worked outside the walls of our house. I told her that the public sports facility was private, and that we could not use it.

"We can't go to the sports center across the street," I said. "It is private, and you must be part of a team," I said. In reality, the opposite was true. The sports

204

center was a public place for the community, whereas it was Petropolitano that was selective, choosing who entered its gates. She felt ambivalent and did not give me an answer.

But then within a few days, Catherine, completely unaware of my ulterior motives, said she wanted to join the volleyball team too, as well as play basketball. Unexpectedly, I had an ally, so we joined forces. With the two of us constantly begging our mother to give us membership at the club, she finally accepted and gave me sufficient funds to sign up for the club and pay the monthly fees.

I waved my brand new membership card at Cristiane.

"We are half way there!" I said.

While Catherine did join the volleyball and basketball teams, I never set foot on the court. My mother made it clear that the membership was for sports only and that we were not allowed to attend balls and nightclubs, events she was now aware of, given the long discussion she had with Miguel a few weeks earlier.

I wanted to be honest with my mother. I wanted her to give me her blessing to go to the club without having to hide it from her, but she had been clear about her inflexibility in allowing us to go out at night. Still, I had come so far. I tried again. I asked her to let us go to the club with Cristiane, chauffeured by her dad.

"Isa, I already told you no. The answer will always be no," she said with an exasperated voice. "Don't ask me again."

I did not.

Except for refining timelines and meeting spots, Cristiane and I followed our plan almost every week. As needed, we added some nights when the club hosted special, themed events, such as the black and white ball, where even the lightest shade of another color would deny one's entrance, or Carmen Miranda balls, where outfits had to have fruit prints or coconut shells for bikinis, as well as headpieces in the shape of fruit. During carnival, I managed to go to all three evening balls.

A routine of sorts set in for the next few months: school in the mornings, traipsing through downtown streets in the afternoon, weekend nights at the club. I took great care never to push the boundaries to the point of arousing the suspicion of anyone within my household. I was on high alert at all times, ensuring nothing blew my cover—which included keeping my escapades hidden from my sisters. Now that we all had our own rooms, they did not suspect I spent most weekends away from mine.

This also included some restraint while I was out. I avoided drinking altogether, refused to try drugs, and pretty much stayed away from boys. The latter mostly because I had no idea how to behave around them, having been so bereft of opportunities to even talk to one. It did not bother me, though. I had what I wanted, which was freedom to see and experience the world—at least my little world in an ensconced city in the middle of the forest. Despite my disinterest, there was a lot of talk about boys, mostly because Cristiane, her sisters, and mine most certainly were interested in them.

At a Tuesday study group, another classmate and Cristiane's neighbor also joined us. We studied in silence for a while, and I once more closed my book loudly, signaling that I had finished my homework ahead of them. While I did this, I puffed my chest and stated that "I always do everything so fast." And that was true. I generally finished exams and homework before most anyone else did, often spending time watching the clock tick until others caught up.

"Not everything," Cristiane said, and her sister Adriana and my other classmate burst out laughing. At first, it was puzzling, but it dawned on me what their giggles meant. I did not find it funny, but rather, something that I began to feel ashamed of. By the time I turned sixteen years old, I was the only one in my small circle of friends who had not yet kissed a boy.

The regular hazing that my friends gave me about not having kissed a boy made me feel different again. Now I worried about how I would find a boyfriend, with the main objectives being simply to quiet my friends down and not to let that familiar feeling of not belonging, not fitting in, take over me again. Thinking the way to a man's heart was to look better, I invested in upgrading myself a little.

By then, I still did not have braces, but I had spent considerable effort improving my appearance. The last time my glasses broke, courtesy of a stray volleyball at school that struck me in the face, I asked the ophthalmologist to give me a prescription for contact lenses instead. By then, I went to exams on my own, and since prices were comparable, to my mother's chagrin, I purchased contact lenses instead of glasses. For the first time, my eyes were visible, and given that their color was rare, the mention of the green color of my eyes became more frequent. While I had not yet set foot in a hair salon, I no longer allowed my mother to cut my hair with a razor. She was not a stylist, but at least she used scissors. I let my hair grow out, and its weight made it seem less frizzy and wild.

There was little I could do to enhance my clothing choices, and I had not developed even the slightest fashion sense. As long as something fit me, I wore it. Nathalie, on the other hand, had good fashion sense, and when we bought clothes once a year, she chose them and instructed my father on what type of clothes he should bring to us on his annual visits. Cristiane and her sister Adriana were always well put together, having the budget and the parent support. Adriana was much taller than me and Cristiane much smaller. Yet, when they truly disagreed with an outfit I wore, they rummaged through their closet to find me clothes. Even though these borrowed outfits did not fit me well, they were significantly better than what I had.

Still, finding a boy to kiss seemed unlikely. Despite visible improvements in my appearance, the boys in my small high school class did not show the slightest interest in me; plus, most of them had girlfriends already. In addition, I did not know how to talk to boys. It dawned on me that I had never been alone with a man other than my stepfather for as long as I could remember, and I most certainly avoided that situation at all costs as it made me uncomfortable. I felt comfortable with books, my sisters, and now with Cristiane and her family, but no one else. If it had not been for the hazing, I would not have minded not having boys in my life all that much. I was content just to be able to leave the house and walk the streets of the tiny downtown and to go to the club on Sundays.

I had more pressing concerns anyway, which was how to enjoy Carnival for the first time when there would be seven balls within four days. Now that I had tasted some freedom, I would not be content just to attend the one on Sunday and stay at home during the other six.

The Brazilian Carnival, known the world over as a feast for the eyes and the senses—and for more than a bit of debauchery—stopped the country in its tracks during four days of revelry, as well as the weekends leading up to it. Every Brazilian celebrated it. And how one did it, as with so many things in Brazil, depended on one's social position.

The masses descended on the streets where music blared from shops and cars. Drunken neighbors congregated with their drums and tambours to create deafening samba rhythms, accompanied by pulsating bodies and sweat. The block parties went on, even during downpours, from the afternoon until sunrise. There were people everywhere, moving, dancing, and cavorting with one another.

Some families—who were most likely correct—believed the free carnival on the streets, with its sweaty crowds, was not safe. Pickpockets abounded, and the sheer number of people would likely cause any group to separate. Groping was expected. Not only was there no question that my sisters and I would not be allowed on the streets, nobody in my small social circle would dare to do so anyway. Those who did not want to mix with the masses went to clubs, which, objectively speaking, were just as crowded, loud, and sweaty as any street corner, but the likelihood of pickpocketing and groping was vastly diminished.

As the premier club, Petropolitano was the go-to destination in Petropolis for anyone who had the means to join, and this is where the entire city's elite converged during Carnival. The club catered to their membership by lavishly decorating the club grounds, having three different bands playing simultaneously, both indoors and outdoors, during each of the seven balls it hosted.

The first Friday was the black and white ball, and the club bouncers would not allow any of their glitzy clientele to enter the grounds if not wearing the right colors. Then there was a red and black ball, and also one where no black was allowed. The Hawaiian ball and the animal ball rounded out the organized night events. The decorations and the color scheme changed with each event, but the revelry did not. The balls began at ten at night and went until sunrise the next morning, every night until Ash Wednesday.

In addition, there were three matinee balls that did not have a theme, so club members could come wearing whatever they wanted. These were open to children, but the entire membership attended too.

The year I was sixteen years old, Cristiane, her sisters, and her neighbors were planning to wear the same costume for the afternoon balls, to indicate that we moved in a pod. Talk and planning surrounding the outfit was at a feverish pitch.

I helped select our mini dress, a print mixed with yellow and black forms; we hoped it would also help us find each other among the massively tight crowds. While we planned, I was always plotting what I needed to do to actually wear it.

There was no way around this one, I considered. After much thought, I saw that I needed my mother's permission. She was well aware of Carnival, as the entire country shut down for it. That is, I could not cloak my escapade this time by claiming to go shopping or doing anything useful in the afternoons.

My sisters wanted to experience Carnival too. I decided that the only way to obtain my mother's permission would be if we all pleaded together—even though I had hidden my previous outings from them.

So my sisters joined in for the first time on the insistent pleas so that we could go to the matinees at the club.

"We will look out for each other, Mom."

"It will be safer if the three of us go together."

"We will stay together throughout the event and be joined by even more girls," I said, referring to Cristiane, her friends, and her neighbors who also planned to attend.

My mother resisted at first, but we were determined that she would cave eventually, worn out with the repetitive nature of our pleas. As we expected, our relentless requests wore her down, and after much begging and cajoling, she said yes.

My sisters and I yelped with glee. This time, my mother even gave us money to purchase the simple, yellow and black dress and gave us permission to attend all three afternoon matinees.

I thought this victory was worth missing the evening events, so I did not sneak out to attend the evening events that year. During the first ball on Saturday afternoon, we gladly dressed in our carnival gear and took the bus. By then, I no longer felt overly stressed nor anxious about leaving the house without permission, having practiced deception so many times on my night outings. Yet, that first time leaving the house to attend a party without having to hide and scheme gave me a heady feeling. It was just so much better than hiding, pretending, and lying. That alone was almost as much fun as the ball itself.

There were nine of us between Cristiane, her sisters, her neighbors, and my sisters. We met on the other side of the gate from the club's entrance, easily spotted in the crowd with our bright yellow dresses.

"We are the nine sisters!" we squealed at one another. "And we will have fun!"

The nine of us stayed together during the first afternoon of jumping, dancing, and screaming. As the ball wore on, some of us left for short periods of time, but we all met again at its end. We returned to our respective homes, the same way we came: my sisters and I taking the bus, with Cristiane and her group with Miguel.

The next day, we repeated these steps over again.

This time, though, our check in at the start was brief, with most of the girls quickly disappearing in the crowd. I stayed close to whomever was left, and that varied. Sometimes it was Cristiane, other times one of my sisters, but they quickly met friends from their school that they preferred to hang out with rather than with me. I left the melee to take a break from all the jumping and dancing and momentarily looked around the crowded, festive ballroom. The place was teeming with sweaty people, jumping and screaming the samba songs from the top of their lungs. Many were kissing, passionately and endlessly. Not too far away from where I stood, I caught a glimpse of Cristiane kissing a boy I did not recognize. I was surprised as she had not spoken about that boy before.

Not having much to do, I looked the other way, only to spot one of Cristiane's neighbors also kissing someone. I then looked for the other six yellow dresses in the crowd, and they were all, including my sisters, accompanied by boys. I stood alone in the crowded room, unsure of what to do. Here I was, having arrived surrounded by eight other women, yet facing the likely prospect of spending the rest of the afternoon and perhaps the entire ball tomorrow alone.

That everybody was coupled up was not surprising. By the third day of Carnival, the party mood and the level of alcohol and excitement increased among all revelers. And it wasn't just my friends, it was pretty much everybody else.

I tried dancing alone, jumping with the crowd, but that felt awkward. I decided to roam instead. I left the main ballroom and went to the adjacent one, which contained a band, party streamers, and loud percussion drums. I felt people's sweaty bodies press against mine. Feeling discomfort, I had the urge to go outside to cool down. I walked around the grounds a couple of times, slowly navigating the crowds of people who spilled over to every inch of the club, which was now crawling with humanity. I walked around the tennis courts and towards the main pool area on the other side of the club. Moving about required navigating crowds of happy, coupled-up people. I looked at my watch. It would be at least another hour before the matinee was over. Not wanting to keep walking, I sat on the steps leading to the main ballroom. That way I could at least people watch and wait for the ball to be over.

Unexpectedly, a gangly boy with curly auburn hair sat next to me within a few minutes.

"Hi," he said.

"Hi," I said back.

"Do you want to dance?"

I was exhausted and sweaty from having danced non-stop for two days. My first reaction was to say I was not interested. But I looked around and saw that there was no one with me, and there probably would not be for a while, until the other girls got tired of so much kissing and joined the group again. It was either dance with this boy or stay alone for a longer period of time. Dreading the alternative, I accepted his offer.

"Sure," I said.

He took my hand, and we returned to the dance floor. We jumped to the beat of the drums and sang when there was a samba song that we both recognized. After a while, he came towards me and planted an awkward, sloppy kiss on my lips. It was surprising. I stepped back at first, ready to protest. Quickly, though, I realized that this was my opportunity to quiet my friends' jokes about not having kissed anyone. So we kissed again. I did not particularly like it. But I was elated to be kissing someone finally. In the midst of it, I thought that I needed to ensure one of my "sisters" saw it. I looked around for the yellow and black dresses in the crowd and moved towards the one I had spotted. I made sure I kissed that boy in front of her. I wanted Cristiane's neighbor to witness that moment.

A few moments later, Cristiane showed up.

"Isa, who is that boy you just kissed?"

"I don't know," I responded.

"You kissed a boy you don't know?"

I loathed to admit it, but I had no information about him. I did not want to make up a name, in case she knew who he was. When Cristiane came over, he walked away.

"Do you know he is fourteen-years-old?" she continued.

"No."

I did not even know his name, so how would I know his age? I felt the pride of my first kiss evaporate. I had just given Cristiane fodder for more jokes.

"You kissed a boy you don't know, who is younger than you?" she repeated, but now laughing. "You are so crazy!" she said, staring at me. "I think he probably had a bet that he had to find somebody to kiss!" she said, without hesitation.

My heart sank as I realized she was probably right. She turned around quickly.

"Cristiane, where are you going?"

"I have to go tell the others!" she exclaimed. The pulsing crowd engulfed her as she went in pursuit of more yellow and black dresses to gossip about the news.

I did not return inside to go find the boy. Before the ball was over, he walked towards me, smiling. Whether he had made a bet or really liked me, it no longer mattered. By then, I was surrounded by the sea of yellow dresses, and I did not want to acknowledge him, so I turned my head away, trying to disappear in the crowd. I held back tears of shame and joined the small gathering of girls with the same dress for one last session of dancing before the matinee ball was over.

My first kiss, the one I had heard my sisters describe as a marvelous experience, was a disaster. I decided I would never again kiss someone I did not know. I would wait until I met a boy I liked first. But deep inside, I was glad that I would once and for all silence my friends' hazing about being slow to attract boys. I had no interest anyway.

And I soon learned that having a boyfriend meant nothing but trouble.

Chapter 40

BOYFRIEND

*T*he girls in my class were constantly gossiping about boys. The principal's daughter began dating one of my classmates, creating a mini-scandal, given how her father prohibited dating at school. Yet, that did not stop her from disregarding school rules right in front of everybody. Couples were forming all around school. It was only a matter of time until this would spill over to my family.

Nathalie should have known better than to tell my mother about her new boyfriend, having grown up in the same household as me and having witnessed Lauro's treatment of Walter, who did not even manage to step one foot into our driveway.

"Nobody has experienced a love like ours," Nathalie often said about her relationship, as if this was the only explanation we all needed to support her love story.

Questioning the status quo, or rebelling against it, was not in Nathalie's nature. As the first born, she obeyed the rules, even when they so obviously harmed her. She had not figured out about my sneaking out, and it must not have occurred to her to do something our parents would not allow. She had been accepting of our home situation until having a boyfriend made her want to break out of the limitations of her life too. So she asked permission to leave the house. When my mother asked why, she told her so that she could meet with her boyfriend in the afternoons.

My mother grew angry, raising her voice: "You will leave this boyfriend."

"But, Mom, I love him," Nathalie responded.

"You know nothing about love. Nobody has a boyfriend until she turns eighteen," my mother said.

Lauro hovered over this scene with a look of utter hate and jealousy in his eyes. He also raised his voice, blaming my mother for this situation: "I told you what would happen if your daughters went to a school with boys." He reminded her how he had been against Nathalie leaving the all-girl school to join me at EPA.

"You will not see this boy again," Lauro joined my mother in saying.

Nathalie, not realizing what she was saying, responded, "Yes, I will. He is in my class."

My mother, seizing this information then said, "If you keep seeing this boy, then you will no longer attend EPA. I will send you right back to Santa Isabel. Or take you out of school altogether!"

With nothing left to say, Nathalie rushed upstairs, slamming the door to her room. My mother was visibly upset, and I, having learned that it was not worth being around when my mother or Lauro came unhinged, left to walk around our yard.

Nathalie had observed me getting what I wanted by repeatedly asking for the same thing until I wore my mother out. So she decided to use the same strategy. She, again, should have known better. Her constant asking was essentially a confirmation that she still had her boyfriend. Instead of more freedom, my sister—and Catherine and I—actually received more restrictions. My mother, assuming that any outing meant a chance to see the boyfriend, forbid Nathalie to do anything.

Nathalie was seething with anger and desperation.

"Isa," Nathalie would tell me, "nobody can love a person as much as I love Binho."

Not having had that experience, I could not relate to what she was saying, so I tried to be more logical.

"Well, I am sure other people love their boyfriends a lot too," I said.

"Not like I do," she reiterated.

She proceeded to tell me how her boyfriend and classmates went out often to nightclubs, to ride bikes, or to eat a hamburger together. She feared that because she did not join them, one day Binho would leave her.

Yet, he did not leave. Nathalie and her boyfriend stayed together month after month, despite seeing each other only during school. And the longer their relationship lasted, the stronger Nathalie's resentment grew.

Upon realizing that our mother would not help her, she stopped asking for permission to go out. She decided to accept the restrictions of her life—that is, until she caught me leaving the house one night.

"Where are you going?" Nathalie's voice surprised me, coming from the darkened veranda where I was tiptoeing my way to the door. Her voice frightened me as I had momentarily thought I had been caught. When I noticed it was simply my sister, I relaxed, but not fully. It had not been my intention to let more people into my plan because I feared that Nathalie would want to come along. I had no desire to share my strategies. I had managed to go dancing unnoticed for more than a year. Whatever help Nathalie needed, it simply could not be worth risking my hard-earned freedom.

I did not respond.

"Where are you going?" she repeated. She at least had the sense to whisper her threat: "If you do not tell me, I will go call Mom."

"Don't tell her," I said.

I sighed heavily and told her that Cristiane was waiting for me outside to take me to the Petropolitano for a night on the town.

"In your pajamas?" she asked.

"No, I am wearing party clothes underneath." I showed her, opening my oversized plaid shirt.

Her eyes opened wide with excitement as she understood the possibilities for herself.

"How long have you being doing this?"

"A long time," I said wearily. "Can I talk to you about this tomorrow? Cristiane is waiting for me." I knew full well that I had about one minute to make it to our meeting spot before Cristiane would go on without me.

"No, I need to know now!"

I missed the outing that evening and accompanied Nathalie to her room instead so that the two of us would not be caught on the veranda after hours. I told her everything: how I waited for everybody to go to sleep; how I jumped the fence; how I had a deal and a meeting place that changed regularly; how Cristiane's father would pick me up; how her sisters would do my makeup; and how I made sure to return home before anybody was awake. I told her everything, but I also said, "I cannot take you with me." Then, feeling guilty about not being helpful, I added, "Because there isn't space in the car."

Nathalie never blamed me for not sharing this secret with her—despite how often she shared with me her despair about not being able to see her boyfriend after school. The only possibility she envisioned was what she could do with Binho going forward.

"I have no interest in going with you," she said with a smile.

"You need to be extremely careful and not get caught!" I said, sounding slightly desperate.

"Don't worry," she said.

I returned to my room, feeling troubled that my secret was out. I knew that Nathalie would never tell my mother or Lauro about it. But I simply did not trust that Nathalie would be as careful as I was. I worried that my jumping days were numbered.

It did not take long for Nathalie to begin jumping the fence too. We never went together. I hardly talked about my plans with her, and I did not know when she went, but go she did.

Despite my fears, neither my mother nor Lauro seemed to have the slightest idea that their daughters jumped the fence quite regularly. I was sure that if my mother found out, I would have known by her anger and the swift punishment that would follow.

Yet, my mother knew a woman in love when she saw one. Having been madly in love once, too, she realized that Nathalie would try to find a way to go meet her boyfriend, despite her being forbidden to do so. So my mother asked our gardener, Tom, who spent a lot more of his time outside in the garden than she did, to monitor and report to her whether he saw any of us, but in particular, my older sister, leave the house.

Tom's patrol of the grounds meant there were many nights when I had to miss going out with Cristiane, as she stuck to our deal to drive away if I was not at our meeting point at the designated time. We tried leaving slightly later, but while she wanted to help me, she did not want to miss out on the balls—neither did she want to tell her father that the noose was tightening around my escapades.

Each night I was left behind, my resentment about my life resurfaced, and now I added Nathalie to the list of people I felt anger towards. And it was not only because I could not leave the house under the cover of the night. Given Nathalie's persistence in dating her boyfriend, my mother looked for ways to restrict her movements, and by extension, mine.

Suddenly, my mother enforced restrictions that had long been forgotten. I had to justify whenever I left in the afternoon, even when simply paying bills. I had to return on a specific bus, unless I had a good reason, such as an unreasonably long line at the bank or post office, for having missed it. The absolute worst was my mother's announcement that she was cancelling our membership to Petropolitano club, which she had willingly funded for the past year.

I panicked. I needed the membership to use the club. Cristiane could not simply take me as a guest multiple times. Losing the membership simply could not happen.

"But, Mom, what about Catherine's volleyball?" I asked innocently.

"She has played enough. She no longer needs to play volleyball," she responded.

Catherine, previously so accepting of our lives, protested: "Why can't I play? I don't have a boyfriend. That's not fair!"

My mother and Lauro did what they always did, making rules without giving reasons to explain their decisions. "I don't want you to go to that club," my mother said.

"Why not?" I asked. "We haven't done anything wrong."

"Your sister Nathalie meets that boy of hers there," she said, providing the real reason for this sudden cancellation. "Besides, why do you care?" she asked of me. "You hardly use it. It is your sister who plays there," she said dismissively, knowing full well that I did not play in any of the sports teams at the club.

I could not contradict her by saying that, indeed, I used it plenty. So I chose to stay silent at that moment.

Soon, though, I launched my relentless begging tactics. I did not stop talking about how important that membership was, how we needed to keep it, and how I wanted to play tennis. This time, however, there was no begging or convincing her. Nothing else mattered to my mother more than ending my sister's relationship. When it came time to pay the bills the following month, she gave me the exact amount of money needed to cover all our other expenses. She had also changed the location where she stored her stash of cash, so I did not have ready access to money as I once did.

The membership was too expensive for me to appropriate sufficient money all at once with the spare change I typically stole for slices of cakes and shampoos. That month, I took a bigger risk. One day when my mother was out in the yard, I went into her room, locked it from the inside, and searched every nook and cranny of her unkempt bedroom to find out where she kept the cash. I was careful not to disturb the location of the piles of magazines and knick-knacks that she stored on her desk and in her closet. The room itself was clean as our maid kept it that way. I kept looking at the yard below to ensure that nobody was coming back. It took me a couple of tries, but I eventually found that she moved her money to a shoe box that she kept in her closet.

Whenever I could do so unnoticed, I entered my mother's bedroom and took a couple of five- to ten-dollar bills. That way, if she ever counted the money, she would not think that so much of it was missing. The membership was about eighty-five dollars for an individual pass, so for the most part, I could amass the needed amount over the month without raising suspicion. The family membership was easily twice as high, and it would have allowed my sisters, or at a minimum, Catherine, to keep playing volleyball. Helping them, however, was not on my list of priorities. I felt the current situation was mostly due to

Nathalie's insistence on keeping her boyfriend. I also blamed her for jumping the fence every so often as it eventually threatened my ability to do so. Keeping Catherine on the membership would mean that my mother would sooner or later question how she kept playing, so I set my goal to fund an individual membership only. My sisters, if they had an interest to take risks, could figure it out on their own, I reasoned.

For the most part, the stealing was so incremental that it went unnoticed. My mother, every so often, would make generic comments, such as, "Where does all of our money go?" I knew, however, that this was more of a frustration over the high cost of living than because she suspected flighty hands appropriated some of it.

Even so, whenever she said so, I felt a deep level of discomfort in my gut. Yet, I did nothing and shrugged my shoulders. I tried to avoid commenting, except when I felt that not commenting might give me away. Then I would mumble something to the effect of, "It is inflation. The prices change every month. Everything is always more expensive."

Despite being able to appropriate some cash, I had to make tradeoffs to ensure I had enough for the club membership. I stopped visiting the bakery for my slice of cake when paying bills in the afternoon, and I reduced the number of hair conditioners I bought and used. Luckily for me, Nathalie and her boyfriend stayed together, despite all the restrictions and tension that relationship brought to all of our lives. My mother, so concerned about Nathalie, barely paid attention to what I was doing. While it was riskier, I scanned the yard, ensuring that Tom was not there, and eventually resumed my life of jumping fences, joining Cristiane and her family most weekends at the club. Yet, despite all my efforts, it was Catherine who somehow found out that I still went to the Petropolitano on a regular basis.

"Can I use your membership card to go to the club?" Catherine asked me one day.

"How do you know about that?" I responded with a mixture of surprise and frustration that my cover was blown.

"I just know," she said.

"No, you cannot," I said.

"How did you get your card anyway? Our memberships have been cancelled," she inquired, not without a note of resentment in her voice now that she could no longer play on a team.

"Cristiane takes me as a guest," I lied.

"You are lying. I saw that you have a card."

"How?"

"I just did," Catherine said unhelpfully.

I felt bad for my sisters, but I also felt it was not my responsibility to figure out a way to help them. Nathalie had been clumsy in her attempts to go see her boyfriend; I knew helping my sisters would mean a bigger risk for me. Both my sisters still talked to and feared Lauro. They acknowledged his presence and continued to give him power over them. I felt strongly that they were not my problem. Besides the incredible support Miguel and Cristiane gave me, I had no examples of people helping each other. If I felt guilty, I do not remember. All I remember was feeling upset at my sisters because they were trying to come up with their own plans and would likely be sloppy with their efforts, creating plans that might conflict with mine.

BREAKUP

espite all the pressure to separate them, Nathalie and her boyfriend kept their relationship alive. That is, until the day she came home sobbing.

We had learned to bottle up our emotions, so Nathalie crying in front of all of us was an unusual sight. She did not answer my mother's attempts to figure out why her older daughter was crying.

When we were dismissed after lunch, Nathalie ran to her room and closed the door.

I knocked softly.

"Nathalie, can I come in?"

She opened the door.

I sat on her bed, and she hugged me. She did not wait until I asked what was wrong.

"Binho kissed Rosemarie!" she told me, her chest heaving with the pain of that statement.

Rosemarie had been Nathalie's best friend and classmate. She apparently was a constant companion of Binho during the many outings he did without my sister. Rosemarie tried to apologize to Nathalie, to tell her that it all meant nothing, but Nathalie would not hear it.

My mother typically did not enter our rooms. But she must have felt either worried or curious about Nathalie's state, and she had heard our voices coming from my sister's bedroom. So she entered the room, without knocking or being invited in.

"What is going on, Nathalie?" she asked.

Nathalie shot her a look of pure hatred.

"She broke up with her boyfriend," I said unhelpfully.

Nathalie looked at me as if I had betrayed her. She did not want to give my mother the satisfaction of knowing that what she had hoped for finally came to pass. My mother simply said, "Good. It is about time." And she left the room.

"Isa, I can tell you nothing! Why don't you just keep your mouth shut?" she said, letting some of the anger and frustration she felt spill over to me.

How could I tell my sister I did not want to betray her, but that at the same time, I felt that if my mother knew Nathalie and Binho were no longer together, then the restrictions and the policing she had imposed around us would potentially let up?

I tried to articulate a response, but Nathalie was too distraught. "Just leave, Isa. Just go, and leave me alone. Because that is what I am—all alone."

I left. And I resumed my life of attending school, stealing incremental amounts of money, and jumping the fence.

Nathalie moped around the house for weeks.

It seemed that we all had found a new status quo in our lives. That, however, did not last all that long. Within a few weeks, Nathalie turned eighteen.

As we did for all birthday celebrations, the five of us gathered around the table to sing happy birthday and eat the cake our maid had baked.

"Did you make a wish?" I asked Nathalie when she blew out the candle.

"Yes!" she said.

"What was it?" I asked playfully, knowing full well that she would not share it.

"I am moving to Los Angeles."

Silence fell in the room, all eyes upon my beautiful sister.

"I talked to my father this morning." She meant our biological father, who had called that morning to wish her a good birthday. "And he invited me to live with him."

My mother took no time in starting the vitriol. "Your father doesn't care about you. He hasn't been here more than ten times in the last ten years," she said, stating a fact we knew well.

"Then I will see him more often now," Nathalie responded calmly.

"You will not go!" my mother said, with the voice she had used so many times to deny us what we wanted.

"You cannot stop me. I am an adult now. I no longer need your permission."

The air felt stiff and heavy. We all felt stunned; nobody made a move to cut the cake into slices, and nobody wanted to stay in the room once my mother's fury started.

My mother had, for so long, vilified my father and spewed vitriol about Carroll, telling us how awful he was for abandoning us, for not providing enough money for our sustenance, and for having a mistress, that she honestly did not expect that my sister would ever choose to live with him. We had no way of knowing whether my mother was right about my father being a monster. But Nathalie decided that anywhere else was better than here.

In the weeks that followed, my mother redoubled her efforts to criticize my father and Carroll. He abandoned us. He was cold. He was selfish. As Nathalie showed no signs of changing her mind, she made offers to change the circumstances of our lives.

"Now that you are an adult, you can have a boyfriend," she told Nathalie. "You can see your man whenever you want," she said, as if she was giving Nathalie a gift after forbidding her from seeing her boyfriend the previous two years.

"I am sure I will find a boyfriend in Los Angeles."

"But you have a boyfriend here," my mother said.

Nathalie shrugged her shoulders, indicating that the boyfriend she loved so much was not enough of an anchor to keep her in this place.

"You can go to Petropolitano whenever you want, now that you are eighteen," my mother continued emphatically. At that, my ears perked up. Maybe if Nathalie was allowed to go, then so would I.

"I don't want to go to Petropolitano," Nathalie responded. "I want to go to Los Angeles."

Nathalie's visa came through within a few weeks, now that she was an adult and did not need a parent's approval for her paperwork. Once the visa was approved, she booked her flight within two weeks.

There was a lot of commotion the day Nathalie left. My mother cried hysterically, not believing that Nathalie was actually leaving. Lauro, Catherine, and I accompanied her to the airport. My mother, who hardly ever left the house, stayed behind—not even leaving to say goodbye to her first born who was about to move abroad. She waved us goodbye from the middle of the street. She told me later that when the car turned the corner, she fell to the ground, screaming, and pulling her hair. The neighbor assisted her in returning to the house so that she would not block traffic as she wailed for the loss of her daughter.

Nathalie had no tears in her eyes. She crossed the immigration line smiling and so disappeared from our lives. She called briefly once she arrived in Los Angeles to tell us she arrived safely. Beyond that, we did not often speak with her. She wrote letters, the intervals between which became increasingly longer, telling us how much she loved her new life. She included pictures of her smiling in Los Angeles and from her trips to Utah, in front of Bryce Canyon, and Las Vegas. She never complained about anything. She made it sound as if living in the United States was close to living in paradise.

As she had done with every correspondence that my father ever sent us, my mother rushed to open Nathalie's letters when they arrived—even if they were not addressed to her. Every time a letter came, her despair and sadness increased about her daughter's departure. She became listless during the weeks following her firstborn's departure. She cried for no reason.

"Why did she leave?" my mother asked me often, not comprehending what role she had played in Nathalie's departure. Could my mother truly not know? I looked at my mother incredulously, wondering how it was that the answer was not obvious to her. I tried once or twice to explain that she, and especially Lauro, were to blame, but she would cut me off, not believing a word I had to say.

"But you have had a great life . . . You were never missing anything. You went to the best schools. What reason did she have to leave?"

Nothing I said assuaged her misery.

Deep inside, I wanted her to stay miserable and realize that unless something changed, maybe I would end up in Los Angeles with Nathalie too. So whenever the subject of Nathalie's departure came up, I used it to my advantage.

"Well, she wanted to go out," I stated, "but you never let her."

She was quick in her reply. "Nobody is going out to a nightclub full of perverts," she said.

I held my fury and desire to tell her that there was a pervert within our house.

"She wanted to see her boyfriend!" I pushed a little more.

"You are not to have a boyfriend before turning eighteen. I told your sister that she could see her boyfriend when she turned eighteen."

"But by then, Mom, it was too late."

Chapter 42

CAUGHT

Despite her despair and lack of attention to Catherine and me, my mother did not lift her iron fist on our schedule once Nathalie left. This proved she did not recognize in the least that all the restrictions my sister faced were the main reason she left us. So, I had no choice but to keep to my normal routine of lying and jumping the fence.

So a few months later, I joined Cristiane at the club and was just returning home as the sun was rising. I jumped the fence quietly to reach the house and went towards the door that I had left unlocked the previous evening. This time, however, the door knob did not budge. The front door was locked. *They must have just made sure that all doors were locked for the night,* I first thought, not at all worried about the possibility that perhaps that door was locked for a reason. I had thought of a Plan B. I always left at least one window unlocked, as well, in case my parents thought to go to the yard after I had left for the night and locked the door when they came back in. So I moved towards the side of the house to reach the window. Yet, the previously unlocked window did not lift up. It had been locked too. Plan B failed.

I felt a tightness in the pit of my stomach. Even though I had not opened any of the other windows the previous night, I went along the entire first floor of the house, trying unsuccessfully to open each possible entrance to the house. My mind raced to figure out if there was another way in, but every single window and side door was locked. The only way into the house was for someone to come out first. Not wanting to face the brunt of my mother's wrath, I decided against knocking on the door as the sun was rising. Maybe I could still avoid discovery if I hid and waited for somebody to come out. Perhaps then I could somehow enter the house unnoticed. I moved towards the small area next to our front door that had a two-person rocking bench. The dawn was setting in; I had danced all night and felt exhausted. A mattress covered the metal squares of the bench. It would serve just fine as a make-shift bed until somebody within the house left.

I barely had time to make myself comfortable. Within a couple of minutes, the bright, outside light went on, blinding me momentarily and shedding light into the dark corner of the yard where I was hiding. The front door slammed, giving the signal that whoever came out of the house had a purpose and probably not one that would suit me. Screams cut through the silence as my disheveled mother made her way towards the pergola area where I lay on the rocking bench.

"Where have you been?"

I quickly sat up on the bench, but did not stand up. There was no point in pretending to be asleep, but I thought it more prudent not to move towards where she was. There was no time anyway. With her quick steps, my mother's large figure towered over me within seconds. Had I bothered to look at her face, I would have seen bloodshot eyes, either from lack of sleep, deep anger, or too much crying. It was probably from all three. She grabbed me by my hair and pulled me back towards the house.

"Where have you been?" she repeated while shaking my head, this time expecting an answer.

My head throbbed with pain in my scalp as she did not let go on my unruly strands while she screamed, pulled, and shook me. I did not answer, focusing more on the pain than on what she was saying.

"Where did you go?" she repeated again, raising her voice even higher so that I would finally pay attention.

"Petropolitano," I managed to respond.

"Who took you?" she continued screaming without letting go of my hair.

"I took the bus."

I had rehearsed this line.

"There are no buses at this time of night!" she said.

The reality of that statement had escaped me. I had grown so accustomed to the idea that I would never be caught, that it did not occur to me to think through what I would do in case this moment were to happen. The buses stopped running by eleven each night. It was clear that the bus was not how I went out or got back.

"There was one today," I stated somewhat defiantly, knowing that I was in deep enough trouble that this additional lie would make no difference. I did not want to compromise Cristiane, and lying about my mode of transportation was the least of my concerns.

"Do not lie to me," she said, shaking me a little harder. "Who took you?"

The pain on my scalp felt intolerable. Realizing that my mother would not let go of my hair until I told her a more convincing tale, I told the truth through gritted teeth.

"Miguel," I said.

My mother felt a sense of panic. She did not know who Miguel was. She had not thought I had a boyfriend, so focused she was in making sure that my sister Nathalie did not have an opportunity to go see hers. She thought that the message that boys were not welcome in our lives until we were adults had been clear. At that moment, she felt more worried that a boy took me out than the fact that I had been out all night.

"You will never see that boy again! I told you that you cannot have a boyfriend!"

"But he isn't my boyfriend!" I protested. "He is Cristiane's father."

Whether she found this revelation more disturbing than if I had a boy my own age helping me leave the house, I did not know, but she let go of my hair.

"You will never leave this house again!" she stated emphatically.

I was too tired to think through whether this was a threat she could enforce. But I knew she meant it at the time. There was no point protesting, and all I wanted was to sleep. I held my head to soothe the pain from all that hair pulling and to verify whether there was any hair left.

In theory, I was to be grounded for an indeterminate period of time. Indeed, I was not allowed to leave the house for the next week, except to go to school. Her ability to maintain that punishment was limited by the fact that, by then, I did all the errands for the household. The week I was grounded, the bills went unpaid, and the supplies on our shelves dwindled. It was unclear why my mother did not ask Catherine to run these errands instead. Her need for me to keep the household humming was larger than her need to teach me a lesson. After about ten days, she asked me to go to the bank that afternoon. Rather than remind her that I was grounded, I took the opportunity and merrily left. Soon after, I recommenced my basic routine of attending school in the mornings and dallying in the streets in the afternoons.

As my mother had no choice but to relent on my punishment, she found other ways to redirect her anger and frustration. She tried a different tactic that she knew would hurt me. She couldn't control me, but she thought she could destroy my friendship with Cristiane, the culprit who enabled me to challenge her authority and leave the house.

"Give me Cristiane's phone number," she demanded of me.

"I don't have it," I lied.

"Yes you do. Give it to me. Now!" she screamed.

I stared at her but did not budge, nor did I give her the information.

Instead of staring at me, she picked up the phone book and found the information I had not been willing to share. "I am going to tell that bastard of a father never to mess with my family again!" my mother muttered as she combed through the thick book, searching for the information she sought.

My mind raced. Cristiane was my first and best friend. I needed her to stay in my life. I remembered clearly how I had lost Walter's friendship when he dared show up at my door and was shown how unwelcome he was at my house. I expected Cristiane to scurry away just as quickly once she realized how menacing my parents could be. That phone call simply could not happen.

Yet, I could not devise a way to prevent my mother from picking up the phone receiver. After wishing for a phone for most of my life, that day, I loathed the fact that we had one.

"Is Miguel there?" she asked with a sweet voice once someone picked up the phone on the other side. I hovered nearby, placing myself close to the phone cord so that I could at least control the damage by perhaps unplugging the phone, should the conversation become unwieldy. Seeing me near her, my mother gestured to me: "Go away!" When I did not, she raised her voice, much louder: "Go away!

I walked out of the living room and stomped on the stairwell to give her the impression that I was going upstairs to my room. When she turned her back, I tiptoed back downstairs, went to the veranda next door, and placed myself behind the wall. She could not see me, but I could hear her well. By the time I began tuning in to the conversation, I heard threats about calling the police. Cristiane was in the same room with her father when that call came, and she later told me the other half of the conversation. Miguel, a respected and decorated military man, knew more of the inner workings of police work than my mother gave him credit for. "Go right ahead," he responded. "Where is your daughter now?"

"She is here, of course, where she should be."

Upon hearing that I was in the house, Miguel continued, "What are you going to tell the police then? That I kidnapped Isa? She is at your house at the moment!" he exclaimed. "You go ahead and do that, and I will then charge you with libel."

Caught off guard, my mother changed tactics. She responded that she would sue him instead of calling the police.

"For what?" he asked. When she couldn't come up with an answer, it was his turn to talk.

"Do you know why I drive Cristiane to Petropolitano?" he asked.

Before my mother could utter a reply, he continued: "Because I know where she is. Now, did you know where you daughter was?" When he did not hear a response from the other line, he continued, "Who do you think is right now?"

Miguel had four daughters. He knew that keeping them cooped up at home was not the solution for protecting them from the dangers of the world. Allowing them to become street smart, on the other hand, would. "So, you go right ahead and call the police and sue me. But if your child is found dead on the side of the street because you don't know where she is, then what good will that do you? I will tell you. That will put you in jail, for being negligent to your child!"

Not able to articulate a response to this onslaught of logic, my mother hung up the phone. She was visibly flustered and upset. I tried to scurry away from the room before she could reach me, but I was not fast enough. "Isa," she called, before I could walk away. I sighed in frustration, not believing I had been caught again. The familiar anxiety and heart thumping returned as I turned towards her, but not before putting my hair in a bun, just in case.

"I am sorry," she said and then walked away.

DISCOVERY

y days of jumping the fence ended the day I got caught. Tom, the gardener who had ratted my escapades to my mother, was now on near-constant guard. Miguel, after learning my mother caught and subsequently punished me, refused to take me to the club again without my mother's express permission. Cristiane, despite her willingness to do it, knew better than to continue supporting me in my escape.

That summer when I was sixteen years old, my father invited me to come visit him and Nathalie in Los Angeles. My mother, still hurting from the fact that her oldest daughter left her, forbade me to go. She also wished to punish me further for jumping the fence, talking back to her, and no longer speaking with Lauro. She made it clear that I lost the right to travel that year.

Not wanting simply to tell my father that I would not go because she forbade me, my mother called my father directly—for the first time since we moved to Retiro—to tell him that I would not travel to the United States that summer because I did not deserve it, was verging on delinquency, and was rude to her. She neglected to say that it was also because I ignored the stepfather my father did not know we had.

As my mother had never allowed me to travel before, I had not expected to obtain permission this time either. Yet, I felt a bottomless pit of resentment as I heard my mother speak on the phone with my father, without giving me a chance to defend myself. I felt anger and hatred towards my mother and Lauro. I resented my sisters, who were so careless in their own efforts to break free that they ruined opportunities for me to do so. I also felt a fair share of disgust towards Tom, the gardener.

I avoided everybody in my house and ensconced myself in my room whenever I could and mostly spent my afternoons studying. After a few days of this solitude, I rejoined the family on the veranda again, where the larger windows let the sunlight in and provided a view of the tree canopies, valley below, and surrounding mountains. Yet, even then, I mostly read silently, not wanting to engage with anyone in my house.

Yet, my mother, noting my disinterest in engaging with her now, respected my silence and would sit quietly next to me. After a few days, she addressed me, using a different tone. It was softer, more measured, more pained. She did not admonish me nor did she have any interest in learning much about my life. My mother, having lived as a recluse for so long, just wanted to talk. But she mostly wanted to speak about herself—about her life, her past, and most importantly, the deep pain caused by the loss of her eldest daughter.

These were often monologues. Sometimes she talked while I did my homework, never needing a prompt to talk more. She often repeated the same stories, sometimes adding more details than the previous time.

During these afternoons at home, I learned facts about our family that I had never heard before. I heard about my mother's life in Egypt and then France before her family boarded the ship for the transatlantic move to Brazil. She spoke of her decision to board the ship to Brazil with her family decades earlier that took her away from France and the love of her life, Jean-Robert. She spoke of the tears she shed during the two-week voyage across the Atlantic Ocean, mourning the love she lost, stuck between wanting to stay behind with her lover and following her family to a distant land. My mother told me that she had met Jean-Robert again, but that the disappointment of that meeting made her close into herself. She looked for love elsewhere, which she found in the arms of my father. She spoke of her marriage to my father, one that she entered into because she wanted to erase the pain of losing the love of her life. She spoke of the disappointment of having daughters, when her life plans revolved around having sons. She told me of her desire to live in France, whereas she found herself trapped in Brazil. She told me of the loneliness she felt by having a husband who was quiet, cold, and often absent. She often mentioned how she disliked the life she was now living. She became hardened by a life and circumstances that she did not choose and couldn't control. She tried to control her life, but life controlled her. She tried to do the best by her children, but she did not know how. Eventually, the weight of the responsibility and her inability to take reins where it mattered manifested itself in a total lack of control. She found the cult; she found a lover; she released the reins of her life and stopped considering the consequences of her decisions. She must have reached the conclusion that whatever she did, it did not matter. So she chose to do nothing at all.

She did not ask much about my life, but that was preferable to me. I had no interest to share what I did to counter the restrictions she placed in my life. I mostly felt I did not have much to say. My life was so mundane and uneventful. I mostly let her talk about whatever she wanted to speak about.

We formed some type of a bond over these afternoons in the sunny room. Sometimes I put my book down and just listened to her endless stories. I began to understand my mother better. She had somebody to talk to, and there was no subject she would not speak about. Except one. She never questioned her choice to come to Shangrila with Lauro. She never said one word of criticism about the stepfather she brought into our lives.

That also suited me well. I had absolutely no interest to hear about Lauro. I had not exchanged a single word with him since the day, two years before, he sent my first friend packing as if he had leprosy. It was difficult to behave as if Lauro did not exist, but in the face of my disdain for him, he receded to the background of my life. He sulked around corners. He left the room when I entered it. He eventually avoided me almost as much as I did him.

Our mutual dislike, however, did not prevent Lauro from speaking of me to my mother. Apparently so much so that one afternoon my mother broke her silence on the topic of my stepfather and brought his name up in one of our conversations.

"Isa, stop this coldness. Talk to Lauro. He misses speaking with you."

"I do not see why I should. My life is going quite well without him in it," I responded.

She was caressing my hair while speaking to me, but she stopped and made me look at her.

"Why are you so cold?"

"I am not cold," I said.

"Yes, you are. I see it in your eyes."

When I said nothing, she continued, "Lauro told me that you never talk to him. That you are never affectionate to him, when all he wanted was to love you."

Although I no longer feared my mother's death if I told anyone what had happened years earlier, I had not spoken about Lauro's abuse to anyone. I had not seen a need for it. Cutting Lauro out of my life gave me the power to distance myself from what had happened. I did not spend time considering it or thinking about it. And I certainly had not considered my mother's reaction should she ever learn, as I knew Lauro would never confess his acts. And I would not volunteer the information either. I knew my mother unflinchingly defended and supported Lauro, so I had no reason to assume she would believe me or do anything about it that would be helpful to me.

"Look at how sad he is," she said while stroking my hair. "And he loves you so much; he is your dad!" she said, emphasizing the last word.

Despite my silence, my mother did not drop the subject. She insisted on talking about Lauro and my need to overcome my whims so that I could let him back into my life. As she spoke, the hatred I had long buried under the cloak of ignoring Lauro's existence surfaced again.

The only way to stop my mother from continuing to talk was to say something. Yet I resisted. But her statement of Lauro's paternity triggered me.

"That parasite is not my father."

"He is better than your father!" my mother said, raising her voice. "He has done so much for you. He does so much for me," she said as she enumerated how Lauro had driven us to school, done the shopping, taken care of us—all while my bastard of a father abandoned us to live with a mistress in the United States. She went on to describe how my father had further destroyed our family by robbing Nathalie from us.

I stood up, almost shaking, and turned to face my mother.

"He is not any of that. He took us to school because this vermin had nothing better to do with his time, living off the money that my real father earns."

"Isa, watch your mouth!" my mother warned me, not liking the turn the conversation had taken.

I now faced my mother, who remained seated while I hovered over her.

"He is a horrible person. Besides, what affection can he possibly want from me?"

"You could kiss him good morning," she answered.

I scoffed, with all the hatred I could muster showing through in my red, flushed face. "He does not want a good morning kiss," I said, feeling increasingly irate. "What he wants is to kiss my breasts!"

A look of horror settled upon my mother's puffy, red face.

"No," she uttered almost in a whisper.

I shrugged my shoulders in frustration, realizing that I had shared a long-dormant memory that I never wanted to relive again. I felt a sense of frustration as I was sure that my mother would doubt the veracity of my claim.

"When was this?" she said, getting up.

I could see she was flustered, but I had gone this far. I might as well keep talking.

"It started when I was thirteen," I said.

"How come you never told me?"

"I thought you would die."

My mother's eyes enlarged.

"Surely I would not die," she responded, assuming perhaps that I meant that she would feel upset.

"Lauro told me you would die if I told you, if I told anyone."

My mother's guttural scream pierced the air.

That scream beckoned Lauro to enter the living room to intervene in our conversation. Unaware of what we had been speaking of, he walked directly towards me, grabbing me by the shoulders and shaking me while screaming, "What did you do?"

I did not have time to answer.

On the table laid a leather purse with metal buckles that Lauro used to carry around whenever he left the house. My mother seized that purse and hit Lauro on his face with it.

"You bastard!" she shouted.

Lauro screamed in pain and let go of me.

He turned to my mother. Unexpectedly, after seeing Lauro take the mantle of a dictator and boss everybody around the house, he did not react to his wife's slapping. He must have understood the reason for my mother's anger. Rather than fight back, he placed his arms around his head to protect it. As my mother continued lashing him with the leather purse, he lowered himself towards the ground, until he was crouching on the floor. And I saw my mother, in a frenetic, mad moment repeatedly slam him with the leather purse; the buckles hitting his back. Lauro did not even scream anymore; he just accepted his punishment.

My mother, completely blinded by anger, betrayal, and madness, did not stop until her arm tired.

When she let out the worst of her anger, she herself fell to the floor, sobbing. I stood in the corner of the room, staring at these two completely helpless people I once feared so much, now prostrated on the floor. Their bodies blocked my way out of the room, and frankly, I had no intention of missing this just turn of events, despite my utter disbelief that I had just witnessed justice.

My mother, in a moment of sanity, looked at me with bloodshot eyes and realized that I was still there. She waved her hand at me.

"Isa, go."

Feeling frozen, I did not move.

"Just go," she repeated meekly. I knew she truly meant for me to leave.

I stepped around my mother and Lauro, who stayed behind on the floor, with my mother crying and Lauro curled in a fetal position in case his beating had not ended.

I left for the front garden. Feeling restless, I opened the gate and walked towards Cristiane's house, at a loss for where else to go.

On the way, I stopped by a small botanical garden brimming with colorful orchids. There, I sat on a bench, enjoying the solitude among the greenery and blooming flowers. My heart beat rapidly, with a mixture of elation and horror at the scene I had just witnessed. At that moment, I recognized that while my mother had certainly failed me numerous times, she defended me the first time I truly asked for help. The beating of my stepfather for the atrocities he caused linked me to my mother in a way that we had never experienced before.

For the first time in my life, I felt a little less alone in the world.

I caressed an orchid stalk, taking deep, slow breaths.

After a long while, I walked back home.

Chapter 44

SUMMER VACATION

*A*t first, there were no apparent changes in my life. As we had so many times before, we all behaved as if nothing significant had happened, despite the unprecedented violence my mother bestowed on Lauro. We never again spoke about the beating incident. Lauro continued to hover around the house and behaved much as he always did, lurking in the background, hoping to be noticed. My mother's relationship with Lauro remained unchanged. Whenever my mother and I spoke, we avoided the subject of my stepfather. She never asked me details about what I had revealed to her. It was as if it never happened.

Only once she made a statement to the effect of "now I understand why your sister wanted to move to the United States." Until that moment, perhaps my mother felt utterly shocked about my sister's decision to move. After constantly demonizing my father and Carroll, my mother never expected that either Nathalie or I would choose to live with them, so convinced was she of the veracity of her own words. My mother, so oblivious to her reality, never allowed herself to comprehend the misery she allowed to fester within our home.

While she never openly admitted it to Catherine and me, losing Nathalie engendered some reflection on the triggers that led to Nathalie's unflinching desire to leave. Understanding that if nothing changed, she might also lose her two remaining daughters, my mother relented her iron fist.

Within a week of the beating incident, when I left to pay the bills in the afternoon, she surprised me by saying, "Just make sure you are home for dinner. You know how dangerous it can be to walk around in the dark."

My mother had just given me carte blanche to return whenever I wanted, provided it was safe. No woman would want to find herself walking the streets alone at night. Despite my yearning to be free to move as I chose, I understood and agreed with her advice. I hid my surprise, left for the day, and tested my mother by taking a later bus home. She made no comment.

Within a few days, she asked me, "How is studying going?"

"Good," I said.

"How come you are not studying with Cristiane on Tuesdays anymore?"

I refrained from reminding her it was because she had forbidden me. I stayed quiet.

"She has a swimming pool, doesn't she?"

"Yes, she does." Ignorant of the reason for the question, I quickly added, "But I never use it. We just study all the time." I lied, not mentioning that we plunged into the pool almost every afternoon while at Cristiane's.

"Maybe you should next time," she said.

I realized my mother had just given me permission to resume my afternoon study sessions with Cristiane. So that is what I did.

My mother also offered to pay for the Petropolitano club membership, completely unaware that I had kept it active for the past year. Catherine resumed playing volleyball at the club, and she allowed me use the club's pool on the weekends.

She balked when I asked to dance at the nightclub. She tried to convince me that it was not a good idea by enumerating all the horrible influences and negative energy that we would be exposed to. Realizing the threats of darkness did not faze me, she relented, allowing Catherine and I to go out in the evenings, provided we had a chaperone.

I felt astonished, but did not seek confirmation, just in case this largesse was temporary. Instead, I left the room and picked up the phone to call Cristiane.

"Cristiane, I can go to Som Petro with you this weekend."

"I wish you could, Isa. But I don't think my dad wants to have your mom screaming at him again."

"She won't scream this time. I promise," I said.

"No!" she said, flabbergasted. "Did she give you permission to go?"

"Yep, want your dad to talk to her?"

So my mother gave Miguel her verbal permission to drive me to the club with Cristiane, as long as he would accompany us.

For the following year, I joined Cristiane every Sunday for a night out of dancing and fun, leaving all dressed up in front of Lauro and my mother, freely entering their car that stopped in front of our iron gate. I never again needed to jump the fence.

The following summer my father once again invited me to visit Los Angeles. This time, though, he extended the invitation to my sister Catherine as well. Theoretically, the previous year was my year to visit, and this year was Catherine's turn. Since I had missed my turn last year, he offered that we both come for the summer.

This time, my mother signed our passport request and allowed us to go.

"I was afraid," she confessed to me years later, "that if I let you visit the United States, and you saw life in America, you would never want to come back to our life here in Petropolis. But then I let you go because I was afraid that if I did not, you would leave for good, just like your sister did."

My mother's fear was rooted in her belief that my father was wealthy and lived an opulent life—a common misperception most Brazilians held about foreigners, most particularly Americans. My mother felt that once we experienced such wealth, we would no longer accept the relative simplicity of our life in Brazil. My mother did not have much fight left in her to forbid us to do much, and she was curious how Nathalie was doing. She felt that if Catherine and I met Nathalie in person, we could give her more reliable news.

Yet, I felt I had been cheated of the opportunity to go to Los Angeles on my own to be with my father. I felt that by joining us, Catherine would take my father's attention away from me. Thus, I resented that my father invited my sister too.

I protested to my mother that it was not fair that Catherine should go too.

"Why don't mind your own business?" Catherine said.

"It is not fair that she goes!" I told my mother. "It's my summer."

"Your father invited both of you," my mother responded.

"But it is my summer!" I repeated.

"Your summer was last year," Catherine said. "Too bad you messed it up, and Mom did not let you go," she said, referring to my mother's often-repeated reason for denying my trip the previous year due to my behavior.

When my father called to organize the trip, I told him I did not want Catherine to travel with me.

"Why not?" he asked.

"Because it is my turn," I said.

"I don't see how your sister joining us makes it not your turn," my father said.

"But it is my summer!" I said, again somewhat frustrated that nobody understood that I did not want to share my father's time, and the spotlight, with my sister.

"Well, Isa, if you don't want to join your sister, you can always stay in Brazil this year too. Catherine has an invitation from me, and she is coming."

I lost the battle.

When summer arrived, both Catherine and I boarded our first flight to Los Angeles to join my father, Carroll, and Nathalie for a month.

My father's living conditions did not match my mother's outsized expectations. He lived in a suburb of Los Angeles, in a standard, middle-class, three-bedroom house that was perhaps less than half the size of our current home in Retiro.

I had not spent more than ten days with my father in the previous nine years. I may have seen Carroll a maximum of three times. If it were not for Nathalie, being at their home would have felt completely awkward, and we often did not quite know what to talk about.

Nathalie seemed happy. She did not yet speak English well, even after a year in the United States, and did not have friends. But she had a job working at a retail store and felt relieved about no longer living in Brazil. She expanded on how coming to America was the best decision she had ever made and said that I should join her the following year when I turned eighteen.

I had planned to join my sister, but I did not feel all that comfortable in my father's home. Los Angeles was such a different world from our small city in Petropolis, with its people-free avenues and large distances. Los Angeles was impressively large, but at the same time, it felt empty and soulless.

We played tourists. We visited Disneyland, where I pinched myself for actually being there, realizing a dream every Brazilian child, including myself, had. We watched Duran, my favorite band, live in concert. We visited Santa Barbara and Santa Monica, which, while nice, were cities with a beach, not too different from what I felt Rio was like. The other days were mostly spent at home, playing at the gated community pool and lake.

The highlight of the month for me was visiting the UCLA campus. I had walked many times by the large, colonial building of the Catholic University of Petropolis. Also I had driven by the tall, multi-story buildings of UFRJ, the top university in Rio de Janeiro, on our way to visit my grandmother in Rio. But I had never experienced a university setting quite like UCLA. It was unthinkable to me that a campus could be as sprawling as the entire city of Petropolis—or so it seemed to me. The main quad, with the large lawn surrounded by majestic and historic brick buildings, seemed something that could only be dreamed of. I could not fathom that such beauty existed. The library alone, with its beautiful stained glass and wood panels, was larger than most buildings I had ever seen. I felt such a sense of awe; I could hardly express myself, so overwhelmed I was at the sheer magnitude and beauty of that place.

It was in the middle of July, yet the campus was bustling with students rushing about with their books and backpacks. As I looked upon the students, hurrying from one place to another, I felt an unfamiliar feeling, the twinge of envy mixed with awe. I looked at those passing by me and could not help but wonder whether these people realized how lucky they were to be at UCLA, to be American, to be free! I felt a strong desire and deep longing to be one of them.

"I want to study here," I blurted out, turning to speak with my father.

"Then you will," my father said happily, noting that one of his biggest regrets was that he never attended college. He said he would be proud of me if I attended this school.

Carroll, a bit more realistic, immediately intervened and noted, "It is hard to obtain admission here. It is extremely competitive."

I turned to Nathalie, who was then attending the state university. "How come you do not go to school here?" I asked.

"It is too competitive to study here," she said. "Plus, I will attend Northridge State University. It is just as good."

"Is the campus as amazing as this one?" I asked, looking around to the beautiful brick buildings surrounding the large, rectangular grassy area of the campus quad.

"Not quite like UCLA," Nathalie responded.

"Then I don't want to go to Northridge," I said. "I want to attend UCLA."

"You have to study quite hard to gain admission here," Carroll interjected.

"I always study hard," I responded.

"Then maybe you can," my father said, trying to be supportive.

A few days later, Catherine and I packed our suitcases, preparing our return to Brazil.

"Isa, can I speak with you?" my father asked me.

"Sure," I said, pausing from stuffing my suitcase with the trinkets we had acquired during the trip.

I followed him to my bedroom so that we could have some privacy talking.

"How was the trip?" he asked me.

"It was great," I responded excitedly.

"What did you like most?" he asked.

"I thought it would be Disneyland, but actually it was UCLA! I never thought a university would be this beautiful and be large like a city,"

He asked a few more questions about my experience that summer. We exchanged happy banter for a few minutes. I also reiterated how much I wanted one day to attend UCLA, to be part of a school that impressed me so much.

"How come you did not want your sister to join this trip?"

I stammered a bit, not feeling like I had a good reason besides telling him that it was my turn and my summer. I had relaxed this insistence throughout the month I had stayed there, but there were a few times during the trip that I pouted about my sister being there with us.

"Your turn was last summer," my father stated.

When I did not respond, he continued, "Your mother tells me that your behavior was such that she did not think you deserved to visit then."

I felt hollow inside and a dull pain in the pit of my stomach. How could I explain to my father that I had been a rebel with a cause, that my mother was punishing me for ignoring a stepfather whose existence I was supposed to keep hidden from my father? Not feeling I could defend myself without admitting the lies we told for so many years, I stood silent.

My father took this silence to mean I had recognized the validity of his point. He continued on with what he actually wanted to tell me.

"Well, I feel disappointed in you."

I pursed my lips, biting them to control the tears I knew were coming. I could have managed, except that this was not the end of what my father had to say to me.

"You have become a selfish person, Isa. You just think about yourself. Did you stop for a minute to empathize with how your sister was feeling about you not wanting her to come here?"

I remained silent, biting my lips. He continued.

"You pouted most of the trip, while Nathalie and Catherine were just having fun. You made it hard for everybody. I am not proud of your behavior, and I expect better of you."

I could no longer contain my tears. My father's disapproval weighed heavily on me. I did not know what to say, so I remained silent, tears rolling down relentlessly on my puffy, reddened cheeks. Perhaps feeling uncomfortable with my tears, he left me alone in my room.

I stayed in the room for a while, not knowing what to do. I did not want to come out because my father and my sisters were in the living room, and I most certainly did not want to let them see me feeling so distressed and humiliated. I remained alone for a couple of hours, drying out my tears by staining the blanket with them. Eventually, Nathalie entered the room, and I pretended I was just fine and busy packing.

I left the room and came to face my father, who, as every other adult in my family, behaved as if no significant conversation happened between us.

Catherine and I boarded our flight to Rio de Janeiro the next day. My father, Carroll, and Nathalie took us to the airport. My father hugged me tightly when I left to board the plane, but said nothing more.

Once on the plane, I asked Catherine whether Pappy had spoken to her too. "Yes, he did," she said.

I felt relieved. Maybe my father had not only scolded me, but my sister as well, equalizing the hurt I felt.

"Pappy said he was proud of me!" she said, beaming and going on and on about how much praise my father had lavished upon her about her behavior during the trip.

"What did he say to you?" Catherine asked me, noticing that I had tears in my eyes as she recounted all the praise she received.

"He told me he was proud of me too," I lied, not wanting to admit to my sister that my father had instead expressed his disappointment in me.

I felt convinced, after that fateful conversation, that my father would no longer want me to come live with him the following year when I turned eighteen. Yet, I kept this doubt from my mother, and upon returning to Brazil, Catherine and I spoke animatedly about Disneyland, the fifty different varieties of cereals available in American supermarkets, and the UCLA campus, knowing full well that I would not attend college there and instead, would seek placement at a university in Brazil.

My mother felt wary of my unbridled excitement about UCLA. She feared that I would follow Nathalie's footsteps and leave soon. After years of not caring about my grades, my mother became unusually interested in my education. She told me that she would provide me with all the resources and freedom I needed to pass the "Vestibular," the entrance exam to the university system in the state of Rio de Janeiro. I could take any classes I wanted. I could come and go as I pleased. I could do whatever it took for me to be successful at securing a place at the best university in Rio de Janeiro. And that's an offer I took to heartily, as I felt the gates to my American dream had closed.

THE EXAM

I met Claudio, a senior in high school, after my summer trip to Los Angeles. He was much too tall and much too skinny, but he paid attention to me at school. One afternoon, while walking a side street that ran parallel from the main road in Petropolis, I entered the clothing shop where he worked.

"I am leaving in about an hour," he said. "Can you wait for me, and we can go have a snack together?"

I looked at my watch. I was expected at home in an hour, by six o'clock. Still, my mother had, in theory, lifted my curfews. I decided to take a chance and wait for him.

We went to the local bakery across the street from the store where he worked. He then walked me to the bus stop. "I will wait here until the bus arrives," he said because it was already dark, and in Brazil, it wasn't safe for anyone to be out alone. We stood next to each other, and I felt nervous to be standing next to this tall man without knowing what to say to him. He turned to me to say something, but instead, he kissed me.

"This must be the first time you've kissed a man," he said after.

"No, it isn't!" I protested, remembering my ill-fated first kiss during Carnival the year before.

"Well, I think it is," he said, smiling. "But don't worry, I will teach you how to do it," and he proceeded to kiss me again.

The bus came much too soon.

"I have a boyfriend!" I announced to Catherine upon arriving home that evening.

"You do?" she asked me, surprised. "Who?"

I described the boy, who, hours earlier, I hardly ever thought about.

Claudio and I met again a few days later at school. He was the first man with whom I had a proper conversation. Or perhaps, not quite a proper conversation—not knowing exactly how to talk to him, I felt it safer simply to agree with everything he said.

"I like to work out," he told me, although it would be hard to tell by looking at his slim physique.

"I do too!" I responded.

"I like to lift weights," he continued flexing his paltry arms to show a negligible bulge in his biceps.

"I like it too," I said, although I had never seen a dumbbell in my life.

Not surprisingly, the relationship ended within a week. Claudio told me I was boring.

I spent the following weekend at home as I did not have a boyfriend to go see. Catherine, seeing me sulk around the house, inconveniently asked, "Where is your boyfriend, Isa?"

"I no longer have one," I said quietly, hoping she would drop the matter without asking too many questions.

"Already?" she retorted. "Who has a boyfriend for only a week?"

Apparently, I did.

My two experiences with kissing boys had not been pleasant nor interesting. They invited the ridicule of my sisters and my friends. Dealing with boys was not something I was good at, did not enjoy much, and honestly was not interested in. Since Nathalie left, I had a degree of freedom I had wished for my entire life. And I did not want to use that freedom in the relentless pursuit of men in which everybody else engaged.

Seemingly overnight, my sister Catherine and Cristiane's sisters and neighbors all had boyfriends, and they naturally occupied the free time they once spent with me with those boys. To adapt, I spent my time traipsing around Petropolis on my own. During one of these walks, I saw signs for a piano class. I came home and asked my mother if I could take piano classes. My mother, pleased that I was finding things to do that would keep me involved in pursuits other than chasing men, agreed to pay for classes. My piano teacher managed a chorus, and despite my questionable singing abilities, I soon joined the chorus too.

Even with my now busy schedule, my mother suggested one more activity.

"You must take a typing class," she said.

"Why?" I asked, doubtful of the usefulness of such an idea.

"So that you can have a job as a secretary."

"But I do not want to be a secretary," I said.

"Well, what else will you do? You should still take a typing class, just to make sure you are prepared," she insisted.

Seeing it as an opportunity to leave the house even more often, I registered for the typing class too.

Big signs hung on the windows above the typing school, advertising college preparatory courses, which I, as a senior in high school, thought I should take. I expected this course would be a harder sell to my mother. To begin with, the course was expensive. The biggest hurdle, however, was that the classes were held in the evening. And despite all my freedom, I still needed to return home by nightfall, or at about six o'clock—not only to respect my mother's rules, but also because it was simply unsafe to be outside alone after dark. Yet, I felt it was worth the risk.

"Mom, there is this college prep course I want to take."

"Do you need it? Don't you have good enough grades?" she asked.

I was slightly surprised to realize my mother knew of my academic performance.

"It doesn't matter, Mom. Everybody else will take this course, and all these people will compete with me for a place in college."

I knew my mother felt insecure about the future and that she wanted to ensure I would attend college nearby—or at least closer than Los Angeles.

"Besides, it is practically a requirement that I take the course to be accepted at the universities in Rio," I said, knowing my mother knew nothing about how college admittance worked.

"How much is it?"

"It is expensive," I trailed and then told her the amount of money. Her eyes widened, but she remained quiet.

"It will get me into UFRJ!" I said, naming the Federal University of Rio de Janeiro, the most prestigious and competitive public school in the state of Rio de Janeiro.

My mother quickly realized that UFRJ was in Rio, which was an hour away—far, but a lot closer than UCLA. So she agreed.

"There is one more point," I said.

"What is it?" she asked suspiciously.

"It is at night . . . but Cristiane will also take the class. Her dad can bring us home so that I don't have to take the bus," I quickly added. I knew taking the bus late at night was not prudent. To my surprise, my mother agreed. Now, suddenly, between all my after-school classes and commitments, I only returned home to sleep.

The first test of whether these prep courses were worth the investment in time and expense came at the entrance exam for the private Petropolis Catholic University, the only university in Petropolis itself. I had no interest in attending that school, but since everybody else took the exam, so did I, believing that it would be good practice for the Vestibular exam.

My picture was splashed on the front page of local newspapers the day the results were announced. I placed fourth among the fifteen thousand students who sat for the entrance exam.

With this high placement, I felt arrogant about my chance to secure a spot at UFRJ. The only path to the university was through a statewide, four-day exam taken by every high school senior in the entire state of Rio de Janeiro with any aspiration to go to college. The grade on that exam alone decided which school one would attend. Hundreds of thousands of students took the exam. I had been at the top of my class since I could remember. I had placed fourth among thousands. I decided to select only UFRJ as a school choice as surely I would nab one of the sixty spots available for economics majors.

Cristiane thought my plan was foolish.

"Isa, you never know; you should add more schools just in case."

"Cristiane, really?"

"If you don't secure a spot in UFRJ, then you have to wait another full year to take the exam again," she said, almost in a panic. "Or we can just stay here in Petropolis, together," she added, referring to the Catholic university where she had placed fifteenth.

"Do you truly just want to stay here?" I asked Cristiane, with a tone of surprise in my voice.

"I do. Our families are here," she responded.

While Cristiane had a close, supportive family and feared what life would be like away from them, I longed to put as much distance as I could between my family and me.

Hearing her concerns, I added additional schools to my list of options, simply by selecting a box next to the school of choice. I added four more, not considering what I would do if I were to place in one of them.

The Vestibular was such an important exam that the answers to the test questions appeared the following day in the newspaper. Students rushed to the newsstands to review the previous day's answers to gauge how well they were doing. After the first day of exams, my confidence increased as I compared my answers to those listed in the newspaper for the Portuguese and math subjects and knew I had done well. The second day was a repeat of the first, now with the geography and history tests.

The third day, we sat for the chemistry and physics exam.

I completed the exam fast, as I had the previous two days. Rather than hand it in immediately, as I typically did, I paused after I answered the last question. I felt an instinct to revisit my answers to the descriptive chemistry questions that required drawing a chain reaction of how two chemicals combined. That section of the exam accounted for 40 percent of the day's grade.

I looked at my answers and—unusual for me—felt doubtful that I had appropriately addressed the question. It seemed too easy, as if it was a trick question. I believed that for such an important, decisive exam, the answer must be more complicated than what I had written down. So I erased my first response and tried something else. Not satisfied with it, I also erased the second answer, to try a third way. It felt anxious and uncertain; it was an unfamiliar feeling not to know the answer to an academic question. The anxiety paralyzed me, rendering me unable to think. When the bell rang, noting that time was up, my exam paper was almost torn from all the erasing, and no discernible chemical reactions were written on the page.

I felt an utter sense of despair deep in my gut, knowing I failed that exam because I had not completed the answer.

The next morning, I woke up earlier than needed for the fourth and final day of exams so that I could buy the morning newspaper that would show the chemistry exam's correct solution. Upon opening the newspaper, I felt my knees weaken and had a horrible compulsion to throw up. The first answer I had written, but later doubted, was correct. I felt so distressed that I showed up for the fourth, final day of exams feeling queasy, which surely influenced my performance on that day of exams too.

I arrived home sobbing.

"Why are you crying?" Lauro asked as he was sitting in the living room when I opened the door to the house.

I momentarily forgot that I had not spoken with him for the past two years. "I failed the exam."

"You are a loser!" Lauro said, seizing on my vulnerability.

I should not have engaged with him, but I felt so distressed, I took his bait. "I am not," I said indignantly.

"You are. You are a stupid girl who thinks you know something, but you are nothing. You know nothing!"

I did not want to believe him, but at that moment, I did feel stupid and ignorant. How could I have erased an answer that was correct? What if Lauro had just stated the obvious truth? Rather than ignore him as I had done so successfully for years, I protested, "No, I am not." I could only whisper; perhaps I was internalizing what he was saying.

Seizing on my weakness, Lauro got closer to me and grabbed and pulled my long hair.

"Ouch!" I screamed.

Lauro did not let go of my hair. I kept screaming, not so much because Lauro was dragging me through the house by my hair, but because I felt so angry at myself.

He shouted a barrage of words that I do not remember, making sure that his face was close to my ear so that I would hear the words clearly. I screamed louder, out of anger and to drown out his voice.

Upon hearing my piercing screams, my mother burst through the door. At the sight of her, Lauro dropped my hair and left the room.

I stayed where I was, hugging my legs and sitting on the floor near the front door. I was crying, partly because my heart was full of renewed hate for Lauro, but mostly, I cried for my failure to seize the opportunity I had to attend the best school in Rio. I felt that no matter what I did, I was destined to have my dreams squashed and to have all those around me put me in my place: my stepfather, who clipped my wings my entire life; my dad, expressing his disappointment in me; and now even the admissions process. I felt like a failure. I did not know who I was if not a top student. My academic performance had defined me for so long; I could not understand how I had failed. My mother sat next to me and held me tightly until my supply of tears dried up.

"You did well on the other tests," she said. "I am sure you will still go to UFRJ."

I shook my head. What did my mother know about anything? She never left the house, never realized any dream, and never completed a day of hard work in her life.

"You know nothing, Mom," I said, feeling deflated.

It took four unbearably long days for the school placements to be published in the thick newspaper, which held the name of each of the thousands of students who took the exam that year. It gave the student's name, the overall placement among all test takers, the university where he or she placed, and the major.

I knew that only a miracle would place me at UFRJ, but I thought I had a chance to attend my second choice, a school with a better geographical placement in the heart of Rio, UERJ, the state university. But I did not place there either.

Next to my name was RURAL University, named for its focus on agricultural majors and for its remote location in the middle of nowhere—between Rio de Janeiro and Sao Paulo. Unlike my first and second choice schools, RURAL did not even have an economics degree. Instead, I was to be a mathematics major. Most students who went there focused on agriculture, animal husbandry, and chemistry—now my most-hated subject.

Given that the school was at least a three hour bus ride from Rio de Janeiro and from Sao Paulo, almost all its students lived on campus, an almost unheard of situation in a country where most lived with their parents until the day they married. And because it was one of the few schools without parental supervision, the university had a reputation as a hotspot for drugs, sex, and alcohol.

With the choice of attending RURAL or the Catholic School in Petropolis, I knew my mother would insist that I attend the Petropolis Catholic University, a safe, nearby choice that required no moving.

Yet, I did not want to go there. I did not want to stay in Petropolis. I was still seventeen, so I could not move to the United States yet—an option I was no longer sure I wanted anyway.

I set my target on attending RURAL.

"What?" Cristiane asked me incredulously upon hearing my choice. "Of course you are not doing that!" she stated. "It does not even have an economics major," which was the subject we both decided to study in college.

When I did not appear dissuaded, she called her father Miguel to join us in the living room.

"Are you thinking about going to RURAL, Isa?" Miguel asked me. "I would not let Cristiane go," he added.

"How come? You let Cristiane go everywhere!" I asked, surprised.

"But to RURAL I would not. And I am surprised that your mother would let you go."

"I didn't ask her yet," I said, "but if she does not let me, where would I go?"

"You can join me at the Catholic University here in Petropolis," Cristiane responded.

I valued Miguel's opinion, but unlike Cristiane, I did not want to stay close to home. Despite the freedoms I now enjoyed, I could not wait to leave the house and never have to face Lauro again. Going to a hot spot of threats I had not experienced was definitely more appealing than staying in my house. Although I managed to distance Lauro from my life, he still lurked around, and as the exam episode provided, I could not fully let my guard down around him.

If Miguel, who was so permissive with his daughter, would not allow her to go, I figured I had no chance in convincing my own mother to support my school choice. So I prepared for a fight when I approached my mother about discussing schools.

"Going to RURAL is a fantastic idea!" my mother exclaimed, unexpectedly.

Taken aback by her willingness, I thought I should explain about the school's reputation as a place where everything my mother tried to protect me from occurred on a regular basis.

"Mom, you do know about the school's reputation, right? About drugs and alcohol?" I trailed.

"I raised you well," she stated. "I trust that you will make the right choices."

Unlike everybody else, my mother did not concern herself with the school's reputation. Her focus was ensuring I attended a school in Brazil—even if it took four hours and three buses to arrive on campus and even if it was a hot bed of drugs, alcohol, and sex. At least I would be home on the weekends. And once I started university, I might become less inclined, she must have thought, to join Nathalie in the United States.

"You are free to go," my mother stated.

I packed what I needed for my first week away from home. I filled a small suitcase with clothes, packed a bag with cheese and cabbage, and carried within me hope and anticipation for this next journey. I boarded the first of three buses, the one to take me to the Petropolis bus station. From there, I boarded the bus to Rio de Janeiro for the hour-long ride in an air-conditioned luxury bus. From there, it would be another two hours in a regional bus, driving over a bumpy and dusty road to the big unknown.

I had never felt more excited in my life.

RURAL

I first set foot at RURAL on the day classes started. The campus was beautiful, peppered with yellow-colored colonial buildings, which had a regal air to them, despite the fact that they were not well maintained and were covered in chipped paint. The main building featured a tower with a large bell and a lush garden courtyard. Given that is was an agricultural-focused school, it had large pastures and landscaped areas between buildings, and the land was full of fruit-bearing trees. The highlight of the campus was the lake, nicknamed Fertility Lake, given the many pregnancies that supposedly originated there.

Besides a small, dilapidated town near the school, which had a supermarket and a fast food restaurant, the nearest town was at least one hour away. The phone systems were unreliable and mostly nonexistent. There was one pay phone to serve the entire school, a school in which most students were living far away from home. Long lines formed to use the pay phone for collect calls to family. I tried to call home once a week, but with the combination of long queues and frequently dropped calls, I essentially only spoke with my mom on the weekends when I returned home. That is, I was completely free of parental oversight for the first time in my life. At first, I did return home every weekend, taking the three buses required for the four hour route home. After a couple of months, however, I returned home every two weeks.

From what I could tell, the rumors were true; RURAL was indeed a hotbed of drugs, alcohol, and sex, although it was also academically challenging. While I did not have parental oversight, I knew that if joined the melee, it would be hard to extricate myself from it.

In maintaining a conservative lifestyle while at RURAL, I did not experiment with drugs and did not smoke nor drink, despite how easily available all of this was. I did not want my mother to say, "I told you so," if I found myself mired in a world of drugs and alcohol. I was sure if I dove into that world, I would drown. Mostly, I wanted to prove to my mother that her fears, which caused so much restriction in my childhood, would prove unfounded. I was not, at least initially, worried about the sex part, given my historic inability even to talk with boys.

The freedom I felt to be away from home, completely free, unsupervised, and independent, was heady enough for me. It was a better high than any drug could have given me.

When I got off the bus on campus for my first day of classes, I did not know where I would sleep that night. I had not thought this lack of foresight about lodging would be an issue. The packet with instructions about our first day said that freshman should check in at the school office to receive a lodging assignment. It seemed all freshman followed these instructions closely; there was a long line at the Housing Office, filled with dazed-looking students, gradually realizing that a place to sleep that night was not altogether guaranteed.

It was my first introduction to how things are done in Brazil. There exists a formal process, and then there is the Brazilian way, a round-about way to get what one wants involving short cuts, knowing the right people, and often bribes. Not understanding any of this yet, I naively stood in line, waiting my turn to receive a dorm assignment.

Unbeknownst to me, seniority ruled RURAL's housing system. There were not enough university-assigned dorm beds for all the new students. So, many ended up "crashing" in someone else's residence or sleeping on a couch, sometimes for years. Those who were homeless the longest had the priority as seniors graduated and vacated rooms. If I were to rely on the formal system, I had better spend my time scrambling to find a mattress to claim in some stranger's dorm, rather than remain in line.

As I patiently waited in line, a third-year student named Marcelo began talking to me.

"This is my first day here," I said excitedly.

"Shhh," he gestured as he placed his index finger over his mouth, the universal indication that I was to say no more. "Come with me!" he beckoned.

Before I could protest that I would lose my place in line, he picked up my luggage, and in an instant, we were outside the crowded hall. I felt that I had no choice but to follow as I was now more worried about losing my luggage than my place in line.

"I will lose my place in line," I said.

"Don't worry. I will get you a place to sleep," he said in a normal-toned voice once I joined him outside.

I did not feel concerned about this turn of events. Perhaps it was that I was too naïve to be concerned about a man taking my luggage uninvited and beckoning me to follow him with promises of a bed that evening. I did not know yet who to trust, and mostly I felt that I should follow anyone who offered to help me.

We walked for about ten minutes towards the women's dormitory, a non-descript, cinder-block, single-story building with whitewashed walls. He knocked on a door. A woman about my age, with long, flowing brown hair and a wide smile opened the door.

"Hi, Kaiza," he greeted her, "I found you a roommate." Marcelo presented me to the fellow student.

While I was still standing at her front door, she gave me a thorough look and asked me a couple of questions.

"OK, you can live here. Come. I will show you the room."

She led me through the cramped hallways towards my room—or rather, my quarter of a room. It was a two-bedroom apartment, with four single beds in each of the rooms. The bedrooms were separated by a bathroom, with four stalls in the middle, and a diminutive kitchen. As I learned later, my dorm was one of the most coveted spots on campus as other campus options were more crowded and remote than my centrally located apartment.

None of the other six girls who lived there were in the room at the time. I placed my luggage down on the bed Kaiza said would be mine as I gladly accepted the offer.

Kaiza then abruptly left. "I have to register you in the Housing Office," she said, "before any of the other girls give the spot away!"

Within less than an hour of my arrival on campus, I bypassed the entire seniority system and found myself a home at school.

As I later learned, Kaiza and my other six roommates did not want the Housing Office to assign someone to live with them randomly. Thus, they were all prowling the housing lines for potential new roommates. Marcelo, Kaiza's close friend, agreed to help her with this task. Kaiza stayed behind to vet whomever came through. I never learned why they picked me and did not care to ask. I got a housing spot within minutes of arriving on campus. I did not realize how precarious my situation was, arriving without prearranged lodging. I felt glad to have a bed and seemingly nice roommates. In Brazil, shirking rules was a way of life. I never questioned the morality of bypassing the housing allocation system. I was just glad to have a place to stay. I was ready to go off and live my college adventure.

"I will show you around campus," Marcelo offered. Nobody else was in the apartment, so I planned to unpack my small bag, but instead, I agreed to join him. He walked me to his car. The fact that he owned a brand new, gold-colored vehicle as a student made him a mini-celebrity on campus. The vast majority of students, and of Brazilian youth in general, did not own cars. The few who did usually received hand-me-downs or used cars from their parents. People gawked at Marcelo's car and nice clothes. That he was nice to everybody and gregarious helped him become one of the most popular men on campus. I did not yet know any of this the day we met. That day, he became my tour guide, driving me around the large campus, showing me the lake, the various colonial buildings, and the vast grassy areas in between them. After a lengthy tour, he drove me to the little dilapidated town nearby so that we could have a hamburger.

"You cannot possibly think about eating at the school's cafeteria!" he stated decisively, making it clear that I would never see him stooping so low as to eat the school-provided fare of runny beans with rice. "I come here to Bob's Burger at least twice a week. And you will come with me!" he stated with confidence, without asking me whether I agreed to this plan.

Thinking about the head of cabbage and ball of cheese I brought to sustain me outside of cafeteria food, it was not as if I had better options. That first night, Kaiza also joined us for dinner, as did another of Marcelo's friends.

Just like that, within a day of arriving on campus, I had a roof over my head, a new set of friends, and I was already living a few adventures. Overnight, I felt accepted into a completely new world. For someone who had been so sheltered, my first days at RURAL were incredibly liberating. I was immediately captivated by the opportunities of that world. It was the first time in my life I remember feeling completely happy.

I woke up the next morning with Marcelo knocking on my door. "Let's go have breakfast!" he said happily, and our second day of exploration ensued. I attended my first classes after breakfast, and he waited for me outside the classroom after my last class for the day, having checked my schedule earlier that morning. He continued showing me around and introducing me to his friends. After dinner, he drove me to Fertility Lake.

It was a beautiful, large, and calm lake, surrounded by expanses of grass and dotted by large trees that provided shade and some semblance of privacy—an important feature as the crowded dorms and the wide open spaces on campus provided little privacy to couples. There, Marcelo moved towards me and leaned in to kiss me.

I had essentially no experience in courtship, and perhaps naively, it did not occur to me that Marcelo would want a return on all the time he had invested in me over the previous two days. Marcelo had been wonderful and thoughtful, and I did owe him my place at Kaiza's dorm. He provided me with an instant network of friends to hang out with, and most importantly, he shielded me from the pranks and humiliation many incoming freshmen experienced during the first days of school. Had I known better, I would have realized that he would make a great boyfriend. But at that moment, all I could think about was that for the first time in my life, I felt absolutely free: free from parental supervision, free from oppression, free to do whatever I wanted, with whomever I wanted, whenever I wanted. I may not have had a lot of experience with relationships, but this was Brazil, and I knew enough about the macho-oriented culture to know that men called the shots. The last thing I wanted was another person to control me and tell me what to do. I simply did not want a boyfriend.

As he move towards me to kiss me, I put my hands on his chest to slow him down, and I said no in a whisper.

Marcelo was not expecting this. Marcelo's star was high on campus. He had not experienced rejection, ever.

I intuitively knew that having Marcelo around would keep me safe. I knew that I was not experienced enough to handle RURAL's culture and reputation for wild partying on my own. As he had proven over the past two days, Marcelo would protect me from pranks doled out to freshman, including being smeared in paint, having to shout obscene remarks from the middle of the school fountain, and having to march naked (or almost) into the lake. I would have a tour guide. I would have a friend.

At the same time, my need for some space to learn who I was and could be was more important than a relationship. Plus, I felt scared of men in general. My stepfather abused me. My real father abandoned me. My mother, so concerned with preventing me from going to nightclubs went into detail about how awful men can be with women. I had never had a proper male friend. Marcelo had, so far, been my most positive experience with men, but I knew that I did not want to date anyone, even someone as wonderful as him. It seemed more honest and safe not to kiss him, so I did not.

We left the lake in silence. He drove me back to the dorm he found for me. At some point during the ride he asked me, "Why do you not want to be with me?"

I don't remember giving him an answer. As I opened the door to leave his car, I felt sad. I thought this was the end of our short-lived but great friendship. I had been so happy the past two days. Now I was feeling miserable again, as I had felt on so many days of my life.

I cried myself to sleep.

The next morning as I was brushing my teeth, Kaiza came to see me in the bathroom. "You have a visitor!" she said, smiling.

"Who?" I asked. She left me by the row of sinks without answering.

Marcelo was standing at the door.

"Want to have breakfast?" he said, as I incredulously looked upon him standing in front of me.

"Sure," I responded, uncertain about what a man, whom I thought I would never see again, wanted to do at breakfast after I had refused to kiss him. Uncertain of what was happening, I joined him, not only for breakfast, but to hang out with him whenever we both had some free time. We became inseparable.

Marcelo smartened me up. He showed me the ins and outs of the university, introduced me to great people, and protected me from the not-so-great ones. Whenever I was in doubt about anything, I asked him. He seemed so wise and caring; he quickly became my world. Soon, the weekend separations when I typically returned home to Petropolis became unbearable, so we talked on the phone. One day I asked my mother whether Marcelo could come visit.

I remembered the shame and humiliation I felt when Lauro treated Walter like a street dog four years earlier. I would never allow the same treatment to this man, with whom I was falling in love. My mother, elated that with a boyfriend I may find a reason not to move to the United States, embraced Marcelo as if he were her own son. Even Lauro had the decency to greet him and treat him with some respect, upon orders from my mother, I was sure.

Marcelo spent most of the first visit successfully charming my mother.

Soon after, my mother, whenever I called or returned home without him on Saturdays, the first question she asked me was, "So, how is Marcelo?"

"Mom, I am your daughter! Will you not ask me how I am doing first?" I protested lightly. But then I would laugh and tell her all about what happened the previous week.

INVITATION

I woke up on my eighteenth birthday with a call from my father.

"Happy birthday!" he exclaimed. "How are you celebrating your day?"

"Thank you," I said. "I will have a cake."

"You should—so that you can celebrate. You can now move here and join your sister."

I was unsure whether my father would invite me to come live with him, given that I failed to seize the opportunity to move to the United States four years earlier. Given his reaction then, I assumed there would not be a second chance. Yet, while earlier I felt certainty that this would be my path, now I was no longer sure.

"I want to come," I told my father over the phone, trying hard not to betray the conflict I felt bubble up within me.

I had not expected to feel conflicted about this choice. Since the trip to Los Angeles the previous summer, I often daydreamed of attending UCLA. But now I was happy with my life. I had freedom. I had a different home at RURAL. I had friends. I had everything I ever wanted, yet the lure of the opportunity—and the memory of my father's disappointment four years earlier when I told him I would not go— was still fresh. I knew the visa process would be lengthy. The move, if it did happen, would not be for a few months still. Who knows what would happen in a few months? I had learned enough, however, that I knew not to close a door where one opened for me.

"I will start your application process then," he said enthusiastically.

"When will it be ready?" I asked, mostly to calculate how much time I would have left at RURAL.

He hesitated. "I don't know yet. The fact that we applied before and you did not come will complicate the process. It may be a few weeks; it may be a few months," he said.

"Will they accept me at all?" I asked.

"You are my daughter. I am now American. We will find a way."

Chapter 48

CHANGE

I had no updates on my visa application status, except for the occasional chasing of documentation needed for my application. As weeks turned into months, my efforts towards moving to a different country became a secondary focus in my life. I was fully engaged in my life at RURAL—as if I would stay there for as long as it took to graduate. I studied hard for my classes, made new friends, and spent most of my free time with Marcelo.

However, within a few weeks, my friendship with Marcelo frayed at the seams. Marcelo and I kept our relationship platonic. As I became more comfortable at school and more settled in my new life under the umbrella of protection Marcelo provided me, I branched out. I made my own friends and engaged in activities he was not too interested in joining, such as taking aerobic classes and finally learning how to swim at the campus pool. Without him, I attended the Thursday night parties most students enjoyed before we all made the trek back to our homes for the weekend.

I met Paul at one of the Thursday parties and felt giddy by his masculinity and the attention he gave me. We were talking about nothing important when he leaned down and kissed me. I reciprocated, thinking it was about time I learned how to kiss a man properly. I did not enjoy the experience in the least as Paul was a heavy smoker and the unfamiliar taste of tobacco lingered in my mouth. I did not want to kiss him again. About two weeks later, I found somebody else with better mouth hygiene, and we kissed for most of the night, as publicly as most couples did in a place without teachers or parents.

Marcelo only infrequently attended the Thursday night parties. But that night he saw me making out with another man. I felt so sure of the strength of our friendship, that I did not consider Marcelo's feelings. We were friends, and he would soon find somebody else to kiss.

Yet, I should not have felt so sure. After seeing me kiss another man, Marcelo made himself scarce. I deeply felt the loss of his constant presence. Only by missing him did I realize the outsized importance he had in my life.

Wanting to repair our rift, I sought him whenever I could during our normal, common free times, trying to recreate the normality of our friendship. He no longer seemed interested. He was too busy, he said, with studying, supporting professors on chemical experiments, and being a huge man on campus. Previously he had taken me along, but now he said that there was no place for me in his life. After his constant rejection, my pride was pierced, and I stopped looking for him.

Once Marcelo was no longer a fixture in my life, RURAL seemed cold and uninteresting. I went home on the weekends and sobbed in my mother's arms, searching for answers to why Marcelo actively avoided me. Many people on campus, used to seeing Marcelo and I glued to one another, but realizing that we were on our own these days, smelled some gossip and constantly asked what happened. I continued spending time with Kaiza, but she hesitated in sharing much information with me, as she remained one of Marcelo's closest friends. She felt conflicted about the state of our relationship, not knowing who to support. Kaiza thus stayed out of the way and was often unavailable as she spent increasingly more time with her own boyfriend. Not knowing what to do to fix this situation, I resorted to what I usually did during times of uncertainty by isolating myself at the library, surrounding myself with books. Yet, no longer content to receive all my sustenance from reading, I sought to fill my time with other people. Slowly, despite my heartache, I made plans and had fun with my new friends who accompanied me to the Thursday parties, kept life interesting at school, and soon took over all the free time I had previously given to Marcelo.

Just as I was feeling more settled into this new routine, I received a letter from the US Consulate and a happy phone call from my father. My visa had been approved. I was awarded a US Green Card, the ticket to the future that allowed me to study and work in the United States.

My father excitedly told me that all I had to do was choose a departure date. "But I am in the middle of the school year," I said.

"That's irrelevant. None of the work you are doing in Brazil will matter here," he said, dismissing my concerns, assuring me that I should have no qualms about quitting school before the semester was over. "Plus, you need to arrive here in time to register for summer school." This timeline determined my travel dates. I was to arrive in Los Angeles no later than late May so that I could start summer classes in mid-June at a community college next to my father's house.

Late May was only a few weeks away. I was not ready to leave. Irrespective of my ongoing heartbreak, I loved life at RURAL. There was so much happening every week. Even Cristiane, who I would still see most weekends when I returned to Petropolis, and her family commented how I seemed happier, more confident, and grown up.

Yet, the logical part of me saw that RURAL was not where I should be. It had been an after-thought in my school-list selection. I wanted to major in economics, not math, but RURAL only offered the latter. I certainly did not want to stay in Petropolis. Then there was the lure of UCLA. All these factors carried a lot of weight, the most important of which, though, was my belief that I simply could not disappoint my father again, as I did four years earlier. I had already not gone to the United States once before after my visa was approved. I could not refuse the same opportunity again.

I set my departure to the last possible day in the window of time my father gave me. He asked me to arrive on the weekend so that he could pick me up at the airport and to come in May. So I set my departure date for May 28, the last Friday of the month.

I returned to RURAL after speaking with my father and promptly started announcing my departure. Once Kaiza learned of my travel plans, it did not take long for the news to reach Marcelo's ear.

He did not seek me. Marcelo and I had not spoken to each other in weeks, yet I felt I owed him proper notice of my departure and a goodbye. Plus, I wanted to see him. I swallowed my pride and walked up the stairs towards his dorm apartment complex, located on the top floor of a three-story building. Despite feeling nervous, I knocked on his door. I expected our meeting to be brief and free of emotion.

Instead, Marcelo became furious that I would actually leave in a few weeks. "You can't leave!" he said, standing up.

"I did not think you would even notice," I said, making a jab at him. I wanted to remind him that we were not in each other's lives anymore.

"Of course I will notice! I always know where you are."

"You do?" I asked incredulously, not knowing quite what to make of this information.

"I just did not think you would leave."

"I told you the day we met that I would one day move to America."

Marcelo, however, as my mother, never thought the day would actually come. But here it was. We could have argued about it; instead, he came towards me, hugged me tightly, and kissed me. It was a desperate kiss, a reflection of the simmering sexual tension we had experienced for way too long.

After that kiss, it was as if the period of not speaking to each other had never happened. We were inseparable again. For the following three weeks, I felt a degree of happiness and elation that I had never experienced before. Yet, deep inside, not believing that I truly deserved this happiness, I assumed that Marcelo chose to be with me now because he knew it was temporary and that in a few days, I would be gone forever. I did not allow myself to believe that Marcelo truly wanted to be with me. Thus, despite the happiness I felt, I did not consider changing my travel plans.

Marcelo never asked me to stay anyway.

Much too soon, my departure day arrived.

As I did not want Lauro to drive me to the airport, I took a taxi to the intercity bus station, carrying two large suitcases with all of my life belongings. There I boarded the air-conditioned bus to Rio de Janeiro. Marcelo met me at the chaotic bus station and drove me to the airport.

My mother hugged me tightly while we waited for the taxi to arrive at our house. Tears streamed down her face, and she caressed my long hair. She later told me that when she saw the taxi turn the corner, taking me away from her, she fell to the ground in the middle of the street, as she did when Nathalie left, sobbing, thinking that she would never see me gain. She acutely felt the loss of her second daughter and asked God why it was that she was losing her daughters to the father who had abandoned us. But I did not know this while I made my way to Rio de Janeiro, full of excitement and anticipation about flying internationally—and about going to meet Marcelo and many friends who had planned to see me off at the airport.

Ten friends, including Kaiza, Cristiane, and other classmates, came for my send-off. They brought cards, balloons, and a stuffed bear. They hugged me, cried, and wished me luck. As I was about to cross the security line from where I would say goodbye forever to these people, I began crying—but not because I felt sad. Rather, it was because, as I looked towards my friends, I recognized I had achieved that for which I longed: friendship and the sense of belonging that comes with it. I shed tears of gratitude. Here I was, surrounded by people who loved me and felt sad about the prospect of losing my friendship. I felt so happy to be surrounded by friends, love, and good cheer. As I left, Marcelo kissed me hard, in front of everyone, who loudly cheered us on.

Suddenly, I no longer wanted to leave. I wanted to stay right here, with this man who I finally found a way to love, with these friends who took me so long to find. I looked around and realized I had all I needed already. Why would I ever want to leave? Yet, that thought only occurred as the airport officer pulled me away from the arms of those who loved me.

"You have to go," he said abruptly. "You will be holding up the plane," he continued as he rushed me towards the immigration line. I waved goodbye to the love of my life and to my posse of tear-stricken friends. Crossing the immigration threshold, I could no longer see them. I walked in a daze towards the airplane bound to Los Angeles.

During the flight, I poured over the many letters and cards I received. I felt again a mixture of elation and horror that I had left my friends, and their love, behind. I hardly slept. I had a one-way ticket to a new life. And that new life did not include Marcelo, nor Kaiza, nor Cristiane, nor anyone who mattered to me. I had hardly seen my father in the past ten years; I hardly knew him. I loved my sister, but I was used to a life without her.

Then I saw the flat and dry landscape of Los Angeles as the plane descended— so different than the lush mountains I had lived in. When the plane landed, I felt awash in panic.

What did I do? I thought in horror. Suddenly, I longed for the airplane to turn back and take me back to Brazil. I did not want to start a new life in Los Angeles. I wanted the life I already had. I began crying, and I could not stop, even as I handed the bulky envelope with the US Green Card papers to the immigration officer.

"Welcome to the United States," the serious-looking woman, who reviewed the documents I presented to her, said with a welcoming smile. That was the tipping point. I could not smile. When I saw her stamp my passport and take the papers I had brought to gain entrance to my new country, my soft cry became sobs.

My father, Carroll, and Nathalie were waiting for me at the arrivals lounge, with big smiles, waving little American flags, happily welcoming me to their life, to their home, and to my new country. I cried more upon seeing them too. They all thought it was because I felt so happy to have finally arrived. When the tears did not cease so easily, they thought it was because I must be sleep deprived, jet lagged, or confused.

Nathalie came to my room.

"Why are you still crying?"

"I don't want to be here."

She sat next to me on the bed and brushed my hair out of my face.

"But here is so much better than our little life in Petropolis," she said, widening her eyes.

"Marcelo isn't here."

"Who is Marcelo?"

I told her about Marcelo, my friends, and what I left behind.

"You will get over it. I also had a boyfriend and friends, but I never looked back."

"It is different," I retorted. "Your boyfriend was not the love of your life."

"Yes, he was!" she responded. "For a while, anyway . . . besides, it is an adjustment," she continued sensibly. "Give it a little time. You will see; you will be happy here."

My father also thought all I needed was time to adjust to this new land, and soon I would feel well. They babied me for the first day, taking me to an ice cream shop and showing me around town. Beginning on the second day, my father only addressed me in English.

My knowledge of English the day I arrived in the United States was to count to ten and name the colors. I could not hold a conversation or even say basic phrases.

"I don't understand, Pappy," I said when he asked me what I wanted for breakfast. "Can you translate?"

He did not. Instead, he repeated the question while pointing to a box of waffles.

"It is the best way for you to learn," Nathalie said in Portuguese.

"Don't translate," my father interrupted. "The faster Isa learns English, the better it will be for her."

My father thought the sooner I adapted to my new life, the sooner my tears would stop. But during these first few days, I did not comprehend what anyone told me. I looked expectantly towards Carroll, hoping some maternal instinct would kick in and that she'd help me, since she also spoke Portuguese fluently after three years living in Sao Paulo. She did not.

"You need to hear English from an actual American," she said, "so I will speak English with you because it's even more important that you hear my native accent than your father's cute, but French, one."

Carroll added yet another idea to teach me English as fast as possible: "You need to watch TV. The language is dumbed down a little bit, and the commercials are repetitive. It will be good for you. You will learn English in no time by watching a lot of TV."

Studies I read later indicated the contrary, that language is not acquired through TV viewing, but rather through reading. I loved reading and had grown up seeking books. My previous exposure to TV was so limited, that experiencing the constant noise of a TV on all day grated on my nerves. Since Pappy and Carroll watched a lot of programming in the evenings, there was not much I could do about it then, but I decided that I would turn it off during the day.

It turns out, that was not an option.

Carroll's mother also lived with us, a fact that nobody shared with me until I met her on the day I arrived in Los Angeles. She was a wheel-chair bound octogenarian. Apparently, it was Carroll's turn to take care of her mother, after she had worn out her welcome with Carroll's two other siblings. Carroll's mother, unable to read well with poor vision and unable to do much of anything else, watched TV all day long.

Growing up, I had resented my mother intensely for forbidding TV viewing, but now, surprisingly, I resented Carroll's mother even more for having it on all the time. I was not used to that constant noise, and I hated it.

I asked her to turn it off; she refused.

I complained about the TV noise to Carroll.

"Well, what will she do otherwise?" Carroll asked. "It isn't as if she can go for a walk," she added sarcastically.

"She could read instead," I suggested.

"She is too old to read," Carroll said dismissively.

"Can we compromise then?" I asked. "Half day with the TV, half day without?"

"What else will she do during the half day? Stare at trees?"

But what about me? Did anyone care about what I would do?

I did not drive, so I could not leave the house, especially in Los Angeles, a sprawling city that required driving. The community where we lived did have a pool, a tennis court, and even a small lake. And while I used these facilities, without company, they were not enjoyable. I did not have any money of my own. Whenever I could, I read books by the pool and spent some time every day exercising, often running outside. But I could not spend up to ten hours a day at these locations, so I had to return home.

My father suggested that when I was able to understand English better, I could register for summer classes at the local community college. But I had to be ready within a month when classes started. If I was not ready, I would not start school until the fall semester.

Horrified at the prospect of spending all summer stuck in the house with Carroll's mother and her blaring TV, I redoubled my efforts to learn English as quickly as possible. I read every magazine my father had subscriptions to— *Time, Newsweek*—reviewing every single page, including all the ads. I underlined words I did not know, looked them up in the dictionary, and reviewed the list with my father or Carroll in the evening.

And I watched TV, too, at least one hour every day. At first, I hardly understood a word. Within a few days, though, after paying attention to commercials, some words began to be clear. Even with Nathalie, I made an effort to speak only in English.

Nathalie was my only friend. She spoke English pretty fluently by then, and she translated whenever my father was not within earshot. She wasn't around often, however. Besides attending college at Northridge State University, she also held a job at a clothing store at the local mall. My father and Carroll left home before eight o'clock and did not get back until early evening. When everybody returned home at the end of the night, it did not necessarily mean much of a change from the boring, long days. Nathalie arrived home tired as she worked until the store closed. My father and Carroll wanted to watch TV after a brief dinner. After spending a year at RURAL surrounded by people, feeling mentally stimulated and even distracted with all the drama surrounding my love life, my current situation felt like I had moved backwards in my life's development plan. I felt disappointed and alone and imprisoned at home. We lived on the edge of the San Fernando Valley in Los Angeles. In a city focused on driving, the scant buses did not even go near our home. There was nowhere for me to go.

After the first two weeks, I realized I had left one kind of prison for another. My dreams about life in the United States did not include being housebound with an elderly lady I did not get along with, listening to the TV blare all day long.

In order to fill the time during my long days, I wrote letters, long letters detailing my boredom in Los Angeles and how I missed my life in Brazil. I wrote to Marcelo first, but then while waiting for a response, I filled the time by writing to everybody else too: my mother, Cristiane, Kaiza, and my other friends at RURAL. Within days, I received the first responses from friends. Marcelo's fist letter was long, reporting how he could not sleep because he missed me continuously, that he had never imagined he could think about someone twenty-four hours a day as he thought of me. He wrote about the hole I created in his heart. Rather than give me solace, the letter made me cry, harder than the day I landed in Los Angeles—if that was possible. I wept for losing the love of my life.

I wrote back the next day. He replied within days. Soon we established a pattern. I mailed a letter every Monday so that I could include whatever I did on the weekend. I received a letter from him on Tuesdays, also indicating that he mailed a letter on a fixed day of the week. We were one letter behind in our responses, but it did not matter. What mattered was that we kept our connection.

These letters were meant to give me comfort. Instead, they delayed my acceptance of my new country as my bond to Marcelo and my link to Brazil had strengthened, rather than weakened.

Within a month of my arrival, summer school started, occupying some of my time. I enrolled in two courses at Pierce Valley Community College, a five minute drive from my father's home. As relieved as I felt to now be attending school, I could not believe that I left Brazil and my remote but good university to attend an unheard of local community college.

"I would like to take summer classes at UCLA instead," I told my father.

"That is not how it works. You can't just show up and take classes there."

"What do you mean?" I asked.

"But you can't just take summer classes at UCLA. You have to earn admission first. And you are not ready to go to UCLA yet," my father said.

"Why not?" I had partly come to America so that I could fulfill my dream to attend UCLA. It was upsetting to learn suddenly that this option was out of reach.

He explained that I needed to take the SAT and apply for admission. But I had missed the exam date and the application deadline. Plus, the exam was in English; that fact alone was an insurmountable barrier. I was only learning to understand English. I certainly could not take an exam written in that language. Besides, Pierce College was located within five miles from my new home, so my father or Nathalie dropped me off and picked me up. UCLA was one hour away, which might as well be another country since I did not yet have a way to get there. No less important, Pierce College, even with the astronomical out-of-state fees, was significantly cheaper than UCLA.

"One day you may transfer there," my father said, trying to cheer me up as he saw how deflated I felt upon learning this new information.

Transfer? What did that even mean?

"Ask someone at Pierce how you can do it," my father said.

So I did, with my sister beside me as a translator.

"When can I transfer?" I asked the counselor.

"It depends. You need good grades. But also, you need to do extracurricular activities," which was a word that even in Portuguese, I did not know what it meant. "If you achieve all this, then in two years. But there are no guarantees. You have to be one of the best."

My heart sank. Two years was a long time.

Upon seeing my disappointment, my father explained that this was a well-trodden path by many to get to university. He reviewed the Pierce College catalog with me to guide me on what classes to take. He was scant help, though, never having attending college himself. So I selected courses that seemed interesting and signed up for an economics class, as this was my desired major. I also chose an oceanography class, lured by the fishing field trip listed in the catalog.

As my schedule was at the mercy of Nathalie's or my father's availability, I often spent interminable hours waiting for them to arrive to pick me up. Despite the inconvenience, I felt grateful to be out of the house and preferred the relatively quiet library on campus over the blaring noise of TV at home.

Sometimes, however, I came home before lunch because Nathalie dropped me off before she left for work. Now that I needed to study, I again asked Carroll's mother to turn off the TV for a few hours so that I could do my homework. I needed silence to decipher the complex economics and oceanography books, written in English, so that I could complete assignments and prepare for exams. My requests were instantly dismissed.

"How can you possibly tell an old lady in a wheelchair not to watch TV?" Carroll's mom mumbled. "Study at the library while you are at school," she said, more sarcastically than helpfully.

My dislike of Carroll's mother grew. So I applied the only technique I knew to deal with those with whom I would rather not interact. I ignored her. She became a fixture of the house, not a person to engage. My relationship with Carroll, already fragile, soured through my open hostility to her mother. I did not consider Carroll's feelings nor anybody else's, so caught up I was in my own feelings and challenges. I hardly considered what disruption it must have been for Carroll, my father, or even Nathalie to have me intrude in their lives, wanting to change how things were done in their house.

Yet, Carroll never once criticized me, nor reprimanded me on my behavior. Most importantly, she never alluded to how my appearance in their home changed everybody's life—and not necessarily for the better.

At first, my summer classes were unbearably difficult as I hardly understood what the teachers said. Within a month, though, I was mostly fluent. Yet I was already behind and found it difficult to understand complex concepts, a scenario which became increasingly more frequent as the quarter wore on. For the first time in my life, I felt incompetent academically. I could not follow the lectures nor comprehend what the professor said half the time. I certainly did not contribute to the class discussion, a concept which, in itself, was foreign to me. In Brazil, asking questions was akin to doubting the professor, so silence reigned in classrooms. But in Los Angeles, everybody talked. Not only that, the professors encouraged questions. Feeling self-aware of my poor English and strong accent, I remained quiet. I strove to catch up. I spent my free time reading, either my school books or magazines. Yet, by the time I mastered one lecture, I felt lost again in the next class. Never having set foot on a boat before, I felt sea-sick during the oceanography field trip, earning no marks for the effort.

Not surprisingly, I received the worse grades of my life for my midterm exams. I cried over my poor grades.

Carroll attempted to console me. "You should find it impressive that you got a passing grade. Look at you! You just got to America a month ago. And you are studying economics, in English. If I were you, I would be proud," she said, smiling.

"I am not proud," I said. "Having a C grade is nothing to feel proud about!" I said emphatically.

Until then, I had been the highest ranked student in my class. But in America, I was one of the worst.

"Well," Carroll said, speaking pragmatically, "schools in Brazil are not of the same caliber as the ones here."

With that statement, Carroll confirmed it would be an uphill struggle from here on out. Due to my upbringing and origin, in America, I might not even rise up to become average. My poor performance on the midterm exam weighed heavier on me than Marcelo's heartfelt letters full of longing for my presence. The grades hurt more than the loneliness I felt as I waited the interminably long hours on campus for someone to pick me up—more than the frustration of having to leave the house to find a quiet space to study or of living with people I disliked.

Two months after my arrival in Los Angeles, I concluded that I disliked the life I led. I felt lonely. I felt imprisoned again, this time because I could not drive and there was no bus to take me out and about. Again, I did not have friends. I missed my boyfriend. I felt like a failure and pessimistic about changing my academic performance.

I romanticized all I left behind in Brazil. I thought about Marcelo and his kisses, and I missed the laughter, warmth, and love emanating from Cristiane and Kaiza. I even missed my mother, who seemed more concerned about me than anyone else in my American household.

I had built in Brazil what I longed for my entire life, and I left it all behind. And for what?

I had made a terrible mistake. I should not have moved to the United States. I wanted, no, I needed, to return to the place I called home.

Chapter 49

CAMPAIGN TO GO BACK

I rehearsed the words repeatedly in my head. The hardest part would be facing my father—and deciding when and where to say it. My father was hardly ever alone. The house was too small to afford any privacy, and whenever we went out, we went as a family. I could have asked him to join me on a walk with the family's poodle, but he did not enjoy walking. That would not be a good plan either, because I did not want to have anybody asking questions in case we returned home visibly upset or puffy faced.

When I first came to Los Angeles, the aura of grandeur I attributed to my father quickly dissipated. While he was successful by Brazilian standards, he was essentially an average, middle-class, company man who liked structure, predictability, and no drama. He had an average house in an average neighborhood with an average job and an average life. He had never been an expressive person. He was a father by biology only, as he also was struggling with how to parent a teenage daughter he barely knew. He treated me kindly, as he would any adult stranger who lived with him. He did not seem to have any friends. He listened to classical music using headphones so as not to interfere with the TV watching, and mostly, he restrained his emotions.

Yet, despite his outward coldness, I began to love my father, not so much for the opportunities he was affording me, but for the person I learned he was:

honest, hardworking, responsible, and loyal. He quietly went about his day. He managed to see the world and rise to a management position when he had never attended college. He supported my academic and professional dreams and often said there were no limits for those who work hard. And I retained the unexplainable need to make him proud of me.

It had never occurred to me to blame my father for abandoning us in Brazil. I was not angry that he chose to see us one day a year when he had a full three weeks of vacation and took at least two extra days just to fly to Rio de Janeiro. My father did not know how to be a father. He must have felt that as long as he paid the bills—as he did not know the hardships we faced—then his duty as a father was met. He must have felt that since he was building an opportunity for us for the future, then what may have occurred in the past was not as important or was, at least, forgivable.

On that particular day, I worried about how disappointed he would feel once I told him I wanted nothing of what he built for us, that I would reject the opportunity he gave me to create a life in the United States. How could I tell him that, in my opinion, this life was not as good as the life I was building in Brazil, where I may not have the same opportunities, but where I had love and friendship?

I knew this would be a hard conversation. Thus, I carefully selected a location where my dad would not dare overreact and where nobody else in the household could hear our conversation, nor offer an opinion.

"Can you just tell me now?" he asked me when I requested an appointment with him at his office.

"No, not now," I said, scanning the noisy house to ensure nobody overhead us.

My father, who perhaps understood more than he let it show, shook his head and said that I could meet him the following day. His office was not too far from Pierce College, and while it rare to see anyone walking outside of the school campus, I walked for half an hour to meet my father at a modern-looking, dark-glass-covered building in a commercial office park.

"Come on in," he said when the receptionist escorted me to his office.

I sat down, facing him, and considered whether I should make small talk first. However, I could not manage to say anything. I looked at his immaculately kept desk and then towards the trees that flanked his window. I had rehearsed this conversation so many times, yet I felt hesitant now the moment was upon me, unsure of how to start. The signs of anxiety began to set in: the sweaty hands, the fast-beating heart.

My father said nothing. He patiently waited for me to say what I had come to say. After a few uncomfortable minutes, my eyes filled with tears, and I just blurted out my request: "I want to return to Brazil."

My father must have known that something was amiss, given my request to come meet him at work. However, he must have thought it was a smaller-scale problem, such as more complaints about the TV situation, or worst-case scenario, complaining about Carroll's mother. Seeing how he widened his eyes and the sadness that overtook him, he certainly did not expect my rejection of the lottery-ticket of life he had given me.

"Why?" he asked. He never needed to say much.

I tried to remain composed, but I could not. Amid tears, I rambled on about not wanting to live with my step grandmother, how I was failing at school, how I hated the TV noise, how I felt imprisoned since he would not trust me to drive. I spoke of every reason I could think of, except the primary one. I had never shared information about Marcelo with my father. As far as I knew, he did not know I had left a boyfriend behind. As he had done our entire lives, he did not ask about the emotional aspects of my life.

He tried a logical approach, providing solutions to each item on my long list of grievances. Did not like the TV? We could institute a rule to turn if off more frequently, such as during dinner. Could not drive? He would sign me up for driving lessons so that I could learn more quickly. Did not do well at school? I could slow down and take fewer classes so that I could have more time for each. Did not like the grandmother? He balked at that, knowing that pleasing me would upset his wife, but told me he'd try to think of a solution.

I just shook my head at his suggestions.

"Thank you, Pappy, but I still want to leave."

It became clear to him that I had already made up my mind and that nothing he said would change it. He stopped suggesting solutions, remaining quiet for a few, interminable minutes.

"It is July and the middle of the summer quarter," he said. "I expect you to finish your summer classes."

That was another five weeks away.

"But I will make you a deal," he continued. "If at the end of the quarter you still want to leave," he paused, looking straight at me, "I will buy you a return ticket to Brazil."

"OK. We have a deal," I said.

I knew then that I would soon have a ticket to return to Brazil. But since I could not start RURAL again until September, and I needed time to write to everyone first about my pending return, I thought I could wait another month.

My father hugged me tightly, in a manner that I was not used to, but he let me go. We drove home together in silence.

He must have certainly shared that conversation with Carroll. In the days that followed, I noticed clear changes that led to some improvements in my life. The TV was sometimes turned off, without me having to ask. Carroll's mother naturally was not happy with this change of situation and complained about it. My father, normally so calm, so composed, one day uncharacteristically lost his patience. "It is because of you that my daughter wants to leave!" he screamed at her. "The TV will stay off," he stated, in a tone that left no doubt he had the final say in that discussion. That uncharacteristic outburst left all of us feeling awkward and uncomfortable, but nobody rushed to deny my father's statement.

I immediately penned a letter to Marcelo, sharing the news of my return. While the travel date was not yet set, it would surely be in September. His response arrived sooner than expected. He revealed his excitement about my return, although he did question whether returning was wise.

In the subsequent weeks, I continued posting a letter every Monday. Yet I noticed the replies did not always land in my mailbox on Tuesdays. They still arrived, but a few days later. Our pattern had changed. Rather than assume it meant something, I thought instead of the multiple explanations for the delay, and while I noticed the change, I put little weight on it.

I felt happier—although it was no longer clear if this happiness stemmed from my imminent return or from feeling increasingly more comfortable in Los Angeles. By the end of the summer, I spoke English fluently. While I could not say I had friends, I was friendly and now talkative with my American classmates. Nathalie, feeling sad about my departure, showed me around Los Angeles on her days off. We went often to the beach, spending long days together, learning more about each other, and creating bonds that we did not have as children. Pappy and Carroll, set on showing me that life in America could be great, planned fun outings to Disneyland and Magic Mountain, a roller coaster park.

I completed my classes at Pierce College, earning C's in both of them.

"I am proud of you," my father said.

I did not feel proud at all, but I felt it would be futile to protest.

"These were hard subjects. You did not speak English. It is amazing you passed the class at all!" my father continued.

My father meant to cheer me up, but there was nothing he could say that would achieve his goal. I could not see that, indeed, it was an achievement to complete difficult classes when two months earlier I could barely count in English. At the time, I felt these grades were immutable; that is, I projected that they were a reflection of how I would perform going forward, ignoring that with a little more effort and time, I would be just fine. But then, I felt like the C's were a judgment on who I was and how I stood compared to others in America. All I saw was the immediate failure. When summer classes ended, I returned to my father's office to discuss our deal.

"You made a decision, I am sure," my father said, starting our chat.

"I have," I said. "I still want to leave."

He remained quiet for a few seconds.

My father did not try to change my mind.

"We had a deal," he said, looking straight into my eyes, "and I will honor it."

The following day, he handed me plane tickets with a departure date set for early September.

While reviewing the plane tickets, I noted a second ticket for a flight from Rio back to Los Angeles in early December.

"Pappy, these are round trip tickets," I said, with a tone of surprise in my voice.

"I know. I bought them," he stated calmly.

The concept of returning to the United States at the end of three months seemed unimaginable. I had no intention to move every three months. My home was in Brazil, where I had friends, was loved, was successful academically, and where I was about to live a great love story.

"You are wasting your money, Pappy, because I am not coming back," I said with a tone of finality.

My father did not seem affected by this answer or attitude.

"If you have not learned anything, at least you could learn the value of insurance."

I shrugged my shoulders, thanked him, and waited for him to drive me home, where my first action was to write a letter to Marcelo announcing my departure date.

Pappy and Nathalie drove me to the airport. Nathalie cried, feeling sad and upset about my decision, especially now when we had learned how to be friends. My father, however, was composed, as if he was dropping me off for a weekend away, not sending me to a different country where it may be months or years until we met again.

"Have a nice trip," he said, hugging me tightly.

"I am not coming back, Pappy. You know that, right?" I confirmed once he released me from his bear hug.

"Then you will not have a use for the return ticket, right?" he said, with a faint smile.

"Right," I said as I left to board the plane that took me back to Rio de Janeiro.

THE RETURN

arcelo greeted me with a hug when I emerged from immigration at the airport in Rio de Janeiro.

"Why did you come back?" he asked.

I looked at him surprised. Surely, he knew why. Did I have to say it? I returned to be with him. I—that is, we—were in love. I thought we had something special.

I, however, did not want to admit these truths to him so boldly. I would rather hear him say these things, to make me feel more at ease around him and to validate my decision to return for him.

"I did not like America," I blurted out, instead of telling him the truth.

He laughed, betraying his surprise at this statement.

"Everybody likes America!" he responded.

"Well, I am not everybody," I said.

We remained quiet.

He drove me up the mountains for the hour-long trip on the scenic highway from Rio that meandered through the mountains to Petropolis. We had so much to say after almost four months apart, yet we mostly rode in silence.

As we approached the area near Shangrila, I had an urge to see it.

"Stop!" I asked him, surprising both of us.

I had built no happy memories in Shangrila, and until then, I had never longed to set foot there again. Yet at that moment, I felt the sudden impulse to visit the farm, to relive memories. The old caretaker still lived there and let us in. I walked through the small patch of grass peppered by fruit trees. I looked up to the round house and its tower.

On the surface, Shangrila seemed no different, yet I knew deep inside that it was. Some of the homes on the property were occupied by different neighbors. Some trees had been felled. The previously whitewashed round house was now yellow.

I thought aptly that this was how I felt too. There was not much difference between Shangrila and my situation. Marcelo and I looked the same, yet we had changed. It was imperceptible on the surface, but there existed an awkwardness between us that had not been there before.

Upon leaving Shangrila, he asked me again, "Why did you return?"

Instead of speaking of my dreams for our future, I spoke of how the constant noise from the TV grated on me, about Carroll's grumpy mother, and about my poor grades from summer school. I also explained how I missed the chaotic nature of Brazil, especially compared to how empty of people Los Angeles felt and how much I missed everybody. Never once did I speak about my longing for him. He nodded in silence. And in silence we remained until our arrival at my mother's home.

My mother rushed towards me, tears flowing freely on her face. She hugged me tightly. After a few minutes, I noticed Lauro standing in the background, waiting for my mother to release me so that he could welcome me. It seemed he expected a hug as he opened his arms wide. Before he could close the distance between us, however, I turned away, as I had done so many times before, behaving as if he did not exist. At that slight, the smile on his face evaporated.

My mother nudged me with her elbow, trying to be friendly while saying, "Come on, Isa; let it go."

I did not move.

Marcelo, not used to such open animosity, filled the vacuum by shaking Lauro's hand. Right after that, Lauro left the room.

"You must be tired. I will leave now," Marcelo said, turning towards me.

My mother stepped in, saying, "Marcelo, you can't leave. We prepared a feast!" She excitedly described the succulent lunch she had cooked to celebrate the prodigal daughter returning home.

So shocked I felt that Marcelo did not plan to stay, I stood silent, not knowing what to say. He never refused food, much less good food. Not only that, I had just arrived. I returned to be with him. I had assumed he planned to stay the day with me.

"Are you really leaving?" I asked, dumbfounded.

"Yes," he said, "but I will talk to you later."

He left, without kissing me goodbye, without asking me whether I was returning to RURAL, and without a plan for when we would meet next. My mother, trying to diffuse the tension everybody felt, made light of it. Catherine and my mother sat at the table, beckoning me to join as I remained glued to the window, long after I waved Marcelo goodbye as he maneuvered his car out of our driveway.

Lauro did not return. The abundance of food felt strange when there were only three people to eat at the long table covered with meats and sweets my mother had so painstakingly prepared.

My mother, so used to pretending that everything was fine, sat down and cheerfully said, "Let's eat!"

I did not want to eat. I wanted escape to some corner of our house where I could be alone and release the tears that threatened to burst from my eyes.

But I did not cry.

Instead, I sat at the table with my mother and sister, joining them in pretending I felt fine too.

Chapter 51

NEXT SEMESTER

By the time I had returned in early September, RURAL had already closed the semester's registration period, as classes had started in August. I pleaded with the university staff to make an exception. I had been abroad. I had not known the rules. Yet, in the bureaucracy that existed at school, nothing I said mattered.

"You are too late. You can register next semester."

"But that's in January," I said, frustrated. "That is five months away!"

"Yes, indeed, that is right. Don't miss the deadlines next time," the registrar responded, hoping that she was teaching me a lesson.

Upon leaving the registrar's office, I walked towards the library. I sat on the front steps, watching the flow of people rushing to their classes, feeling dejected that I was not to be one of them. What would I do for five months until the next semester started? I most certainly did not want to wait it out in Petropolis. Although my relationship with Marcelo existed only in my imagination, I returned to be with him, and he was at RURAL. I had to stay there.

I hatched a plan.

I went to my dorm room, dreading the possibility of learning that someone else occupied it.

"Isa! Welcome back!" Kaiza said happily.

We hugged tightly. She was expecting me as I had also written to her about my return, asking that we'd be roommates again.

"It is so great to see you, Isa," Kaiza said sincerely.

"Kaiza, is my bed still available?" I asked abruptly.

"Of course it is. Who else was I going to put in here?" she said, hugging me again.

"Kaiza, you are the best!" I said.

After I dropped my luggage and answered Kaiza's barrage of questions of why I had returned, I sought one of my math major classmates who lived in the dorm facing mine.

"Can I get the class schedule?" I asked her.

"Sure, here it is," she said, handing it to me, "but didn't you get it when you registered?"

"I did," I lied, "but I don't know where I put it."

I planned to stay in school, telling no one that I had not registered for classes: not my mother, not Kaiza, not my classmates, and most certainly not Marcelo.

The professors seemed oblivious as to whom attended class. They most certainly did not check attendance records, and therefore, I felt that I could attend classes without being questioned. I created a class schedule based on the schedule of my closest classmate, noted which books she purchased, and asked my mother for money to buy them too.

I attended classes, willing myself to believe that what I learned this semester would help me when I would retake the class later on. For the moment, I ignored that I would eventually need to explain why I would repeat the class.

I spent my days as if I belonged at RURAL. I attended all classes. I joined study groups, pretending to complete assignments I did not hand in and prepare for exams I would not take. No professor ever questioned that my name did not show up on his roster. They barely knew who attended class. When not pretending to be a student, I walked the far reaches of campus, ran around the lake, took swimming lessons, and wondered what could have caused Marcelo's change of heart.

Except for those with whom I corresponded during the summer, most people seemed surprised to see me.

"I thought you moved to the United States!" people said, often hesitantly, given that I was standing in front of them instead.

"I did go," I responded, "but then wanted to come back."

"Why?" they all asked, as if choosing to live in Brazil and attend RURAL in the remote hinterlands of the country was something one would do only if he had no other option.

"I did not like it," I said.

The truth was now blurred. All the pretending was clouding my feelings about how I felt about my summer experience in Los Angeles and about what was happening in my life. I was no longer sure I answered any question truthfully. But I felt too ashamed to admit that I gave up a lottery ticket for a man who clearly and openly ignored me.

"How could you not like America? Everybody loves America!" fellow students insisted.

I shrugged my shoulder, "Well, not everybody."

I would speak at length about the hardships I endured during my summer in Los Angeles, trying to convince anyone who would listen of the validity of my decision. My classmates, many of them used to real hardship in the form of poverty, struggles, and inefficiencies, could not relate.

"Truly? How could you give up the chance to live in America? Do you know what I would give to have the same opportunity?" they would ask incredulously, shaking their heads in disbelief at my foolishness.

I talked so much, trying to justify my actions to the hordes of people who questioned my choice, that within two weeks, my voice grew hoarse. A few days after, I could not speak at all.

RURAL hosted a hot-air balloon festival with people from all over the country coming to see the large objects floating away over the large, calm lake. The whole campus mobilized to make this festival a great success. Picnic tables sprang up on the campus' expansive, pretty grounds to hold a special, invitation-only lunch event, a party which some friends and I managed to crash. The school was a beehive of social activity, which made being unable to speak particularly challenging. It also rendered the recovery of my voice unlikely, as I could not restrain my desire to speak whenever any sound arose from my throat. Yet, even had I not lost my voice, I would not have known what to say upon seeing Marcelo sitting at a table next to me, his arms embracing a pretty girl.

I felt distraught seeing him at the next table, ignoring me while doting on somebody else. Marcelo did acknowledge my presence and asked me a question I could not answer as my voice failed me, my throat and my heart hurting. I felt frustrated at my inability to speak and confused about Marcelo's behavior. A month earlier, he had sent me letters, painstakingly written with cut outs of words and letters from a glossy magazine, stating the depth of his love for me and his despair for my move to the United States. Yet, here he was, in front of me, barely acknowledging I existed. I felt miserable, yet I felt too proud to leave, not wanting to give him power by displaying my discomfort in leaving the most coveted party of the entire school year.

I remained seated across the table from him, feeling a knife twisting in my heart as he paid attention to a girl who was not me.

Kaiza, who was seated a table over, noticed the awkwardness of the situation. She tapped me on my shoulder, saying loudly, "Isa, look! The balloons will take flight!"

The balloons were indeed inflating in the vast meadow next to the party.

"Come with me," she continued, laughing. "I want to meet the cute pilot who will fly one of the balloons!"

Grateful for the escape route that Kaiza afforded me, I left without patently displaying the humiliation I felt. I accompanied her to the edge of the lake, away from balloons or any cute pilot she may have wanted to meet.

"Are you OK?" she asked when we were out of sight of anyone from the party.

I shook my head, finally letting the tears fall freely as I stood on the edges of the lake.

These tears were not only because Marcelo evidently created a life for himself that did not include me, but also because I felt invisible to most everybody else too. The previous semester, I was a hot commodity on campus. I was a freshman, the girl with big opportunities who could live the dream everybody had. Now, I was just another person in school, going about her business. I felt other people's contempt for my failure to grab an opportunity where there was one. The familiar feeling of not fitting in, of wanting to belong, took hold of me.

I was back in Brazil, in a place I had thought was my home, but I neither had nor was building anything of worth. My idea of a relationship did not materialize. I was not registered at school, so any effort that semester was essentially wasted. I was floating. I felt lost, and during subsequent days, I wandered the expansive campus on my own, not wanting to study for exams that did not count, yet not wanting to tell my friends I was not studying.

I did not wander for long.

A few days later, I contracted chicken pox. More ominously, I felt a growing lump on my tailbone that made walking painful. Within a couple of days, the lump grew so large that I could not walk at all. Rather than return to RURAL, I stayed in Petropolis, nursing my physical and emotional wounds.

As there were no telephones at RURAL, I could not reach any of my friends during weekdays. But I knew that Marcelo visited his mother in Rio most weekends, as did Kaiza. When I failed to show up at school that week, Kaiza called to check in on me. Within days, the get-well cards from friends poured from my mailbox, wishing me a speedy recovery and updating me on the campus gossip. Every day, I hoped one of these cards would be from Marcelo, as Kaiza surely would have told him about my illness. Every day I felt disappointed that among the numerous letters I received, there was not a missive from him.

The time at home allowed me to weigh the consequences of my choice to return to Brazil, for a man whose behavior I did not understand. By then I had given up that Marcelo and I would actually rekindle our love. Yet, I needed answers.

I swallowed my pride and dialed Marcelo's phone number in Rio on Saturday. Marcelo's mother answered.

"It is Isabelle," I said. "Is Marcelo home?"

"Are you calling me from Los Angeles?" she asked, surprised to hear my voice. Clearly, Marcelo had not bothered telling her that I had been back for almost a month.

"No, I am in Petropolis."

"Are you visiting your mother so soon? She must be happy!" she said, with the wistful thinking of a single mother who couldn't bear the thought of her child moving away.

"No, I live here," I said.

"I thought you moved to the United States," she stated.

"I came back. I did not like America."

I felt I had to explain.

"Really?" she said, without elaborating.

Without wanting to give the long-winded explanation of how I found myself in Petropolis, I cut her off. "Can I please speak with Marcelo?"

"He isn't here," she said. "He did not come home this weekend."

I let out a sigh.

"How are you, Isabelle?" she asked, with a palpable concern in her voice.

I did not want to share much information with her, but her tone of concern disarmed me.

"I am not well. I have chicken pox and a huge, painful lump on my tailbone that hurts so much I can barely walk. My mother is so scared; she thinks I need surgery to walk normally again."

"There is no need to do surgery!" Marcelo's mother said loudly. "Surgery is never the first solution. I have a better option for you. Here is the name of a pomade that will draw the inflammation out and burst the lump."

A burst lump did not sound promising, but it was better than enduring the pain I felt. When I hung up, I asked my mother to go to the pharmacy for me.

"Mom, I spoke with Marcelo's mom. She recommended a pomade to burst the lump," I said hopefully. "Would you please go buy it for me?"

"This is witchcraft! Why would you listen to that woman?" my mother responded loudly. I thought her reaction was party because somebody else's mother had given me advice instead of her.

"Mom, it hurts to walk," I responded. "I just want to try it. Can you please just go and get it for me?"

"It will not work," she responded.

"Come on, Mom, please. I just want to try it," I pleaded.

"No, I will not go. This will not work," she said, raising her voice to tell me her decision not to help me was final.

I felt lonely, so very lonely again. My life had not changed. It was as it had always been. Nobody seemed willing nor able to help me. Who would ever help me? I needed something simple, just somebody to go to the pharmacy, less than half a mile away, to purchase a medicine that could help me. How often had I gone to the pharmacy to run errands for my mother, for Lauro, and for my sisters? But when it was my turn to receive help, there was no one to do it for me.

I got up slowly and looked at my mother.

"I will go myself then."

"You can't walk!" she said.

"I will find a way."

I could walk, just extremely slowly as every step pulled on the lump, increasing the pain. Slowly, I made my way to the sitting room where I knew my mother kept some cash and took enough to buy ten pomades, if needed, and left the house.

Every step was so excruciatingly painful.

After almost an hour, I made it half way through what was normally a ten-minute walk. My tailbone throbbed with pain. I looked around the familiar cobblestone road that led to the pharmacy and bakery, with a mélange of both manicured mansions and dilapidated homes flanking the road, and burst into tears. I cried for the physical pain I felt, but also for the despair that arose within me from feeling abandoned by my mother and my now ex-boyfriend.

I looked through my tears to the path that led me towards the pharmacy. It was so close I could see it. Yet I knew it would take a long time to reach it. I thought bitterly that this was a metaphor of my life. I could see a path to happiness, yet reaching it was difficult and seemingly filled with pain.

After another twenty-five minutes, I bought the pomade at the pharmacy. As soon as the salesperson handed it to me, I took a big swab of cream and placed it over my tailbone lump—even though there were enough people around who may have been shocked to see someone apply medicine on themselves in public. I did not care. I would do anything to heal as soon as possible.

Yet, nothing immediately happened with my lump. It did not burst nor get smaller. It hurt just as much, especially after I had pulled it by walking for more than an hour. I took a deep breath and set out for the hour-long return back home.

Once at home, I felt so much pain from my effort that I lay down on the couch and stayed there for hours, with a book for company. I reapplied the pomade repeatedly as Marcelo's mother advised me. For the next day, my own mother ridiculed me, telling me I brought the additional pain upon myself for listening to someone other than her. I tried to ignore her by concentrating on the book. Not wanting to give her satisfaction, I ensured I did not complain about my misery.

After two days, the lump ruptured. A mess of pus and inflammation poured out, which I noticed more because the pain subsided suddenly rather than due to the stench it caused. I felt so relieved that the pomade had worked that I did not concern myself with feeling disgusted. I could feel the pain dissipate as the pus oozed out of the wound. I could finally walk again without significant pain. By then, the chicken pox had subsided too, leaving a scar on the top of my nose ridge. The scar on my nose, and now in my heart, served as a reminder that it was up to me to make my own life and chart my own course.

During the three weeks spent in Petropolis during my illness, away from the distractions of school and uninterested boyfriends and mostly left alone by my family, I reflected about my life. What did I have? I felt alone and disconnected from the world. I felt grateful that Kaiza and other friends had written to me, but the people who were supposed to care for me the most, my boyfriend and my mother, had not been there for me. Then I thought how foolish I had been to give up a chance for a better life in the United States because I wanted to believe that here in Brazil is where I would find love. I believed it was in Brazil where my friends would rally around me. My mother, who had so decried having lost one daughter that she told me she would do anything to keep me in Brazil, could not live up to her words. It was not in her nature to care for others. And Marcelo, I did not know what to think of him, but I felt certain that I should not tie my destiny to him either.

So I cried again. This time, I wept for being so foolish in my decision making and for the death of the idea that I would find happiness where I was.

After some thought, I decided I could perhaps fix this situation, that it was not too late to start over.

I picked up the phone and placed a collect call to my father.

"Pappy," I said when he answered the phone.

"Hi, Isa, are you well?" he asked, surprised to hear my voice, as I did not usually call him spontaneously.

"No, I am not well," I said. I wanted to tell him about the chicken pox and the lump in my tailbone and about losing my voice and about heartbreak, but words escaped me. Instead, I just said, "I am sorry I ever left. I made a mistake. I want to use the plane ticket you bought for me and return to live with you."

I suppose my father may have thought to himself that he knew I would eventually call, that I had been a fool to make decisions based on young love, and that what he offered was clearly better than what I had. I readied myself for the onslaught of a well-deserved set of I-told-you-so criticism.

"We were hoping you would come back," is, thankfully, all he said.

"Thank you," I said, amidst tears that flooded my eyes.

I had not expected kindness from my father—not when I had clearly disappointed him a couple of months earlier by returning to Brazil; a year earlier for selfishly denying my sister opportunities; four years earlier, when he thought I lied about wanting to live with him; and finally for being ungrateful and unkind towards his mother-in-law and his wife.

This time, I told myself, I would do things differently. This time I would not disappoint my father or myself.

It was only mid-October. My father, wary of having me back in the United States before he could find something to occupy my time, suggested I return in December. "You can't attend school until January, and there is no one who can be here with you. Carroll and I will take time off in December so that we can be with you. This will also give us time to make some changes around here," he said.

Plus, the return plane ticket had already been purchased for early December. Despite having settled on a departure date, I waited a few days to tell my mother I would leave again.

"Don't!" my mother pleaded tearfully. "Not again."

"I am sorry," I said softly, almost as a whisper.

"You will be happy here. Marcelo will see how wrong he has been," she said, caressing my hair as her tears freely flowed. "He will be back; you will see."

I did not cry this time. I let my mother hold me, but I felt no sadness and no conflict for my decision.

"It does not matter, Mom. It is too late for him to come back."

Chapter 52

THE LIE THAT ENDED ALL LIES

*T*here were five weeks until departure. Once the visible spots of chicken pox faded, I returned to RURAL to finish the semester I had not started. My mother did not hold me back and gave me enough bus and lunch money for the following few weeks.

This time, I did not share with my classmates that I was about to leave again. I had come to believe the only reason I made friends was because I had what everybody wanted: a way out. I wanted to see what life would be like if people thought I was just one of them and would stay around for the foreseeable future.

I did not seek to speak with Marcelo when I returned and went about my life as if he did not attend the same school. We frequently bumped into each other, as the common areas in the large campus were somewhat concentrated. As I had done before with Lauro and Carroll's mother, Marcelo became yet another ghost, somebody who existed at the periphery of my life but was not acknowledged. While I still attended classes, I no longer studied for exams I had no intention of taking. I filled my time playing volleyball, learning how to swim in the campus' Olympic-size pool, and attending school parties.

In mid-November, all students received notices to register for the following semester. Thus, many of the ongoing conversations veered towards the classes we would take. Kaiza, although she was majoring in chemical engineering, shared with me the classes she registered for so that I could match my schedule to hers for general requirement subjects.

"What classes will you take?" she asked me, wanting to know the teachers I would have and the classes I planned to register for.

"I am still thinking about it. I did not register yet," I said, noncommittally.

"You haven't registered? You must do it before all the classes fill up, and then we will not be able to take them together," Kaiza responded.

This was my moment to tell my closest friend that I had no intention whatsoever to register for next year's classes, that I was not even registered for this semester, that in a couple of weeks, I would be in Los Angeles again.

Yet, I did not. I did not find the place within me to tell Kaiza the truth: I would not register; I was leaving; all I really disliked about America was that Marcelo was not there.

But it was too complicated. And in the past, whenever life got complicated, I retreated to my shell, choosing silence over truth. I felt that Kaiza would judge me if I were honest with her, that she'd brand me as indecisive or immature—or just plain confused. It did not occur to me that, as a friend, she would have extended understanding and compassion or perhaps even helped me. But I had never experienced that kind of support before. All I wanted was to protect myself from feeling judged by her. Never mind that in two weeks I would have to face her, and everybody, with news of my departure. At that moment, though, I had not yet learned that some people could be trusted. So I invented a story about changing schools to explain why I would not be around in two weeks.

"Well, I am thinking about taking the Vestibular exam again to see if I can change schools and go to UFRJ."

UFRJ was the best university in Rio de Janeiro, the one I failed to attend after flunking the chemistry part of the exam the year before. "I could go there," I continued. "I got the chemistry part right after all," I told Kaiza, after explaining my whole test-exam drama. "Plus, Adriana is doing that."

Adriana was a math major classmate who was transferring to UFRJ because her ill mother needed her to stop the daily, two-hour commute from central Rio de Janeiro to the hinterlands of RURAL.

"What? Do you want to leave me again?" Kaiza said jokingly. "You can't leave. You are back now, and look at how much fun we have!"

"Maybe I will stay, especially now that I found my new Marcelo," I said, referring to a boy I now dated who shared the same name as my ex-boyfriend.

She laughed. "Of course you will stay. You can't leave now! And make sure you register for the same classes as mine. You need to act fast!" she said.

"I will perhaps register later today then," I lied.

The following week, I felt it was time to start telling people about my upcoming departure. I told acquaintances first, feeling their judgment may not affect me as much as that of my closer friends. They looked at me incredulously.

"Isabelle, you do not know what you want!"

"You are crazy, girl!"

"Is it for real this time?"

"But I thought you did not like America!" That was the most common response from those who had previously heard exhaustive explanations of why I had returned.

"Well, I changed my mind," I responded. Or, I said, "It is a good opportunity, and I should try again."

I thought I could control who I would tell when. I had not expected that the news would travel faster than my ability to share them.

The next day, Kaiza stormed into the dorm.

"You are going to the United States!" She made a statement; she did not bother asking a question.

"Yes," I responded.

"When?"

"In two weeks."

"But just last week you told me you were going to transfer to UFRJ or stay here."

"Now I am moving."

"When did you decide this?" she pressed.

I wish I had understood the implications of this question. Kaiza sought a time stamp, one that would forever brand me a liar. I had lied for so long, why could I not just tell this one more little lie? Why, of all times, was this the time I decided to tell the truth?

"When I was in Petropolis recovering from chicken pox."

She calculated that my decision was four weeks earlier.

"But you just told me yesterday you registered for next semester!" Kaiza exclaimed.

"I did not register."

"Are you even registered this semester?"

I had not expected such a direct question. Kaiza probably asked it in jest. I knew she was unaware of my ruse to pose as a registered student that semester.

"No, I am not."

"You are not even registered this semester?" she asked incredulously.

I nodded my head.

Kaiza's face turned redder as she became overwhelmed by the rage she felt towards me.

"You lied to me!" she stated, raising her voice.

I had. And there was nothing I could say now to explain why. I lowered my eyes as tears were welling up at this interrogation, as I felt increasing shame for my actions.

"I am so stupid," she continued. "Here I am, writing you cards so that you can get better, making sure you have your bed here. And you lied to me? All you are is a liar!"

There was only truth to her statements. Yet, they stung. As it so often happened before, my tears turned to sobs. I tried to explain that I did not want to tell her I was leaving because I wanted to feel normal and I believed that people, including her, treated me differently when they knew I was leaving. I wasn't coherent; plus, it did not matter, not to Kaiza anyway.

"I was your friend!" she said as she left the dorm, leaving me behind, crying and trying to figure out what to do to salvage this situation.

A few hours later when she returned to the dorm, I tried to apologize. She completely ignored me, treating me as if I did not exist. I knew that tactic well, having availed myself of it so often in my recent past. I recognized then how harsh it was to be on the receiving end of that punishment.

For the next few days, I tried at every opportunity to tell Kaiza that I felt deeply sorry and that she was important to me. She continued to behave as if I did not exist.

Kaiza never spoke to me again.

Chapter 53

LEAVING SHANGRILA

or two days, I aimlessly wandered the university grounds, trying to make sense of my life. I had imagined that once back in Brazil, I would recapture all that I had built before I left. Yet within a few months, all I had in my hands were shards of dreams I once held. I had lost two of the most important people in my life. I was not attending university. I felt as if I did not have a home. I cried so often that I forgot what it felt like to be happy.

During these wanderings, I recognized why I lost Kaiza's friendship; I had returned the warmth and friendship she so generously extended to me with lies. That I treated such an important relationship so callously would weigh heavily on me for a long time. But at least I understood how my actions caused the irreparable rift with my former friend.

The reason why Marcelo's behavior changed so suddenly was still a mystery to me. Feeling there was no more pride to salvage, as I planned to leave RURAL forever the following day, I found myself standing in front of the door to Marcelo's dorm.

I hesitated for a few seconds. Yet, I had come this far, and I would not turn back.

I knocked on his door. Marcelo opened it immediately, as if he sensed someone was right outside his door.

"Isa!" His voice betrayed surprise in seeing me standing in front of him.

"Hi," I said meekly, waving my hand.

We stared at each other on his front door before he invited me in.

I took a seat facing him across the small, square table where we had shared so many meals before.

We remained quiet, staring at each other for a few seconds. My eyes welled up, and I squirmed on my seat to break the awkwardness.

"I am leaving," I blurted out, breaking through the loud silence.

"Where to?" he asked, genuinely puzzled.

"Back to Los Angeles."

He paused for a few seconds before replying.

"You should have stayed there in the first place."

"You made that clear!" I responded, feeling wounded and defensive.

Silence ensued again. He stared at me for what seemed a long time, but then lowered his eyes as he spoke: "When you left, I thought I lost you forever. I never wanted to hurt that much again."

"I don't understand," I responded, sensing I was about to lose my composure. He loved me so much that he did not want to be with me? It made no sense.

He got up, rising from his seat so that he could be next to me. He took my hand and held it as he began telling me the story of what happened when I left six months earlier.

"I had an affair," he started.

"I know. I saw you with her," I said, referring to the pretty girl he caroused with during the hot-air balloon festival.

"No, not Valeria."

I did not respond. There were more?

Marcelo continued, "She is married. She has a child, a son, who is one-year-old."

I widened my eyes in shock.

"You see, I wanted someone I could not get attached to," he continued, looking at me, as it if was my responsibility that he had chosen an unavailable lover.

My jaw dropped, yet no words came out.

"Her husband found out about us, and he shot her," he continued.

"With a gun?" I asked, horrified.

"What else would he shoot her with? Yes, with a gun," he said sarcastically.

I did not respond, so he continued: "She has been at the hospital these past few weeks, between life and death, and it is all my fault." He ran his fingers through his short hair and continued, "I tried to visit her, but you can imagine that I am not welcome at the hospital." He had tears in his eyes.

It was the first time I had ever seen Marcelo cry.

"I am sorry," he said as he concluded telling me this tragic tale. Now he was the one sobbing with pain, shame, and regret. "I have been avoiding you," he continued, "because I felt ashamed. I did not want you to know the mess I made of my life."

I leaned over and hugged him. We kept our embrace for a few minutes.

I did not know what to say. There was nothing left to say.

I got up and picked up my purse that I had placed on his bed.

As I turned around, we again stared at each other. There was such pain in his dark eyes. But I felt no empathy. I had given up so much for him. I had tried so hard for years to shed all that was dysfunctional from my life. I had felt that Marcelo was a safe harbor from all that was ugly, scary, and threatening. I always believed that with him, I would be safe.

But that sense of safety first showed its cracks when he ignored me upon my return. Then it fully broke when he never contacted me during my illness. But this? This was bringing all that was dysfunctional, immoral, and wrong right back into my life. Life with Marcelo would be dealing with other women, jealous husbands, destroyed families, and disfigured wives. I wanted none of that mess. My life had been messy enough.

I felt the walls narrow in his small apartment. I wanted to break free and depart to somewhere far away. As he saw me move towards the door, he got up. "Please stay!" he said, placing himself between me and the door.

I shook my head and looked at him one more time with my red, bloodshot eyes. "I cannot stay."

Upon hearing this, he stepped aside, freeing me to walk out of his room and out of his life.

Not knowing where to go, and not wanting to explain my puffy, red eyes to the throngs moving about campus, I picked up the pace and walked quickly towards the lake with my head lowered. There I sat for a couple of hours, staring at the glistening surface, throwing rocks into the opaque but still water.

Ripples formed as I threw rocks into the lake. The rhythmic, predictable reaction made me reflect: one single pebble, one single action, causes a wide reaction of many circles. I imagined myself as the rock from which ripples emanated. Who was I? I told lies. I omitted the truth. I stole. And lies—and their destructive impact—reverberated from me. Lies and omissions, so ingrained in my life, brought nothing but distress and destroyed relationships. As a result, I lost a lover, then a friend. I thought of the stress of constantly hiding the truth, of always being careful about what I said to whom, covering one lie with another. I recalled the fear and responsibility I felt for my mother's life if I told the truth, thinking she would die as Lauro had often threatened. I recalled how that fear paralyzed me for a long time, allowing for terrible things to happen to my sisters and me. I never again wanted to feel the pain of losing a good friend. I did not want to feel the responsibility of causing pain to someone else, as I felt to a certain extent that Marcelo's lover got hurt because of me.

It would have been so easy to blame my earlier experiences. But more than anything, I did not want to feel that I was a victim.

I was lucky to have another chance to start over. Nobody knew me in the United States—not even my father or Nathalie knew me all that well. I recognized that this time, I could truly shed my past and leave the person I was behind and try to become someone new. I could become someone who told the truth, someone who did not deceive, someone who trusted, someone who loved. I could become somebody special. I could live my life in a way that I had never been allowed to.

I knew it would take some work to become a better person than I was, but I decided at the lake that I would do what it took to get there.

I returned to my dorm, searching for Kaiza, trying again to make amends, to tell her that I felt truly sorry. I wanted to say that I now understood why she felt so upset with me. I wanted to share my resolution with her that I vowed to change, to become a different person, a better person.

Kaiza ignored me, not giving me the opportunity I sought to explain myself. I felt sad, but it also convinced me that what I needed was a clean slate.

The next day, I boarded the bus with dry eyes, making, for the last time, the long journey from RURAL back to Petropolis.

A much smaller crowd went to the airport to see me depart this time. My mother, who never left the house, made an exception. She and my sister Catherine accompanied me, as did one of my classmates, along with her boyfriend. It was a far cry from the last time I had been at the Rio de Janeiro International Airport with all the fanfare, balloons, and craziness that accompanied my first send-off.

"Will we see you again in three months?" my small entourage joked with me.

"Are you planning to miss your flight?"

"Will you like America this time?"

I took their jokes in stride. I deserved them.

"Yes, I am staying this time. I will stay until I finish college," I responded patiently.

They looked at me skeptically.

"We don't believe you. We will see you right back here in three months," they said, laughing.

"No, you will not. This time I will stay—for a long time."

As departure neared, my little group created a circle around me, and I found myself in the center of a group hug. My forehead touched that of my mother.

My mother fell apart, as expected, as we said goodbye.

As I crossed the immigration line, I looked back for the last time to wave goodbye to my sobbing mother and my small group of friends. This time, I did not feel the same longing to stay or the elation to have been surrounded by friends.

This time, I had a purpose.

When I crossed the security check threshold, I did a lot more than just board a plane. I left behind the person I had been. Now, I would grab this opportunity to start over, to be whomever and whatever I wanted.

I was not quite sure what that new identity would look like. I would have to practice honesty and truthfulness before I could finally shed the survival skills I acquired in Shangrila, which had served me so poorly once we left the round house.

I looked back at the handful of people waving goodbye, feeling such gratitude that they had come to the airport to say goodbye a second time.

"I will be OK," I said, softly but firmly. "I am about to start my life."

EPILOGUE

Shangrila became a coal factory. The owners of the property had three children, all of them died young before their parents: a suicide, a motorcycle crash, and disease. Shangrila was then left without heirs. The farm's caretakers took over the property upon the death of its owners. The whitewashed round house became yellow and half-square. All the fruit trees, including the large avocado tree, were felled to make way for the coal furnace. The landlord's home and former library area became a storage facility, stacked from floor to ceiling with barbeque-grade coal. All the structures on the entire farm became run down and dilapidated. It was an end, perhaps, befitting of a cursed place that certainly did not bring happiness to its inhabitants.

Dobby, the dog, was hit by a car a few months after Lauro bought him from me, remaining paralyzed for the rest of his life.

Nathalie and I moved to the United States when we both turned eighteen, two years apart. I frequently returned to Brazil and became close friends with my mother. Nathalie never returned nor ever spoke with our mother again.

Despite receiving multiple invitations from my father to join us in Los Angeles, Catherine stayed in Petropolis, unable to be yet another daughter who left our mother behind.

I did realize my dream of attending UCLA.

The three of us became resourceful and independent women. I believe this is due to how we grew up, needing to be self-sufficient and resourceful to escape the chains of our restricted childhood. We all became entrepreneurs and founded businesses in the areas where we excelled: Nathalie in art, Catherine in beauty services, and I in quantitative analysis.

For more than two decades, I returned to Brazil annually to visit my mother. Each time, my mother asked that I reconcile with Lauro, who lurked in the shadows as I continued to ignore his existence. On one trip, he challenged the status quo. Then I was the only time I addressed him directly since that fateful day he sent Walter running from my house; I gleefully shared that I regarded him as the lowest form of life that ever existed. Since, despite numerous subsequent visits, he has never tried to speak with me again.

My mother and Lauro stayed together and alone, without the love and support of family, neighbors, or friends, just as they always wanted.

My father never once asked about the years we lived in Brazil. Later, he alluded to his regrets of leaving his children behind when he moved to the United States. He often wondered, out loud, about what could have caused Nathalie's strained relationship with our mother. He frequently lamented about his weak bond with Catherine, a daughter he never learned was not his. For all the years after I permanently moved to the United States, he sought to make amends for having left my sisters and me during our childhood. I saw the deep regret in my father's eyes as he lay dying, wanting forgiveness from his daughters.

Cristiane remained one of my closest friends. Her family welcomes me as if I am one of their own. I am forever thankful for the role Cristiane had in my life. Her father was the first adult I could trust and who protected me. Their support allowed me to have a glimmer of faith that people can, indeed, help one another.

Losing Kaiza's friendship was critical to enabling me to forge deep friendships with others, having learned the lesson that only trust and honesty create a solid foundation for any type of relationship. I tried for many years to speak with Kaiza, yet she ignored my attempts. I did not try again until close to the publication date of this book when she graciously forgave me for lying to her.

Despite my vows never to lie again, my sisters and I kept our story hidden for decades, partly to protect my mother, partly to protect Catherine, but mostly for never wanting to admit to my father and his family that we lied to them for so long. I did consider it, but I never found a good time to tell my family that we had been lying to them for years.

That is, until now.

ACKNOWLEDGEMENTS

I heard the stories of our lives in bits and pieces, repeated multiple times. As we were not allowed to watch TV, we mostly read and talked. Throughout my childhood, I had only heard my mother's side of the story: how my grandparents and my mother moved from Turkey to Egypt, then France and eventually to Brazil. My mother and her family were portrayed as strong and upright people. Whenever she had anything to say about my father's side of the family, they were portrayed as weak and dishonest.

I believed this to be the truth, until at my father's request, I reluctantly met his sister, my Aunt Paule, as a young adult. Upon our meeting, at 4 a.m. at a train station at the tiny village of Thionville in France, Paule took me to her apartment, served me tea, and ignoring my protests that I would rather sleep, proceeded to show me pictures of my grandparents and of my father as a child, telling me their remarkable story: how they went from Lithuania to Poland, then France and eventually to Brazil. That night, not only did I learn more about my father's side of the family, but it made me realize what I knew about them was either false or incomplete. I longed to learn more.

In Brazil, I lived my own story. One that I purposely did not share, even with my closest friends. I felt strongly that I did not want to be defined by my past, nor that I should be portrayed or feel like a victim. In ignoring my past, I set out to create my own narrative, one that did not include my childhood.

However, upon the birth of my son, I felt the urge to capture the remarkable story of our relatives, who moved around the globe, ensnared by world events they often did not willingly participate in. Now, as the only person in my family who knew something about both sides of the story, I felt I owed it to my son to capture the tenacity, resourcefulness, and more than a bit of street smart displayed by my relatives in their journeys. Soon, I drew parallels between their lives and mine, noting that I too became persistent, resourceful and street smart to get myself out of the situation in which fate had placed me.

Thus I started to write my own life story.

This was meant as a private project and for years, amidst child rearing of now two sons, the founding and growing of a company, I wrote. I interviewed my mother and my aunt to fill the gaps. I returned to Brazil and visited Shangrila where I grew up. I retraced my relatives' steps in France. I wrote sporadically. Sometimes I felt a burst of productivity, and other times months went by as life got in the way before I would write again.

Upon my divorce however, I found myself with free time I did not know how to fill when my children spent time with their father. Wanting to fill the emptiness their absence created, I registered for a writing class at Stanford University, as part of their Continuing Studies offerings. My homework assignment was to write and share six pages of a story with my classmates for review and comment. I had never before shared any information about my past, and I hesitated to do so among strangers. I considered writing something else, something less revealing about me. Yet, I had not written anything else, and pressed by time I shared a high-level synopsis of my entire childhood, dreading my classmate's judgment about my dysfunctional upbringing.

The feedback I received astounded me. Not only my classmates had not been judgmental, they hungered for more. They asked for more information about Shangrila, the characters' motivation to perpetrate and allow abuse, and how in the world I found myself in my predicament.

It was then I recognized that my tale was not simply meant for the sake of maintaining family memories. Instead, it was meant for a wider audience, one that could feel inspired by my story.

At the time, I had mastered how to build economic models and spreadsheets, skills I learned through my Economics degree at UCLA and an MBA from Kellogg, at Northwestern. While my spreadsheets helped many clients, they were not that useful in helping me write a book. While pondering this situation, I learned about the Stanford Creative Nonfiction Writing Certificate, which is designed for people just like me, who needed guidance in writing a book. My classmates, Kimberly Wohlford, Barbara Schuster, Jodi Solow, Luanne Castle, Jane Saginaw, Kimberley Lovato, Rebecca Galli, Kristine Mietzner, Jennifer Lou and others with whom I worked for two years, provided invaluable feedback as my story developed.

Otis Haschemeyer stood out among other professors by his dedication to his craft and to the success of his students. The most important decision I made about my book was asking Otis to be my advisor. It was a privilege to work with Otis and with his generous guidance, the book took shape. He helped me figure out where the story begins and ends, how to develop my characters and how to write a book I am proud of.

My mother, Paulette Hodara, planted the seed for this book by constantly sharing stories about her life in France, my relatives' lives in Egypt and Turkey, the early years of my parents' marriage, and the bitterness she felt towards my French relatives. She knew that she would not be portrayed well in this book, yet she offered me her blessing to publish it and happily filled the information gaps during the writing process.

I had only heard negative adjectives about my French relatives, thus I only reluctantly met Paule Gecils, because my father demanded it of me. Yet, we not only spent a remarkable first weekend together in Thionville, later that summer Paule visited me in Geneva where I lived at the time, so that we could continue our conversation over the many delicious meals she cooked for me. Since, we have frequently met around the world, forming a deep friendship. Paule shared my father's family side of the story. She gifted me a book of family pictures, paintings by my grandfather and a timeline of events which touched me deeply and that I will forever prize.

My sister Nathalie Gallmeier read early drafts of the book, corrected factual errors, and served as my compass ensuring that the timeline of events were correct. I felt worried about her feelings towards this book, as we shared many of the unfortunate events of childhood. She disagreed in how I portrayed our father, but she also gave me her blessing and full support.

Cynthia Crosby Wiggin, along with stepping in to read the manuscript to catch errors that nobody else would see, provided keen insight on the book cover, helping to shape it to reflect both the essence of the book and to spark curiosity among potential readers. Dena Hein, Bill Plummer and Addison Polcyn provided input on cover selection as well.

Terry Whalin, the Acquisitions Editor of Morgan James Publishing Company believed in the power of this story. Jessica Foldberg, Margo Toulouse, Nickcole Watkins, David Hancock and Jim Howard of Morgan James Publishing Company worked with me to make this book a reality. Seth Harwood, from the Stanford Continuing Studies, provided invaluable advice on contracts. Angie Kiesling and her staff, from Split-Seed edited the manuscript. Myrna Hasty was fantastic in proofreading.

Perhaps it is not surprising that with a story such as mine, it took a long time to get some things right. Recognizing the fragility of relationships, I initially did not want to share my manuscript with James Polcyn, for fear that he would see a side of me I was not quite prepared to share. Yet, he not only treated my work with utmost care and sensitivity, he became an invaluable supporter of the book and the process, often offering me guidance and strength, especially when I wavered about sharing such a personal story. James is a gift to me.

Leaving Shangrila is a true story. This is also a story that many people wanted me to keep hidden. Not everybody gave me their blessing. I may have upset some. Yet, I heard of a saying that "evil flourishes when good people choose silence." My childhood was proof of it. So many people stood by, choosing to do nothing and say nothing, because it was easier for them then.

I am guilty of it too.

For a long time, I also chose to forget the past, keeping the truth hidden because that was also easier and more convenient. But I decided, a long time ago, at the shores of a lake in Brazil, to only embrace the truth. And more recently that it is my responsibility to break the silence, and to hopefully inspire others to do the same.

Isabelle Gecils
Belmont, California

ABOUT THE AUTHOR

Isabelle Gecils was born in Brazil but it is hard to say what her true origins are with a French father, an Egyptian mother, and Turkish, Lithuanian and Polish grandparents. She is now proudly American. Consequently, Isabelle has an accent in every language she speaks, over time growing comfortable with belonging nowhere and everywhere at the same time, enjoying the freedom this can entail.

Leaving Shangrila, is her debut memoir, about a journey from a life others choose for her, to one she created for herself.

To support the writing of *Leaving Shangrila*, Isabelle completed the Stanford Creative Nonfiction Writing Certificate Program. She wrote *Leaving Shangrila* while living in Belmont, California. She currently lives in Saratoga, California, with her partner, their four sons, and two cats.

CPSIA information can be obtained at www.ICGtesting.com
Printed in the USA
BVOW08s1444170416

444539BV00005B/302/P